He'd identified what he saw as The Problem several months ago, even whispered about it to his friends, risking a leak that could lead to truly disastrous headlines—but it was only now that a plan crystallized, more or less, in his mind, and he realized that it was time to turn a nagging awareness into an act. Time to do something.

In the TV world, as you may know, "to do something" often means "to fire someone." A member of the *Today* show "family" was going down, Jack.

—From TOP OF THE MORNING

"Intriguing revelations."

—TheDailyBeast.com

"It reads more like *Heart of Darkness*, this searing account of life at the top of the television jungle . . . Mr. Stelter pulls back the curtains and exposes a savage corporate world that might have been inhabited by the Sopranos."

—*Washington Times*

"Your wake-up coffee will taste a bit zestier if you sip it while reading this riveting, revealing rundown of the high-stakes world of morning television."

—*American Profile* magazine

# TOP
# OF THE
# MORNING

# TOP
# OF THE
# MORNING

## INSIDE THE CUTTHROAT WORLD
## OF MORNING TV

## BRIAN STELTER

**GRAND CENTRAL**
**PUBLISHING**

NEW YORK   BOSTON

Grand Central Publishing
Hachette Book Group
237 Park Avenue
New York, NY 10017

www.HachetteBookGroup.com

Printed in the United States of America

RRD-C

Originally published in hardcover by Hachette Book Group.

First trade edition: May 2014

10 9 8 7 6 5 4 3 2 1

Grand Central Publishing is a division of Hachette Book Group, Inc.
The Grand Central Publishing name and logo are trademarks of Hachette Book Group, Inc.

The Hachette Speakers Bureau provides a wide range of authors for speaking events. To find out more, go to www.hachettespeakersbureau.com or call (866) 376-6591.

The publisher is not responsible for websites (or their content) that are not owned by the publisher.

Library of Congress Catalog Number: 2013932327

ISBN 978-1-4555-1288-1 (pbk.)

*To my mom and dad, who always rustled me out of bed in time for the morning shows. Mom always watched* Good Morning America; *I always watched* Today.

*✹ ✹ ✹*

*To Jamie, my love, who makes every morning a good one.*

## Ask the Author

I'd like to answer your questions about morning television as you read. Tweet a question to @brianstelter on Twitter or look me up on Facebook, and I'll reply right away.

To read a Q&A of other readers' questions, visit http://brianstelter.com/morning/

# CONTENTS

**Act 1: Operation Bambi — 1**

    1: Operation Bambi — 3

    2: America's First Family — 13

    3: Hands Are Tied — 33

    4: "Here Comes the Storm!" — 49

    5: Denial — 69

**Act 2: Good Morning — 101**

    6: Try Harder — 103

    7: A Hole Dug Deep — 113

    8: Unfinished Business — 125

    9: Hacky Sack — 135

    10: *Morning Joe* — 149

    11: May the Best Booker Win — 165

    12: Invincible — 183

    13: Inevitable — 199

    14: The Call from the White House — 211

    15: "I Am Going to Beat This" — 221

**Act 3: (Almost) Instant Karma — 231**

    16: The New Girl — 233

    17: Total Victory — 257

    18: The Empty Chair — 267

*Afterword* — 291

*Afterword to the Trade Paperback* — 297

*A Note About Sourcing* — 323

*Acknowledgments* — 325

*Index* — 329

# ACT 1

# OPERATION BAMBI

# CHAPTER 1

# Operation Bambi

OH, WHAT A THRILL IT IS to solve, or even to think you've solved, a large, long-standing, and most of all very public problem! So it was with a sense of welling satisfaction, and a growing warmth that spread through his broad bosom like the aftereffect of a double jigger of single malt scotch, taken at the end of one of those five-hundred-dollar TV executive lunches that we're told don't happen anymore, but that most certainly do, at places like La Grenouille and the Four Seasons, every damn day, that a certain producer at NBC came to the realization, in January 2012, that he did after all know how to steer that tsunami-tossed cruise ship of a television enterprise known as the *Today* show into smoother seas.

Yes. He. Jim Bell. Had. The. Answer.

To be clear, this was not exactly a eureka moment for Bell. The forty-four-year-old Harvard-educated son of an attorney at General Electric had at that point been in charge of the most valuable franchise in morning television for more than six years. He'd identified what he saw as The Problem several months ago, even whispered about it to his friends, risking a leak that could lead to truly disastrous headlines—but it was only now that a plan crystallized, more or less, in his mind, and he realized that it was time to turn a nagging awareness into an act. Time to *do* something.

In the TV world, as you may know, "to do something" often means "to fire someone." A member of the *Today* show "family" was going down, Jack.

And so it was, unbeknownst even to the members of the "family," that a plot was hatched, a plot in some ways similar to the plots one reads about in those raised-letter paperbacks one buys at the airport, or sees in old Steve McQueen movies. It would feature clandestine meetings, a Greek chorus of naysayers proclaiming it far too risky, an unstoppable momentum, a cold-hearted exterminator, devilishly handsome men, alluring and dangerous women, and even, yes, a name. Let's call it—as Jim Bell did—Operation Bambi.

If that leads you to think there was something lighthearted or self-effacing about Bell's scheme, it shouldn't. The title was not satirical. Operation Bambi may have been far less important in the general sweep of history, but it was no less earnest an endeavor than the Nazis' Operation Sea Lion or America's Operation Desert Storm.

Still, what are we to think when what is essentially a corporate personnel decision is dressed up with a kind of dashing, pseudomilitary moniker?

Two things.

One is that while morning TV is created mostly for women, it is, even at this late date, quite obviously managed mostly by men—men who like to think in terms of war, sabotage, and, well, embarrassing James Bond–y names for stuff they do in the office.

The other thing we can take from Operation Bambi is a lesson about sleep deprivation. This is something to keep in mind as you read this book, or think about this genre in general. The subtle but sometimes strikingly weird effects of sleep deprivation can be seen everywhere in the world of morning TV, and they make people do...interesting things. Meredith Vieira recognized it when she left *Today* in 2011: "When you're tired all the time, you just don't feel well. It's easy to gain weight; it's easy to get depressed. And there's anxiety." And no amount of money can cure exhaustion. Though many have tried. Network morning TV hosts are, almost by definition, millionaires: several make north of five million dollars a year and one, Matt Lauer, the longest-serving and most successful of them all, makes more than twenty million. They work for producers who make far less, though those producers don't have to do what hosts do: appear alive and alert and attractive on the air every single morning, no matter how sleepy or stressed or ugly they really feel. Not to put too fine a point on it, when you're dealing with a lot of rich folks whose alarm clocks go off at three thirty in the morning day after day, some crazy shit is going to go down.

For example, Operation Bambi.

The tongue-in-cheek name came to Bell honestly enough, when a staffer asked whether removing this person would be like "killing Bambi." The question highlighted something Bell already knew: that this would not be just another ouster. It would be big news, in the business pages of *The New York Times* and in the celebrity weeklies, and, if not handled correctly by both NBC and the victim, a potentially fatal blow to many people's careers. It would be discussed around water coolers, on Facebook and Twitter, in hair salons and restaurants and gyms—wherever plugged-in people, especially plugged-in women, congregate. That's why the severing had to be handled very cleverly, very carefully, so smartly that when it was over, and despite what might get written on TMZ or Gawker, neither he nor his network would seem mean, and the question of jumped-or-was-pushed would remain at least a bit murky. That's why it needed to be not just a "clean break" or pink slip or that classic cop-out, the phone call to the agent, but something layered and nuanced and, well, an Operation. Heck, with a little luck, he might even be able to give a reasonable observer the impression that the victim had been promoted—that the job they'd dreamed about had finally landed in their lap! That they'd no longer have to go to bed at nine p.m., dread the alarm clock at three thirty a.m., or tolerate strangers' questions about their strange sleep patterns!

Elegant executions had been done before. When ABC nudged *Good Morning America* cohost Joan Lunden out the door in the late 1990s, she came out and claimed it was her doing, saying in a statement, "I have asked the executives of ABC to give me a chance to do something I've never done: wake up my own children with a smile, while they're still children." Here's what Lunden now says really happened: "I called up and I said, 'Look, you guys, let's just say I want to leave. I'd rather leave with dignity; I don't want to go to war with you guys; and it certainly behooves you guys not to make it look like you're replacing me with a thirty-year-old look-alike of me.' So we all agreed." And the part about waking up her children with a smile? Nowadays she jokes, "I'm here to tell you that morning with children is highly overrated!"

But viewers bought her statement at the time. In this near-sighted business, that's what matters most. The tearless termination was to the TV executive what the eighty-yard, post-two-minute-warning drive was to the football quarterback: a way to show his mettle. Bell was a pro. He could do this thing.

Of course, there were other possible outcomes as well, once Operation Bambi got rolling. Anyone who remembered the beyond-awkward transition from Jane Pauley to Deborah Norville on that same *Today* show in 1989 knew that the ousting of a familiar TV face—which ultimately was what this operation was all about—could also be horribly bungled. Things often turn out poorly when male television executives play chess with female personalities, moving them on, off, and around the set of a show that three million female viewers think of as theirs. Go figure.

Still, Bell, too, felt inextricably wound up in the *Today* show's fortunes and he might have thought that he could deftly remove the cancer that was steadily killing the show—cohost Ann Curry, as you no doubt guessed a while back—without traumatizing the surrounding tissue. And he might have thought this for a couple of reasons. One was that while his boss, NBC News president Steve Capus, did not agree that Curry should be forced out, Capus's boss Steve Burke did. Burke had a row all to himself on the intimidating NBC organizational chart, a row at the top. Burke was the chief executive of NBCUniversal, the man with the ultimate say over what happened on *Today*. And Burke said he backed Bell's plan.

Another reason for Bell's confidence was reinforced on the show every day, every time Curry stumbled through a transition or awkwardly whispered to a guest. He felt that her sheer badness as a broadcaster was apparent to all, and that a "promotion" to a better job that allowed her to "sleep in" and, of course, "spend more time with her family" would be greeted with a national sigh of relief.

Bell was just doing his job, which was to cure the show of problems as they arose and to maintain it in a state of apple-cheeked health, tasks that, if you consulted the record, he'd carried out admirably since inheriting the show in 2005. Cancer metaphors aside, *Today*, at that point, still had a record of performance that stoked envy throughout the television world. It had been number one in viewers, and number one in the coveted twenty-five-to-fifty-four age group known in industry lingo as "the demo," for more than eight hundred weeks in a row. Read that again: eight hundred weeks. If that sounds high to you, imagine how much higher it sounds to the staff of ABC's *Good Morning America*, who start every week with the knowledge that they are going to get whacked.

The fabled "streak," as everyone called it, had started in 1995 when Jeff Zucker was the executive producer of *Today*. Zucker had taken over *Today* in 1992 at the tender age of twenty-six, at a time when the show was still struggling to recover from the Norville disaster. The idiom "burning the candle at both ends" might as well have been coined for Zucker, as evinced by his rapidly receding hairline. What *Today* enjoyed now was the TV equivalent of Joe DiMaggio's 1941 fifty-six-game hitting streak, a number one record that seemed—to some, for a while—as if it would never be broken. You don't achieve this kind of success by accident. You do it by consistently informing and entertaining your viewers. But wait, there's more! Because this is morning television, you also do it by hoodwinking the Nielsen raters, figuring out sneaky ways to pay guests for interviews, sabotaging the competition, and spending a good deal of time and energy trying to divert attention from your stars' sexual peccadilloes, marital problems, and monstrous personalities. So, like Zucker and others before him and like his counterparts at other networks, Bell was both doctor and witch doctor, fixing what was wrong, but sometimes dabbling in the dark TV arts, or at least looking the other way when his valued underlings did.

Let's put this in perspective. Jim Bell does not under normal circumstances strike the people he works with, or the reporters who cover television, as a cynic, an a-hole, or a backstabber. To the contrary, he is, according to the testimony of many who know him well, a terribly nice guy, the kind who takes the time to e-mail a list of must-eats to a reporter who's drinking his way through Barcelona on vacation. (Let me take this opportunity to thank him again for pointing the way to Euskal Etxea and Cal Pep.) A lot has been made of Bell's physical size (at six foot four, he can be imposing) and his history as a Harvard football player, including by him. At his first meeting with Lauer, he famously described himself to the anchor as "a big guy who likes big challenges." But Bell is also an unusually intelligent man, even if he sometimes conceals it behind his laconic sports-producer persona. He has a polymath's fascination with the wide world of news and pop culture that *Today* inhabits, and a reputation as a straight shooter, inspiring deep loyalty among his senior staff. Though he has struggled at times to lose weight, he seems not to sweat at work. "You'd want him as your platoon leader in the trenches," said one of his deputies. "The guy is just totally unflappable."

Bell cracks jokes in the male-dominated control room with the best of them. He critiques his lower-rated competitors with a smile, almost always seeming to be an inch or two above it all, which he literally is. But by January he was showing signs of being affected by the grind and the burdens of morning TV, and, well, things happen. No wonder, then, that the friend who called him "unflappable" wouldn't put his name to the quote, or that Bell wouldn't put his control room jokes on the record so that they could be printed here. This is a genre that has claimed many victims, starting with Dave Garroway, the first host of the *Today* show when it premiered in 1952, the man whose on-air sidekick was not a smart-'n-sassy woman or a warm-'n-fuzzy weatherman but a chimpanzee named J. Fred Muggs. Garroway, perhaps not the most mentally healthy person to begin with, succumbed to the pressure of filling all that airtime, day after day, in a fascinating way. He saw ghosts, felt he was being followed everywhere, and eventually, long after he left the show, shot himself in the head.

No one was suggesting that Bell was about to go all Dave Garroway on himself or even pull an Arthur Godfrey (in 1953, morning show host Godfrey fired his popular house singer Julius LaRosa on the air; all these years later it still makes for a cringe-inducing moment). But tough stuff had indeed been happening on Bell's watch. The ratings for the *Today* show had started to erode even before Vieira left in June 2011; her exit and Curry's entrance sped up the trend, thus helping the long-suffering second-place *GMA* creep closer to first. As if the vulnerability of the streak, now nearly sixteen years long, wasn't enough to quicken the pulse, the biggest star of the show—Lauer—was thinking about leaving *Today* at the end of his contract cycle. The fact that he was being forced to sit next to Curry was one motivating factor for Lauer—it's hard enough to wake up in the middle of the night when you adore your coworker, and it's even harder when you don't. Lauer was firmly in the "don't" camp. But there were other factors, too, like his wife, Annette, who had stayed with him despite several rounds of very public, very painful rumors about his extramarital affairs. Annette wanted him to retire, and some days he felt the same impulse. This was hard work, much harder than most viewers ever realized. If he left, what would happen to *Today*? Bell had no obvious successor lined up.

Given that Bell faced so many huge problems in such a short time, could anyone criticize him too harshly for coming up with Operation Bambi? Convinced, as he was, that Curry had to go, the operation as he saw it had three parts: a) convince Lauer to extend his contract, which was set to expire in December 2012, b) remove Curry from the chair next to Lauer's, and c) replace Curry with the up-and-coming cohost of the nine a.m. hour of *Today*, Savannah Guthrie. Yes, this was all very perilous, but as still another kind of doctor, Hippocrates, told us, desperate times call for desperate measures.

But what is it that makes morning show people so desperate, so murderous of their colleagues and competitors, so willing to bend the rules? It's all because the stakes are so high. *Today* and *GMA* are the pinnacle of the television profession. For NBC and ABC, respectively, they are the profit centers of the news divisions that produce them; they basically subsidize the rest of the day's news coverage. In the Most Valuable Viewer category, otherwise known as "the demo," every hundred thousand viewers represent roughly ten million dollars in advertising revenue yearly. In other words: convince one hundred thousand more MVVs to watch every day and make ten million dollars. Spur the same number to stop watching and watch the ad dollars evaporate. No wonder the producers of these shows pop Tums as they await the overnight ratings. Their jobs and the jobs of many beneath them hang in the balance. And besides, media moguls don't like to lose.

What people not in the business sometimes don't get is that being number one in the ratings has a value all its own. Not just in the amount that the winning show's salespeople can extract from advertisers—though there's that: *Today* took almost five hundred million dollars in 2011, 150 million more than *GMA*—but in reputation, in influence, in sheer television industry power. *Today* had the upper hand in booking A-list celebrities. It had the clout to insist that a politician talk to Lauer before anyone else. It had the right to call itself "America's first family."

But all of that was at risk now for Bell, Lauer, and the rest of the *Today* show staff, and not just because *GMA* was trying to claw its way to number one. The rules of morning TV were changing as cable TV, the Internet, and cell phones all gave people more choices when they wake up. Why wait for Al Roker's weather forecast on *Today* when the Weather Channel's phone app can tell you whether it's going to rain? What's the point of a sixty-second stock market preview when CNBC's business-minded morning show *Squawk Box* is only a remote click away? There were a dozen morning shows on TV in January 2012, all with specific audiences in mind—conservatives got *Fox & Friends*, golf nuts got *Morning Drive*, Capitol Hill wonks got *Washington Journal*. The most innovative of the bunch was *Morning Joe*, a political chatfest that dismissed most of the conventions of morning TV and won over most of official Washington and media-centric New York. Like *Squawk Box* and *Today* and a third of the Weather Channel, it was owned by Comcast.

Individually, no cable TV show or Web site or app could challenge *Today* or *GMA*, each of which attracted five million viewers at any given time. But cumulatively all the competition was inching closer to—or maybe it's better to say dragging down—the Top of the Morning. In fact, in the very month that Operation Bambi took shape in Bell's brain, January 2012, still another option appeared, a hard-nosed newscast called *CBS This Morning*. CBS had been languishing in third place in the morning show wars ever since there were three networks to choose from. But the fact that the network was still trying after all these years—this time with a completely remade-from-scratch show led by Charlie Rose—was a testimony to the profits and wondrous possibilities of morning TV. And, if you don't get it right, the pain.

# CHAPTER 2

---

# America's First Family

WHAT'S TRULY INTERESTING about this proliferating panoply is not so much that it came into existence—the whole world is breaking down into niches—but that the very numerousness of the options worked to alter the nature of morning TV shows, institutions that have always seen themselves as being in the familiarity industry, and thus have historically been about as open to change as your average seventy-six-year-old Roman Catholic cardinal. Consider, gentle reader, that it's been time to see, in the immortal words of Al Roker, "what's happening in your neck of the woods," for *sixty friggin' years* now.

Actually, Roker, the current *Today* weatherman, hadn't even been born when NBC gave birth to the show. But even on the very first day—Monday, January 14, 1952—Garroway scrawled regional weather forecasts on a chalkboard map of the country and spoke as if he knew the tape would be preserved for history. *Today*, he predicted, presaged "a new kind of television." He was right. Watching the tape today, it's remarkable to see how many now-familiar features of morning television were a part of the original recipe. Not just the weather; even back then there were short newscasts, live shots from other cities, and sidekicks who humanized Garroway and cracked jokes and generally made *Today* feel like a family. There was even a clock in the lower right-hand corner of the screen, next to a ticker of newspaper headlines. *GMA* borrowed the recipe when it came on the air in 1975, though it fiddled with the specifics slightly, opting for instance for a softer, more conversational style and a studio that was supposed to look like a suburban home, not a newsroom. *GMA* was Pepsi to the *Today* show's Coke; the greatest rivalry in television was on. It continues to this day.

In the early part of the 2010s, though, the morning menu became in almost every way noticeably...more so. Which is to say that the fluffy show, *GMA*, became fluffier, the "serious" portions of the long-running shows were spun off into distinct brands such as *Morning Joe*, and the perennially "other" show—whatever it is they are calling the CBS a.m. entry at the moment you're reading this book—became more "other."

Perhaps you noticed that *Today* was missing from the previous sentence. That right there points to the show's single biggest problem. In a media universe that was changing at a revolutionary pace, the *Today* show...wasn't. As one senior staffer memorably said in 2012 when a bunch of brand strategists showed up at *Today* to help retool it, "If I look at the show, I am not sure I'd know what year it is." This from one of the smart people in charge of a show called *Today*.

✹ ✹ ✹

*GMA*, on the other hand, looked very much like, no pun intended, today, and possibly even the future. After a gut renovation in 2011 the pace of the show was faster, the banter between the hosts was snappier, and the hosts themselves were smiley-er, something experts had once thought was not possible. The screen literally looked brighter than it used to be, and the show's stories were, too: in preshow meetings, producers fretted about not broadcasting too much "darkness" as viewers were just rubbing their eyes and putting on their slippers. So while the lurid crime-of-the-day segments at seven thirty were still deemed necessary ("Without them, viewers reject the show," one of the anchors said), they were balanced by viral videos of stupid human tricks and no small number of stories about celebrity crushes and "bags that compliment your body type" and morbidly obese house cats.

Loyalists to *Today* liked to describe *GMA* as smutty, crappy, and, most of all, tabloid. But in the face of such criticism, the man in the *GMA* control room overseeing the renovation, James Goldston, just shrugged. What he was producing, he thought, was what morning TV was supposed to be. "If I had any mission," he said later, "it was to bring more FUN to the show. . . . If it's boring to you, it's going to be boring to the audience. So make it entertaining. You can be serious, you can be very serious, but even if it's serious it has to be entertaining."

No one disputes that the morning shows are supposed to be entertaining as well as informative—look no further than the chimp on the *Today* show set in the 1950s for proof of that. The philosophical battle is over the *mix*—the exact proportions of light versus dark, of You Should Know This versus You'll Enjoy This. With Goldston in charge, *GMA*, aware that You Should Know This was always just a click away, skated as fast as it could to You'll Enjoy This. George Stephanopoulos was front and center, to suggest gravitas, but everyone understood that Bill Clinton's former communications director wasn't, by himself, the reason people came to their party. No, *GMA* got its five million daily viewers by front-loading the show with the fast and frivolous, the criminal and the cute. (In 2013 Jon Stewart called Stephanopoulos a "contractual hostage.") Some of the cutest stories were a weird fit for Stephanopoulos, Robin Roberts, and weatherman Sam Champion, but that didn't matter so much because Ben Sherwood, the man who had put Goldston in charge of *GMA* in 2011, had added two new partiers: Josh Elliott, a hunky import from ESPN, and Lara Spencer, an entertainment reporter who served as the show's social butterfly.

These people not only related well to the viewers, they got along like chums, or so it seemed from the many *GMA* segments in which they relayed stories about their time spent hanging out when the cameras were off. Yes, the members of the team butted egos once in a while, as people with Macy's-parade-balloon-size egos will, but overall adored each other compared to the way the *Today* team coexisted, which was, in a word, tensely: Lauer and Curry rarely if ever saw each other away from the set.

Some journalism professors and surely some ex-viewers cringed at the morn-porn being churned out by ABC. So did some people close to *GMA*, like Charles Gibson, who had co-hosted the show with Lunden in the 1990s and with Diane Sawyer until 2006. Gibson, who could still remember a day on *GMA* when he'd moderated a long debate about the existence of God, disliked what he called the "pop-culture news" format of the current show. But no one could say that the recipe—which was really only a recipe in the sense that "deep-fried Oreos" is a recipe—wasn't working. In the overnight ratings that both networks obsessed about, *GMA*, the perpetual runner-up, was, in late 2011 and early 2012, cutting into the *Today* show's lead, and thus into its sense of invincibility.

Although the difference between the two morning titans was sometimes subtle—*Today* yanked many of its stories out of the same goody bag as *GMA*—*Today* seemed to enjoy it less and second-guess it more. Lauer and Curry often agitated for more meaningful stories about health, politics, and foreign affairs, but with limited success. "I want more spinach and less sugar in this big meal we give viewers," Curry told *Newsweek* in November 2011. "Sometimes I feel personally our balance isn't quite right."

In early 2012 Lauer and Curry continued to complain about

the tawdriness of it all, but neither they nor anyone else on the show went the additional step of conceiving a workable alternative. No one had a vision. The best the cohosts could do was show the viewers, with a bit of body language or a sarcastic smirk, or an occasional *ahem*, that they did not think that the news of a celebrity's engagement or a potty-trained cat was so earthshakingly important. Some in the audience thought the snarkiness was an insult to the amazing animals and the pertinent celebs they, the audience, fiercely crushed on. Most just wanted more dishy/funny/scandalous segments, and sooner, please, obese-cat videos being, if the ratings are any indication, addictive.

If in 2011 the *Today* show was a classic New York City department store, it would have been B. Altman's at the moment when the smartest person then working at that storied Fifth Avenue emporium looked out upon the teeming sales floor and realized that the world had shifted beneath the retail business and something was deeply and horribly wrong. Altman's is no more, and while no one expects Studio 1A, the *Today* show's legendary street-level venue, to become a 16 Handles anytime soon, it was apparent to anyone casting a gimlet eye on the situation that, in contrast to *GMA*, and despite Bell's, and a lot of other people's, best efforts, *Today* seemed a bit lost in the twenty-first century, as if all it had going for it was its rapidly dwindling 1990s momentum. Top NBC executives later called what happened to the show a "slow fade," although no one was uttering that phrase when the fade was just starting to take effect. Still, it seemed to many as if America's first family was going the way of the Mulvaneys in Joyce Carol Oates's *We Were the Mulvaneys*. And now there was something else at the center of the show, something that, if it was a family, was one of those makeshift nineteenth-century frontier families in which the mommy dies and, out of some kind of no-longer-comprehensible hardscrabble necessity, the daddy marries the aunt. All anyone could say for certain was that this family-like thing costarred Ann Curry, who for so long had been but a member of the supporting cast, and that all was not going swimmingly.

But the lack of a vision wasn't the biggest obstacle the *Today* show faced. Visions can be concocted or stumbled upon or co-opted from another show. Visionaries can be wooed over osso bucco. Much harder to come by, the one problem you can't solve by throwing money at it, is chemistry, that elusive quality that most discussions about the medium of television center around. Chemistry is the difference between *Friends* and so many other well-written sitcoms that die in October and whose names we don't recall; it is the reason someone as talent-challenged and un-beautiful as Ed McMahon could have so many millions of dollars to squander at the end of his improbable career. It's important at every stretch of the daily schedule, but ask the pros: if you don't have it in the morning, when the research shows that viewers want to smell the coffee and feel the warmth and hear the happy banter that happens when the highly paid stars are aligned, it doesn't matter what else you're toting, pardner. You're Richard Nixon in 1960, you're Big Brown in the Belmont, you're CBS.

A lot—but not all—of what we mean by *chemistry* is ineffable. You know it when you see it, but you can't say what it is. Tracy and Hepburn had it. John Travolta and Lily Tomlin in *Moment by Moment*? Maybe not so much. Lauer and Couric had it in historically significant proportions from 1997 to 2006, and when Couric left and Vieira slipped in beside Lauer, well, the NBC stagehands still had to spark-proof the couch. Over at *GMA* the crew—Roberts, Stephanopoulos, Champion, Elliott, Spencer—were relatively new to the game, but still so good at it they treated chemistry like a scholarly treatise: first they told you they had chemistry, then they went ahead and had the chemistry, then they told you that what you had just seen was chemistry in action.

The subject does not totally resist description, though. Parts of chemistry, in the TV world, come down to technique: to the questions you ask guests, the way you handle transitions to and from your cohost, the way you read the teleprompter. Perhaps most importantly, chemistry is in the things you don't do when others are speaking. A good part of chemistry, on morning TV, in other words, comes down to principles and tricks that you can learn at the close-cover-before-striking school of broadcasting. If you do these relatively mundane things the textbook way, you minimize distractions and show your viewers and your colleagues that you feel comfortable in your role: *voilà*, the screen exudes warmth and the audience gathers round. In this sense of the term, Ann Curry flunked chemistry badly, almost as soon as she was elevated to the cohost position in the spring of 2011.

What were her faults, exactly, as Bell (and his allies) saw them? Start with the frequent faux pas. Only seconds after Lauer announced on May 9 that Curry was going to be his new cohost, she said, "I feel like the high school computer nerd who was just asked to the prom by the quarterback of the football team."

This wasn't just disingenuous, it was painful to endure. Asked to the prom? The MVP of morning broadcasting hadn't invited her anywhere. He thought she was a perfectly nice human being, but not the perfect cohost—not by a long shot. When Capus, the news division president, told him that Curry was going to be his new cohost, he had said only, "OK, but..." The *but* was that their on-air chemistry had been lacking big-time in the more than two hundred times she'd filled in for Couric and Vieira.

Lauer's opinion was important—by virtue of how much he was paid, it had to be. But Lauer wasn't paid to pick talent, his bosses were. And they—primarily Capus and Bell—didn't feel they had much of a choice in the matter. Curry had been the news anchor of *Today* for fifteen years, ever since her predecessor, none other than Lauer, was elevated to the cohost chair next to Couric. Having been passed over once before, Curry pushed hard for the chair this time and NBC knew she could be trouble if she was passed over again. She might indeed have had a certain Bambi-like quality, as the operation named for her suggested, but, in her own strange way, as even some of her supporters will tell you, she is as ego-driven and career-consumed as anyone who ever stood in front of a tangle of sign-waving tourists, looked into a camera, and said, "When we come back, David Hasselhoff."

Speaking of her strange way, that was another problem. Curry's on-air comebacks to Lauer during her first months as cohost were just plain weird—the conversational Hacky Sack often fell thudding to the rug or, figuratively speaking, wound up in the saucepan put out for Al Roker's cooking segment. You could argue, and her supporters did argue, that this inability to make small talk on TV meant she was bad at being a phony. Yet her honest reactions to comments, features, and news stories also seemed fundamentally off, as if she had been raised on a planet only somewhat similar to our own. Then there was that unsettlingly ambiguous look in her beautiful Bambi-like eyes. As Tracy Jordan said to his psychiatrist in a 2007 episode of *30 Rock*, "Who's crazier, me or Ann Curry?"

Most annoying to her detractors was Curry's "whisper-talking." When interviewing people who had just lost a child or suffered some other severe emotional trauma, Curry would soften her voice to the point that it was virtually inaudible. She offered no apologies for this trademark move. When addressing people in the first blush of shock or grief, "I have a natural tendency to lower my voice," she explained. "It's not even intentional. I just don't want to make them feel that their backs are against the wall." But what about the viewers with their ears pressed against their TV screens?

If you go back and look at the tapes from this period, you'll see

Lauer glancing slightly out of camera range, as if he's searching the wings for the ghost of Couric or Vieira. "He would lob something to her, and he never quite knew what he was going to get back," said a longtime *Today* staffer. "As a result, he just started playing it very, very straight, and then it looked like they had absolutely no rapport.

"At some point," the staffer added, "Matt just kind of gave up."

It's debatable whether Lauer gave her a chance at all. Curry didn't think he did. She told her friends that she tried to soften Lauer up by taking him out to lunch a couple of times, but she didn't feel that he reciprocated her gestures of goodwill. They almost never socialized outside of the office. At first Curry tried to think positive and attributed their lack of quality time to the fact that both she and Lauer had children to attend to. What would you tell yourself, if you were her? Later on she told herself that Lauer, the Alpha Dog, was uncomfortable with her own alpha-ness.

Curry had branded herself years ago as an international reporter, ready and willing to parachute into any trouble spot on the map. She was the first anchor, for instance, to report from Sri Lanka after the devastating 2004 tsunami in Southeast Asia. "By the time everybody else realized how big a deal it was, Ann was already on a plane," one of her former producers said. Curry had strong feelings about using television as a force for good—but what came across as inspirational to some seemed overly righteous to others. And it may have been a particular turnoff for Lauer. "She was so determined to prove that she was a real journalist, she got in the way of herself" by trying to prove how much knowledge she had, said one person who was interviewed by Curry many times on the show. "When television types do that, particularly women, they rarely succeed." A lot of people echoed the sentiment. They said, rather simply, that Curry "tried too hard." And the harder she tried, the more grating and insincere she seemed.

It was Bell's job to fix these problems, or at least address them.

Tape reviews are part of the job for executive producers, just as they are for athletic coaches: with the talent, they look at highlights and more importantly lowlights, pointing out things little and larger that could be done better next time. These get-togethers not only address particular problems, they tell the person under review that she's worth the time and effort; that she's been given a great TV job for a reason, after all. The reviews usually end with both producer and talent feeling better.

But those conversations with Curry barely happened after she started cohosting, even though for a lot of reasons (see above) she seemed like the ideal candidate for a tape review. "She got no feedback from Jim Bell," one of her allies inside NBC News said later. "Ann just became more and more anxious as the days, weeks, and months went by, because she was not getting that kind of feedback." Maybe she *was* getting the feedback, but was ignoring it—that's what Bell's allies said. "He was trying to be constructive," said one who blamed Curry for lacking self-awareness and being in deep, almost supernatural denial.

Everyone agreed on this, at least: Bell didn't always have the best bedside manner. Their conversations sometimes left Curry even more off balance. Pulling her aside after a show in early September 2011, Bell said to her, "Matt thinks you're too happy, too excited."

"Too happy?" Curry said.

Curry stood there for a moment feeling confused. Was she being told to tamp down her natural exuberance? If so, what was she to make of that instruction? Exuberance had gotten her all the way to the top of the *Today* show.

Ann Curry was born on November 19, 1956, on the island of Guam, where her father, Bob, a chief petty officer in the

US Navy, was stationed. He had met her mother, Hiroe, a rice farmer's daughter working as a streetcar ticket-puncher, in occupied Japan after the end of World War II. He kept riding her streetcar until he mustered the courage to ask her out to dinner.

Based on a story Curry recounted in a 2005 book about fatherhood, *Big Shoes*, by her colleague Al Roker, it seems fair to say that she received the perseverance gene from both parents.

"My parents were both 18 years old—kids—and they fell in love," she wrote in the book. "But they had to overcome many obstacles before they married. My father was told that if he married a Japanese woman, his eyes would start to slant, and he would turn into a 'bamboo American.' The military wanted to protect him from making a rash decision at a very young age, so he was transferred to Morocco. Although her family also opposed the match, my mother sobbed, believing she was saying goodbye forever to her one true love. My father did not give up so easily. For the next two years, he wrote to her and sent money to her struggling family. Eventually, he got himself transferred back to Japan. There was a big, tearful reunion. Only when he held my mother did he realize something was terribly wrong—she was almost skeletal. She'd been diagnosed with tuberculosis. The military wasn't letting its men marry women who had the disease, so my mother used her sister's X-ray to get the license. My parents married, and then my mother had surgery performed by a team of American and Japanese doctors. They took out 90 percent of one of her lungs, but she survived. For the next few months, my father nursed her back to health. Her mother, who'd been against the relationship, finally told her, 'You will never find a man who loves you this much—I bless your marriage.'"

The story calls to mind *gambaru*, a Japanese word that Curry's mother taught her, which Curry defines as "Never ever, ever give up, even and especially when there is no chance of winning."

After many moves due to her father's military service, Curry's family settled down in Ashland, Oregon, a town of twelve thousand near the California state line, in 1972. In interviews years later, she recalled being singled out for being Japanese American; in third grade a classmate called her "Jap" and she punched the boy in the mouth.

Curry was the second in her family to go to college, after her father, who started taking classes when she was a teenager. A beneficiary of the GI Bill, he wanted to fulfill his lifelong dream of becoming a teacher. "More than anything else, that pushed me to go," she said in a 2001 *Today* segment about her college years, which were spent at the University of Oregon, three hours north of Ashland. The film *Animal House* was shot there during her senior year, and the man she ended up marrying, Brian Ross, is visible (barely) in one of the frat-party scenes. (The two dated in college, but split up; ten years passed before Ross saw Curry on television in Los Angeles and reconnected with her. They married in 1989 and have two children: McKenzie, born in 1992, and Walker, born in 1995.)

Curry, as you may not be surprised to hear, was the kind of student who protested when the university proposed to close the library at midnight rather than leave it open all night. Infatuated with journalism, inspired by Bob Woodward and Carl Bernstein and most of all Walter Cronkite, she dreamed of being a reporter with compassion and integrity—perhaps a foreign correspondent for *The New York Times*. Some of her professors thought she seemed like a natural fit for television, and although she'd first thought of the medium as too insubstantial and its product too fleeting for her tastes, she took an internship and then a job at KTVL, the CBS affiliate near Ashland, to pay off her student loans. At first the situation did not seem promising. An executive producer there told her that "women have no news judgment" and were too frail to carry a camera. Such nonsense only spurred her to become the station's first female reporter, doubling for a while as a camerawoman for her stories. The station bosses eventually gave her an anchor tryout, but were so disappointed by her first day that they didn't let her try again, according to a 1997 profile in an Oregon newspaper. (Was she already showing signs that she was more comfortable in the field than in a studio?)

Hopscotching, as so many aspiring TV stars do, from small to medium to big TV market, Curry moved north to KGW in Portland in 1981 and then south to KCBS, the powerhouse CBS station in LA, in 1984. NBC News snapped her up in 1990, first to be a correspondent in Chicago and then to host *Sunrise*, the same early-morning newscast Deborah Norville had come from. The role of foreign correspondent was still on her mind. "There are so many stories in out-of-the-way places, and I'd like to write them," she told a newspaper reporter in 1991. "I'm fascinated with the East and the Middle East, places like Afghanistan and Eastern Europe." Over time, though, Curry's career goal changed. After a few years of getting up in the middle of the night to host *Sunrise*, where she bonded with Capus, the show's producer, she started agitating for the anchor job on, of all highfalutin shows, *NBC Nightly News*. ("The dirty little secret about Ann is that she is so fucking ambitious," a longtime colleague of Curry's said.) Tom Brokaw, a *Today* host from 1976 to 1981, had been anchoring *Nightly* for a dozen years at that point, and he was not going anywhere. But when the weekend *Nightly* slot came open in 1993, and Brian Williams got it, Curry called then–NBC News president Andrew Lack at home one night and expressed her rather fierce unhappiness.

The *Today* show was another route to the top. The show's history and enduring popularity made it a crown jewel of sorts inside NBC News, even if *Nightly* was still the newscast of record. "It has always been the best place to work inside NBC News," said Capus, who was the supervising producer of *Today* for a brief period in the

1990s. Since that time *Today* has swollen from two hours to four, with a hugely popular Web site, Today.com, to boot. "It is one of the strongest brands in America," Capus said. "It's like Jell-O or Kleenex—it's the brand name," said Steve Friedman, who ran *Today* in the 1980s. "Everybody in morning television is doing their version of the *Today* show, because it came first."

So it was a pretty big deal when Lack named Curry the show's news anchor in 1997 at the same time that Lauer, the news anchor for the prior three years, ascended to the cohost chair. Curry's assignment was supposed to be temporary, but Lack loved Curry's work—"No one says, 'Back to you, Matt' better," he said—and made it permanent three months later.

Once Curry arrived at *Today*, she seemed to forget Brokaw's chair and focus instead on Couric's by jockeying to fill in every time Couric was away. The tense rivalry between the two women was an open secret; producers who were around the pair at the time said Couric thought Curry was fake. On the air, though, Lauer, Couric, Curry, and weatherman Al Roker were not just a happy family, they were "America's first family," a title NBC memorably attached to them with this jingle:

> *Katie, Matt, Al, and Ann,*
> *first on your TV.*
> *America's first family:*
> *Today on NBC.*

This was the beginning of the golden age of the *Today* show. Though Katie, Matt, Al, and Ann didn't know it yet, the streak had begun. The foursome—backed up by Zucker in the control room—carried the show and its viewers through the death of Princess Diana in 1997, the Columbine school shooting in 1999, the scary but ultimately overhyped Y2K crisis, and the presidential election in 2000. They also ushered in an era of big morning stunts, the best being "Where in the World Is Matt Lauer?" which sent a jet-lagged Lauer all around the world in successful pursuit of... well, basically ratings. Said a very jealous producer at another network, "It's probably the only really exceptional idea that any of the morning shows have come up with in the last twenty years." What it was for Lauer was a pinnacle of his personal and professional life. During the 1998 WITWIML, somewhere on the road from Cairo to Venice to Athens to the Taj Mahal to Sydney, Lauer produced a diamond ring and asked his then-girlfriend, Annette Roque, who had come along for the wild ride, to marry him. It shows you how long ago 1998 was in morning show years that his proposal of marriage wasn't taped and teased and broadcast twice, first at regular speed and then in the form of a joshing slow-motion replay.

By 2000 *Today* had become a ratings juggernaut that made *GMA*'s last winning week, in December 1995, a distant memory. Zucker began his ascent of the NBC food chain, becoming president of the network's entertainment division. The producer who took over *Today*, Jonathan Wald, maintained the show's ratings and reputation through the biggest story to ever occur on the morning TV shift: the September 11, 2001, terrorist attacks. Some days the gap between *Today* and *GMA* was two million viewers wide. But one week in December, three months after the attacks, sportscaster Bob Costas filled in for Lauer and the gap shrank to eight hundred thousand. At NBC "alarm bells went off," Wald said. Three months after that, on the day after ABC televised the Academy Awards, the morning-after show by *GMA* came within sixty-five thousand viewers of *Today*, giving more ammunition to those who wanted to shoot the show down. When asked about the ratings, Wald delivered a classic comeback to the *New York Observer*: "If they get the Oscars five nights a week, they'll have a great shot." Fluke aside, the staff of *Today* took the threat from *GMA* seriously. "We all got together and said, 'We've got to be more aggressive and we can't let any-thing fall through the cracks,'" Wald recalled. "We went back to a couple of chestnuts: women and health; women and money. It wasn't about getting more celebrities or more concerts or any-thing like that, it was 'Let's go back to what this audience really cares about.'"

Couric renewed her contract at the end of 2001 for a then-record fifteen million dollars a year, guaranteeing Curry at least another five-year wait for the cohost chair. It was a long game that she played. On morning TV, familiarity breeds security. Consider for a moment that Curry sometimes filled in when Couric was on assignment or on vacation. Consider, too, the precedent that NBC had set by moving Lauer from the news desk to the cohost desk in 1997. These things instilled in the viewer the expecta-tion that Curry was "in line"—that she would someday succeed Couric, who was making it clear to anyone within earshot of the makeup room that she wanted to do something else when her contract expired in 2006. For NBC there was an inherent risk in this situation: viewers, many of whom had waited and waited for promotions themselves, wanted to see Curry rewarded for her perceived loyalty, and if they saw anything else they might take their eyeballs elsewhere, with disastrous consequences for the show's bottom line.

Curry was not the only person at the network playing a long game. Neal Shapiro, who had succeeded Lack as president of NBC News, also saw Curry's moment of leverage looming sev-eral years in the distance. In 2003, soon after Jane Pauley decided to leave *Dateline*, the newsmagazine she had cohosted with Stone Phillips since its inception in 1992, Shapiro brought up Curry's name at a senior staff meeting with, among others, Zucker, NBC Sports & Olympics chairman Dick Ebersol, and NBC uber-boss Bob Wright. With Pauley gone, Shapiro saw a way to get Curry off the *Today* cohost track without offending the audience. "I said

Ann should be the full-time cohost at *Dateline*, joining Stone," he recalled.

The beauty part of Shapiro's plan was that, while it would have been done partly to head off a public relations disaster later, it had the advantage in the grand scheme of network business of making perfect sense. Character-driven stories of the sort that Curry delighted in were a staple of newsmagazines, and her previous contributions to *Dateline*—exclusive stories about the McCaughey septuplets, for instance—were highly rated. Said Shapiro: "The audience would understand moving to prime time was a great promotion and there would be no backlash against *Today*." And there was this: "By making her a host of *Dateline*, we could open up the news anchor job on *Today* to someone like Natalie Morales or Hoda Kotb"—and start grooming another successor for Couric.

Ultimately, though, Zucker quashed the plan. "He said America loved Ann and that we couldn't disrupt the 'first family of TV,'" Shapiro recalled. "He said that the *Today* show was the most important show we had, and that taking Ann off the show was too big a risk."

Maybe Zucker was right to keep her at the news desk for the time being. Still, that was hardly the same thing as saying that Curry was right for the cohost chair. By 2005, Zucker—who was well on the way to becoming CEO of all of NBC—had squeezed Shapiro out of his job and replaced him with Steve Capus, who had successfully produced *NBC Nightly News* for the four years prior. Separately, he had also hired Bell to run *Today* and Phil Griffin, an MSNBC executive, to oversee the show. When Couric prepared to move over to CBS, all four of these men had a role in choosing her successor—which would have been a Big F'ing Deal for any business, and especially for one like NBC that prided itself on picture-perfect transitions (Pauley to Norville being the exception that proved the rule). And all four were skeptical of the short list of thirty- and fortysomething women who had put themselves forward for the job. Zucker instead pursued the fifty-two-year-old Meredith Vieira. "Following Katie Couric's run at the *Today* show was gonna be one of the most difficult things for anybody to come in and do," he recalled. "And I was incredibly nervous that the next person would come in and fail. I thought it required somebody who had incredible broadcasting chops and tremendous confidence. And as I looked around, it became clear that Meredith was the perfect, and maybe the only, person who could do it."

But he had to talk Vieira into taking the chair while keeping Curry and the other candidates in the dark. One day in October 2005, knowing she was busy and might rebuff a sit-down meeting, he offered to give her a ride from her first job, cohosting *The View*, to her second job, giving away money on the game show *Who Wants to Be a Millionaire?* Her agent Michael Glantz had told Zucker that getting her was a total long shot: ABC had tried and failed to woo Vieira to host *GMA* years earlier. But Zucker went for the ride anyway. He instructed his driver to go slowly since the distance between the two TV studios was just three city blocks, and when Vieira hopped in the SUV, he got right to it. "I know your story," he said. "I know you have gone down this road before, but don't discount this before you think about it." He described the *Today* show gig as a once-in-a-lifetime opportunity, one that she was perfectly and uniquely fitted for. "These opportunities almost never come along," he said, "and you should grab it." Vieira said one of her hesitations had to do with the hours. Zucker had no good rebuttal for that one. But he said that her travel schedule would be limited, and promised that he'd be personally involved. Then she asked why he would pick someone who was three years older than Couric—in television, a business that prizes youth above almost all else, transitions almost always happen in the other direction.

But for Zucker, the unconventionality of the Vieira pick was part of the appeal. He liked that it would surprise people. The SUV pulled up to the *Millionaire* studio and Vieira, noncommittal but not outwardly opposed to Zucker's idea, hopped out. Then Zucker pulled out his cell phone, called Glantz, and said, "I think we have a shot."

Zucker wooed Vieira for several more months and once went up to her home in Westchester to talk through the possibilities. Around the same time, he also tried to steal Kelly Ripa away from *Live with Regis and Kelly*, the *Today* show's main rival at nine a.m. That was a no-go. Vieira, however, was more persuadable. Maybe it was Lauer who sealed the deal: at the beginning of December, while she was still hesitating about the job's impact on her family (her husband, Richard, has multiple sclerosis) and still dreading the early morning hours, he invited her to dinner at his Park Avenue apartment. Vieira wore a white T-shirt, a black jacket, and jeans, but fretted that she was dressed too casually for this all-important blind date. When she saw what Lauer was wearing— jeans and a sweater—she was relieved. He offered her a glass of wine and she thought, "I love him already." Over dinner they talked about the time commitment and Lauer, who already had two kids with Annette and would soon have a third, said he was living proof that the show could accommodate family life.

The Vieira deal was done the following April. That's when Zucker had to call Curry to his office on the fifty-second floor of 30 Rockefeller Center for a "very uncomfortable conversation"— his words.

As soon as Curry saw the direction of the conversation, her emotions started welling up. Zucker said he wanted her to understand that the selection of Vieira was more about what she, Vieira, had—genuine star power—and less about what Curry lacked. But that sentiment, not surprisingly, didn't make Curry feel any better. Through tears, she told Zucker that she was considering leaving the network. He said she could if she chose—but he wanted her to stay.

Curry didn't leave, of course, but she did do something to protect herself. She had her longtime agent Alfred Geller petition for an "out" clause in her next contract. The clause didn't say anything about Curry being guaranteed the cohost seat the next time it came open, as some claimed at the time. But it did allow her to leave the network immediately, and go to work for someone else immediately, with no penalty, if she was passed over again.

# CHAPTER 3

# Hands Are Tied

FADE OUT/FADE IN five years later, in the spring of 2011. In morning television, where the watchword is consistency, a whole lot had changed. Although *Today* still led in the ratings—its streak was now more than fifteen years old, and some staffers had high-school-age children who knew only a world where *Today* was on top—the footfalls of *Good Morning America* were getting a little bit louder. A year ago *GMA* had been a million viewers behind; now it was just six hundred fifty thousand behind. This was doubly worrying to the powers at NBC, since Meredith Vieira had just given notice that she was quitting the show—completely voluntarily, by the way, a rarity in television news.

Who were those powers these days, anyway? Many of the little brass name plaques on the executive floor atop 30 Rockefeller Center had a bright-ish sheen, for Comcast's years-long quest to take control of NBCUniversal had finally succeeded in January, and the new owners were settling in. There was no plaque for Zucker; he'd been asked to leave by Steve Burke, the longtime president of Comcast's cable division, who was the new CEO of NBC. If Zucker had been best described as a programmer, Burke was a no-nonsense operator. He had twenty-two business units to tend to, and more than a few were in bad shape. NBC's prime-time lineup, for example, was mired in fourth place. But NBC News wasn't one of his headaches. It was number one in the morning with *Today*, number one in the evening with *NBC Nightly News*, and number one on the weekends with *Meet the Press*, and it was bolstered by two cable channels, MSNBC and CNBC, that made hundreds of millions of dollars for the company each year. When Burke moved into his suite on the fifty-first floor he had taken one long look at NBC News and thought, "That's one I don't need to worry much about."

So Capus was still the president of NBC News and Bell was still the producer of *Today*. But the news division was on edge nonetheless, wondering who and what would survive in the Comcast era. Vieira's decision to leave had been a real jolt, and not the good kind. For the record it shouldn't have been a surprise, since Vieira, when her contract came due in 2010, had signed only a one-year contract extension. Even Glantz—who got a cut of every one of her paychecks—had told her it was probably time to go. "Some of the usual lightness of Meredith is missing," he'd said to her, according to an interview in *Good Housekeeping*. Still, NBC seemed caught off guard. The network tried very hard to persuade her to stay, "because she was so beloved and the show was doing so well," said Don Nash, who was the senior broadcast producer of *Today*, the No. 2 to Jim Bell. She and Lauer got along famously; sometimes they'd greet each other with "Hey, honey," like an old married couple. But Nash and his colleagues respected Vieira's decision to spend more time with her husband and children. "She has balance in her life," Nash said. "It wasn't all about the *Today* show for her. It was first her family and second the *Today* show, which I think is a really healthy outlook."

Yes, but: now *Today* had to stage another transition, this time without Zucker and with new corporate overlords who knew almost nothing about the show. Vieira wanted to sign off in June, three months before the end of her contract. NBC had to act fast.

But we really shouldn't overcomplicate this. Curry was the only real candidate for the job. Why? Well, for one thing, her Q Score—a proprietary measure of likability obtained by surveying thousands of John and Jane Does, and taken deadly seriously in the TV industry—was twenty-one, nine points above the average for a news anchor. Similarly, when focus groups were shown video clips of Curry at her best—interviewing refugees in Darfur, for instance—the responses showed that she was not just liked but adored by the audience. So did the comments on Facebook, Twitter, and every two-bit TV blog that mentioned Curry. An NBC executive who saw the research and read the comments said offering her the position was a "no-brainer."

Another reason Curry figured to move up was that clause in her contract. Geller, her agent, had passed away one month earlier, but her right to leave if she wasn't picked made the decision to promote her, said an NBC executive, a "nondecision." And on top of all that, Capus genuinely believed she was more than competent, and felt that after fifteen years of dutiful service as *Today*'s news anchor, she deserved her shot. "It was her turn," he said.

Bell wasn't so boosterish. He had reservations about Curry, just as Lauer did—or maybe *because* Lauer did. Just because she was beloved in one job, Bell thought, didn't mean she was right for another. He took some meetings in the spring with possibly poachable outsiders like Megyn Kelly, a rising star on the Fox News Channel. He also inquired about breaking bread with Robin Roberts, though it never happened, according to associates of hers. But those were merely one-lunch stands; ultimately he bought into the talk of this being Curry's turn, even if he didn't fully believe it.

In a meeting with Burke, Capus laid out his reasoning, as well as one other pesky point that loomed over every single move *Today* made in 2011: Lauer's future. Lauer's current contract was due to expire on December 31, 2012, and he had—significantly, everyone thought—declined to proffer any assurance that he was inclined to stay for any number of additional New Years. If Curry, miffed at being passed over a second time, exercised her contractual right to quit without penalty, *and* Lauer left a year later, the *Today* show would be two Familiar Faces short of enough Familiar Faces to be a serious morning contender. Burke did not want to start the Comcast era with that kind of debacle. His conclusion, according to other NBC executives, was nothing if not commonsensical: "If Meredith's leaving and we can't convince her not to leave, it goes to Ann." In other words: a nondecision.

The only one of the players who did not seem certain that Ann Curry would be the next *Today* cohost was…Ann Curry. "She had some misgivings," said Nicholas Kristof, an op-ed columnist for *The New York Times* and a friend of hers. At dinner at Curry's Connecticut home in April, Kristof and his wife Sheryl WuDunn weighed the pros and cons with her. "We couldn't believe that she was even debating this," Kristof said. "How could you be offered the job of cohosting the *Today* show and not leap at it in a nanosecond?"

For a couple of reasons, Curry told them. The first thing worrying her was that the ratings for *Today* were already starting to slip. Beyond that, Curry was also concerned about how the new job would affect her international reporting. "She was afraid that NBC would make it harder for her to go overseas," Kristof said. "She didn't want to be doing fewer of those pieces just because she was climbing one notch up the ladder." Curry wasn't doing all that many at the time—no more than two or three a year. But the stories she did do, about the victims of wars and natural disasters all too frequently forgotten by the rest of the media, were important to the people she interviewed, to the people watching all across the country, and to the reputation she sought to embellish. According to Kristof, she worried that the new assignment would be more prestigious but ultimately less satisfying. "I think the argument that affected her most was that this promotion would make it easier to get those kinds of stories on the *Today* show," he said—she'd have more clout and more control over her day-to-day destiny than she ever had as news anchor. Assured that she could continue her overseas jaunts, Curry said yes to the cohost job at the end of April. Her dream job—that's what she called it—would become her reality.

The producers of the *Today* show were well aware that baton-passings were important, highly emotional moments for viewers. Sudden disappearances could be disastrous; CBS had proven that time and time again. Heartwarming transitions, on the other hand, could be beneficial, bringing in new viewers and ginning up all sorts of positive press attention. Rule of thumb: the word *love* should be used as much as possible in regard to fellow cast members. The word *deodorant* should be avoided.

All this may seem obvious, but the going of Vieira and the coming of Curry provide starkly contrasting examples of the different ways transitions can work.

Vieira went out dancing. The whole show on June 8, 2011, was a love letter to the departing cohost, starting with a sound bite from the Bruno Mars song "Just The Way You Are": "When you smile/The whole world stops and stares for a while/'Cuz girl you're amazing/Just the way you are." There was a ten-minute video celebrating her tenure, mentioning her coverage of news events like the Virginia Tech mass shooting in 2007 and her interviews with figures like Charla Nash, the Connecticut woman whose face was torn off by a chimpanzee in 2009. Fighting back tears after the video, Vieira recalled a candlelight vigil on the campus of Virginia Tech shortly after the shooting, during which students came up to her and asked, "Can we please hug you?" She said, "They watched the show every day. And they didn't have their mothers or their fathers next to them. I realized in that moment what's so humbling about the power of this show to really reach people. And it's such a blessing to have had that ability." Holding her hand, Lauer said, "I'm not sure they would have said that to everybody. I think it's you."

This was all a warm-up for a grand finale, put together with only a few days' notice by a small team of producers. It was an over-the-top lip-synch of "Don't Stop Believing" done live with two hundred staffers. Vieira seemed genuinely surprised when her cohosts, all clad in special T-shirts emblazoned with her name, guided her through Studio 1A, a myriad of hallways, and the control room one floor below, then outside to Rockefeller Plaza. There were Jimmy Fallon, Abe Vigoda (the butt of a running joke on *Today*), and a synchronized dance on the plaza, one that made anyone half-watching at home stop and pay full attention.

After it was over, Vieira, in tears, hugged Bell, who was wearing an "El Jefe loves Meredith" shirt. "Thank you so much, I love you," she said to the staff. Then she leaned into Lauer's embrace. "I love you," she said. As the show went to a commercial break, the staff chanted "MER-E-DITH." The sequence went off perfectly. In response to an e-mail congratulating him on the transition, Bell wrote, "It has been a fun, if draining, week. It's definitely the duck analogy: smooth on the surface, furious paddling beneath the water."

The next morning it was Curry's turn. *Today* celebrated her promotion with an eight-minute-long highlight reel that interspersed Curry's foreign conflict coverage with her hijinks on the plaza and her bungee-jump for charity. All of her cohosts showered her with praise. "We don't own our position, we are caretakers for a certain period of time. And there will be no better caretaker than Ann Curry," said Roker, her closest friend among the castmates.

But something went wrong in Curry's very first minute as cohost. It was a *Today* show tradition, on a new cohost's first day, to replay the announcer's introduction a couple of times and let the new person savor it. The intro is iconic: "FROM NBC NEWS/THIS IS *TODAY*/WITH MATT LAUER/AND ANN CURRY." "Let's take a listen," Lauer said at 7:01, pointing skyward—but the control room played only the words "ANN CURRY."

"That was it?" Lauer asked. Curry put her hand to her face. "ANN CURRY," the announcer said again. The crew started cracking up. "That worked well," the show's longtime stage manager Mark Traub sarcastically said off camera.

This was followed by "awkward Ann moments" of the sort that would plague the relationship between Lauer and Curry in the months to come. Curry must have been sweating while watching the highlight reel of her career, because right afterward she said, "I knew I should have worn deodorant today, this is hard today!" Caught off guard, Lauer mock-groaned and said, "Thanks for sharing that." Then she gave him a halfhearted hug and exclaimed, "Well I'll share some more if you'd like!" Lauer, seeming embarrassed by her inelegant behavior, quickly changed the subject to the oversize glasses Curry, in the video, had just been seen wearing as a local reporter in the 1980s, and repeated a joke that Don Nash, the senior broadcast producer, had said in his ear: "You know, contact lenses have been great for Ann's career."

"I don't actually wear them!" she blurted back. "Which is, you know, why I can't read the teleprompter half the time!" The cast and crew all laughed loudly. As Homer Simpson has been known to say, "It's funny 'cause it's true."

This was a preview of Lauer and Curry's awkward year to come. The day before she started, Curry had told an interviewer, "I'll be dancing with a partner who is Fred Astaire. I've just got to be able to go backwards, in heels. And I do love to dance." You'd never have known it, however, from the way she repeatedly—and seemingly obliviously—stepped on Lauer's toes. "Katie and Matt, it took them a while to get up to the same dance and move in the same steps," one longtime NBC executive said later. "Meredith and Matt, it took them a little while, too. Ann and Matt? They're not even listening to the same song."

Lauer, a discreet and deliberative guy, was careful not to air his discomfort with Curry's promotion in public. But it came up time and time again in private conversations. At the end of their second week together on *Today*, late on a Saturday night, Lauer bumped into Zucker at a party in Bridgehampton, a few miles from Lauer's Hamptons estate. The two men hadn't seen each other in a while. They started chatting about the changes at the show, and Zucker made it clear that he wouldn't have appointed Curry to cohost had he still been in charge. "Yeah, well, you know," Lauer responded, "it's not exactly the way I would have done it."

Bell, in conversations with friends around the same time, hinted that the "out" clause had had a lot to do with the ultimate decision (or nondecision) to make her the cohost. "It was probably a mistake," he told one friend, "but we just didn't want to wake up and see Ann on another network."

Viewers picked up on Lauer's dissatisfaction, maybe through his sour expressions when Curry fumbled her lines or told a strange joke. Some thought his overall performance as an anchor sagged. One day, according to a longtime staff member, he said to a production assistant, "I can't believe I am sitting next to this woman."

It must be noted here that not every day was dire for Curry or for the *Today* show, which remained America's favorite show to wake up with. She did good work: she interviewed the Dalai Lama in July and shed light on the famine in Somalia by flying there in August. Even though she didn't like all the softer stories picked by her producers, she loved the challenge of cohosting; she strove to be one of the best who'd ever had a seat on the famed couch.

But before long Curry wasn't the only one whisper-talking: rumors were spreading that, because of her inability to find a niche on what was increasingly *The Matt Lauer Show*, she was on her way out. In 1989, Deborah Norville, at the start of an ill-fated thirteen-month stint as Bryant Gumbel's cohost, had complained that the staff and the viewers of the *Today* show didn't allow a new person enough time to succeed. "This job is radically different from any I've had before," Norville said shortly after being upgraded from news anchor. "It's a learning experience for me—and I think I can learn. All I can say is, don't shoot me before I'm in the saddle—let me get up there and ride a bit."

Now Curry was experiencing the same thing. When I interviewed her for a short story in *The New York Times* in February 2012, right after she had returned from a trip to the Sudan, she sounded like a woman who wanted more time. "I used to struggle," she said, with the sharp turns that morning TV demanded. "But actually, this time, on my first day back, I was interviewing someone about why neon colors are the colors for spring. I marveled because, I remember, I switched into that gear pretty seamlessly. I felt, sort of for the first time, that I'm getting better at switching gears." Case in point: Curry was calling from John F. Kennedy International Airport, where she was about to fly to Los Angeles to cover the Oscars. There was still sand in her suitcase from Africa.

Curry rambled on for a little while about having a "real chance" to redefine the *Today* show cohost role. I thought nothing of it at the time. But I wondered later if she'd been campaigning, in effect, to keep her job. Did she know that, within months of her debut as cohost, Bell had begun to think about what a succession plan would look like, whom it would involve, when it would roll out? By the end of 2011 he had a specific successor in mind: Savannah Guthrie, the former White House correspondent who had joined *Today* as the cohost of the nine a.m. hour in June, at the same time Curry ascended to the main seven-to-nine cohost job. He'd seen how Lauer and Guthrie clicked when they shared the screen, and he made that happen more often by ensuring that Guthrie was the first, second, and third choice for fill-in when Curry was away. To colleagues he trusted, he said, "I think Matt and Savannah are the best pairing I have."

For a while Bell and his lieutenants wondered if they should let Curry remain next to Lauer, but replace news anchor Natalie Morales with Guthrie, thereby injecting some new energy onto the set. In that scenario, Morales would have been moved to the weekend show. But the idea didn't get very far: NBC, always worried about too much change in the morning too quickly, extended Morales's contract in early 2012, although she wasn't being seriously considered for the top job. Only Guthrie was.

Guthrie, born in 1971 in Australia, grew up in Tucson, the Arizona city where her family settled in 1975. Her father, a mining consultant, suffered a heart attack and died when she was sixteen. She went to college a few miles from home at the University of Arizona and studied journalism, then climbed the TV ladder like Curry and wound up at Court TV covering the Michael Jackson trial in 2005. NBC poached her in 2007 and gave her a prestigious White House posting a year later. People in high places at NBC loved her, though she seemed uncomfortable when told that—a sign of shyness that to many at NBC only increased her charm. Guthrie was important to Bell not just because of the particular talents she brought to the show, or even the way she got along with Lauer, but because she represented an answer to the question "If not Ann, who?" "Not Ann" started a civil war of suits inside NBC. On one side was Bell. On the other was Capus, who was fond of Curry and wanted Bell to give her a chance. Sure, she probably wouldn't last for five years like Vieira did. But Capus wasn't convinced that there was an imminent problem.

Here's the rub: it sounded like his boss, Burke, was, and that was something he had to reckon with in the political scheme of things. Burke, who had blessed Curry's promotion mere months before, now thought Curry was hurting the show. Well, not Curry per se, but her dicey serve: "When Ann plays tennis with Matt," Burke told a colleague, "he hits the ball over the net, and she doesn't always hit it straight back."

When Burke spoke that way, Capus—who'd earned the nickname "Rage" for his short temper—thought Burke was channeling Bell, and he resented Bell for going over his head. The relationship between Capus and Bell was disintegrating.

Things hadn't always been bad between them. Before Comcast took control of NBC in January 2011, Capus and Bell had had a cordial if distant relationship, according to underlings and friends of the two. Capus beamed with pride for NBC News, *Today* included. Since the *Today* show was the main source of profits for the news division, Bell had a lot of autonomy: he was basically the president of the *Today* show ("Jim's attitude is 'I pay the bills around here,'" said one of his lieutenants), but was deferential to Capus when he needed to be. And Capus respected Bell's producing talent and political acumen. But they never really clicked. Capus was the street fighter, the state school guy—Temple, in Philly. Bell was the Ivy Leaguer—Harvard. When Comcast came in, the differences came out. Steve Burke and Bell bonded early on, which helps explain why there was widespread talk that Bell was in the running for Capus's seat or for a top spot at NBC Sports. In August 2011 Burke appointed Bell the executive producer of the Summer Olympics in London, the successor to Bell's mentor Dick Ebersol, who'd had that title for twenty years. Now Bell was in charge of *two* of NBC's most important investments.

Capus didn't quite understand why Burke was so enamored of Bell. Even before Bell began campaigning for Curry's removal, Capus thought it was high time to hand *Today* over to a new producer. But Burke decided to let Bell try to juggle the morning show and the Summer Olympics. Capus was assured that the Olympics thing would be temporary, and then Bell would refocus on *Today*. But he was annoyed nonetheless.

What seemed to bother Capus most was the belief that Bell had undermined him in meetings with Burke. *Undermined* is a strong word, but it was true that Bell had told Burke, "We need to make a change" at *Today*—beginning the process that would become known as Operation Bambi. The Bell/Burke friendship "shaped all the Ann stuff," an NBC executive said later.

Bell's voice seemed to be coming at Capus (and Curry) from any number of directions. In a gossipy feature called "Workplace Confidential" in the January 16 issue of *New York* magazine, an anonymous source was quoted as saying, "If the show's audience doesn't gravitate to Ann Curry soon, could NBC buck its own succession plan, much as it did with Conan and Jay Leno, and have Savannah Guthrie replace Ann? She's got that girl-next-door quality, and Ann can sometimes come off as disingenuous in interviews. And I don't see a situation where they could remove Ann and keep her at the network (she wouldn't be happy staying on as a special correspondent, and she is no longer hosting *Dateline*). There would be nowhere else for her to go. Unfortunately, that's the way those things play out." After the item appeared, Curry went to the *Today* show's spokeswoman, Megan Kopf, and asked if the PR department was ferreting out the source of the blasphemy. It's unclear what she was told, but the real answer was no, it wasn't.

One thing that concerned Bell mightily was the way Curry's performance affected Lauer's. The star seemed disenchanted not just with his costar but with the entire show. Suddenly Lauer, the five-alarmer charmer, didn't have especially good chemistry with *anyone* on the set. While Bell might have denied this, others could sense that the host wasn't trying very hard, wasn't rising to the occasion. According to many of his colleagues, Bell saw the problem as Curry. If she wasn't sitting next to him, "Matt would get the stick out of his ass," Bell told several of them.

Bell may have been right in his opinions, but some of his subordinates thought he was starting to let his anger, and his dread about the ever-improving *GMA* ratings—the ABC show was now about half a million viewers behind *Today*—affect his judgment. One afternoon in January, he called his senior producers to a meeting in one of the NBC Sports conference rooms, a dozen floors above NBC News and thus out of view of the rest of the *Today* staff. Things weren't good: the more closely one analyzed the ratings trends, the more clearly they favored *GMA*.

This mattered beyond the confines of the seven and eight a.m. hours. Sherwood, the ABC News president, and Goldston, the man he'd tasked with turning *GMA* around, were trying, in tough economic times, to expand the news division into new time slots and onto new platforms. They wanted *GMA* to have an afternoon talk show spin-off. They wanted ownership of more hours in prime time. A win by *GMA* would go a long way toward making the division's other dreams come true, just as years of wins by *Today* had expanded NBC News' fortunes and real estate. And now it was all so close. "It just felt that we had the magic," *GMA* cohost Robin Roberts said. "That we had become what the other place used to be."

*Today*, though, was conceding nothing. Tucked safely away in the NBC Sports department with his colleagues, Bell felt he could be frank about what he saw as their single biggest problem—guess who. Bell strongly criticized Curry's broadcasting skills and suggested that she was largely to blame for the weakened state of *Today*. To some of the producers in the room, both his indiscretion and his comments themselves were shocking. One in particular, senior producer Melissa Lonner, spoke up in Curry's defense. Lonner, the only Asian American on the senior staff, and

Curry had vacationed together with their partners; she couldn't possibly sit quietly, especially when Curry wasn't there to defend herself.

"Ann feels like she has no support," Lonner said. "She feels like she's all alone."

But Bell didn't back down. He never explicitly told anyone to stop giving Curry the best segments or to ignore her ideas. But before long his denunciation of Curry trickled down to the lower-level staffers, as he must have known it would. According to one member of the *Today* team, "The message was 'She's dead. She's a dead woman walking.'"

Bell was the prototypical battle-scarred veteran of the morning wars. He had been hired by Zucker, at Ebersol's urging, to produce *Today* in 2005, and had at that time beaten back a fairly serious threat from *GMA*. Zucker liked Bell because he had ample live television experience and had thrived in a big and complex organization, NBC Olympics. Bell began work at NBC in 1990, as a production assistant in an Olympics unit that was compiling profiles of athletes for the 1992 Summer Games in Barcelona. At that time he had no aspiration to run part of a TV network. He'd happened to be in Spain, taking a year off before law school, when a person in NBC's human resources department who knew Bell's dad called and asked him to assist Randy Falco, a top NBC executive, on a trip to Barcelona. Falco had ruptured an Achilles tendon and needed to be pushed in a wheelchair (and occasionally carried up and down stairs where there were no ramps).

Impressed by Bell's intelligence and his propensity for hard work, Falco offered him a job at NBC Olympics. By the time of the next Summer Games, in 1996, Bell was a coproducer of daytime coverage. He continued working his way up the Olympics

ladder and, along the way, produced innumerable football, baseball, basketball, and tennis broadcasts for the network. A talented
and well-regarded guy's guy, he was not only a friend of the
NBC Olympics boss Dick Ebersol but widely believed to be
Ebersol's heir apparent. Bell shared Ebersol's love of old-school
television perquisites—first-class airfare, only the best hotels and
restaurants, and, at *Today*, front-row spots at the show's concerts.
His wife Angelique sometimes tagged along to the concerts and
boogied just out of camera range. "Nobody has loved being the
*Today* show executive producer more than Jim Bell," said one of
the show's producers.

Bell had earned all the perks—he'd repeatedly stopped *GMA*
from stealing first place. Now he was trying to stop it again. He,
in concert with Burke, had not only a plan but a timeline: try
to renew Lauer's contract by April, then try to get rid of Curry
by June, then reintroduce the *Today* family on the stage he knew
best: the Olympics.

# CHAPTER 4

---

# "Here Comes the Storm!"

WHICH WAS A BETTER PARTY, the on-air one that the *Today* show threw for itself on January 13, 2012, to celebrate its sixtieth anniversary, which featured taped congratulations from President Barack Obama and first lady Michelle—or the loud private bash held at the Edison Ballroom the night before?

The answer will depend on how you feel about Hoda Kotb rapping center stage with her ten a.m. cohost Kathie Lee Gifford, and Katie Couric rhythmically grinding against Megan Kopf's PR boss Lauren Kapp.

Yes, the Edison Ballroom was the better party. While the hip-hop artists Pitbull and Flo Rida performed, and the champagne flowed, and a pride of former *Today* show lions like Barbara Walters and Bryant Gumbel looked on parentally from a VIP section above the dance floor, the current stars and their stressed-out producers blew off some serious steam. "No reporters!" shouted Savannah Guthrie, shy as ever, when I tried to say hi. "Me spanking Kathie Lee—that was off the record."

At about nine, a dance band took over, and Capus jumped onstage to play a not-bad rhythm guitar. NBC paid extra for the band to keep playing till eleven thirty, an hour and a half longer than expected. Guthrie, who had no kids at home to worry about, stayed longer than almost any other cast member. "A year ago," she said, alluding to her position as a White House correspondent for NBC and an anchor on MSNBC, "all I knew was Medicare Part B. Now I know Flo Rida!"

The next morning, Friday the thirteenth, as generations of *Today* show hosts gathered to be interviewed in the studio, Guthrie, resplendent in a bright red dress, but not wanting to overstate her role in the proceedings, stood at the very end of the line, just past Natalie Morales. This was a day to celebrate the rich heritage of the show, a day for all those *Today* veterans assembled—Barbara Walters (1966–1976), Jane Pauley (1976–1989), Bryant Gumbel (1982–1997)—to talk about how the show had changed their lives, yes, but mainly to watch the highlight reels stitched together lovingly by the staff—Oh, look, there's me probing for the serious side of Tiny Tim!—and to listen as the Obamas paid tribute to the franchise's importance. "So many Americans start their day right here," the first lady said in a prerecorded piece, "watching all of you as they're getting ready for work and sending their kids off to school." The president picked up where she left off. "Over decades and across generations," he said, "the *Today* show has become a part of American culture. A place where millions tune in to see how their world has changed overnight. That's why we're so pleased to join all of you in celebrating this remarkable milestone." Michelle concluded, "And we know you'll have many more years of success." The Obamas are technically neutral in the morning show wars, though what that means is that they pay roughly equal attention to the Big Two. It's hard to imagine the first couple doing a drop-by on, say, *Fox & Friends*.

"Thank you for your legacy," Curry said to the assembled group after Tom Hanks rolled out a birthday cake. Huh? Anniversary, shmanniversary: in terms of impossible-to-respond-to comments, it was, for her, business as usual. Then all the hosts were shooed outside for a class photo on the plaza. The moment would double as a televised champagne toast to the staff of *Today*, dozens of whom stood to the sides of the assembled all-stars. It was a little after nine a.m.—making this a long morning for the guests who had arrived before six for hair and makeup. Walters, eighty-three, had already left, as had ninety-one-year-old Hugh Downs. When Couric asked Lauer what was coming up next, he teased her: "What, do you have somewhere to go?" Lauer, standing symbolically in the center of the group, huddled for warmth with the woman who had succeeded Couric as cohost, Meredith Vieira. Out here they ducked raindrops and wondered what was taking so long. It seemed one cohost was missing: Curry.

When she ran outside a minute later, a sharp gust of wind blew through the canyons of Rockefeller Center. The raindrops temporarily turned to ice pellets, stinging the faces of the assembled hosts. Curry positioned herself on the periphery of the group, lest she appear to be butting into the center of the shot. But she was the cohost of *Today*—the center was where she belonged. Vieira noticed and shouted "Ann! Ann!" convincing Curry to dart over to her.

The last person involved in the photo shoot to come outside was Jim Bell. He took his place beside Lauer and Curry and nodded to the camera when the control room cut to a shot of him holding his champagne glass high, seeming to savor the moment. One might have reasonably asked why he seemed so purely triumphant, since there was real reason for concern. The week of the anniversary party, the *Today* show averaged 5.54 million viewers, about 677,000 more than *GMA*. The same week a year earlier, the gap between the two shows had been 1.13 million. Total viewership of the two shows had stayed more or less the same, meanwhile, which meant that a substantial stream of *Today* viewers were defecting to *GMA*.

As the icy drizzle started to intensify, the hosts and producers dashed back inside, dropping their half-full champagne glasses on a table by the entrance. Curry, before she went inside, looked up at the angry sky and said, a little bit too presciently, "Now here comes the storm!"

*   *   *

Actually, the dark clouds had been gathering above the gleaming Lauerdome for years. Pretty much everyone in the industry agreed that Lauer was the best male morning show host in history. Capus would say it perfectly later in 2012: "It's as if the man was born to do a program like *Today*."

But he'd been doing it for longer than just about any *Today* host ever had, even Couric. His contract wasn't set to expire until December of 2012, but in 2010, before Comcast formally took control of NBC, Steve Burke had been concerned enough about the waning enthusiasm of *Today*'s longest-running host to reach out to him. Burke had heard secondhand stories about Lauer telling makeup artists and golfing buddies that he was looking forward to waking up when he wanted to, not when his iPhone alarm dictated. "Matt had told people that he was not happy on the show and was not happy with the direction of the show," said one NBC executive. "You have to think about how tired he must be," said another. Lauer's wife Annette, who nearly divorced him in 2006 amid affair rumors, wanted him to quit the morning grind and stop dividing his time between Manhattan, where they had a 5.9-million-dollar Park Avenue apartment, and the Hamptons, where they had a fifteen-million-dollar estate on twenty-five acres. Annette kept reminding him that Bryant Gumbel, his predecessor and best friend, seemed to be enjoying his days in semiretirement.

With two years still left on Lauer's five-year contract, Burke invited Lauer to a get-to-know-you dinner, the first of many that they had in 2010 and 2011. Lauer was honest about the fact that he might want to leave at the end of his contract term—"I've been doing this a long time, and I don't know whether I want to keep doing it," he would say—and Burke honestly sympathized. He just wanted Lauer to know that NBC's new owners respected *Today*, and NBC News, and most of all him.

Lauer in turn wanted assurances that Comcast did not have plans to change *Today* into a tabloid-style show. If that was what they intended, that was their prerogative—but he didn't want to be a part of it. Lauer took his role on *Today* seriously, just as Gumbel had in the eighties and nineties. He saw himself as the keeper of its flame. He had watched the show himself, growing up in the New York City suburb of Westchester, and studied telecommunications at Ohio University in Athens, Ohio, in the late seventies. He interned during his senior year at WOWK, a CBS affiliate eighty miles south of Athens in Huntington, West Virginia. When the station offered him a job producing and writing the noon newscast, he jumped—and dropped out of college four credits shy of a diploma. (The credits were in a classic literature course and he thought he'd find time to finish later, but never did. He wrote a paper about his experiences since college to get an honorary degree in 1997.)

From WOWK Lauer hopped from market to market, with stops along the way in Richmond, Providence, and Boston, but the infotainment shows he fronted kept being canceled—a sequence of failures that left him doubting his future in the television business. Then WWOR, at the time an independent New York City station, called. The station wanted him to host *9 Broadcast Plaza*, a three-hour morning talk show. This show, he said later, "was a precursor to a lot of the lowest-common-denominator talk shows you see on the air now. The producers booked debates on ridiculous subjects, brought in people from both sides, and loved it when those people screamed and stuck their fingers in one another's chests."

Lauer said he probably shouldn't have taken the job. The breaking point was the station's proposal that he read live commercials, the same way *Today* cohosts had in the 1950s. After he resisted he was fired, but not before Ken Lindner, a TV agent in Los Angeles, was so impressed by one of Lauer's interviews that he flew to New York to meet Lauer in the flesh.

"What would make your heart sing?" Lindner asked Lauer at their lunch meeting.

Lauer joked that his heart would sing if he stayed employed for more than thirteen weeks at a time. Then he answered honestly: "I'd like to host the *Today* show or be Larry King."

Well, if that's the goal, Lindner thought, you're on the wrong track. Lauer needed a hard news background, breaking news experience, and the kind of credibility that you're not going to get on shows like *9 Broadcast Plaza*.

In retrospect, then, the pink slip from *9 Broadcast Plaza* was a very well-disguised blessing. Lauer spent the subsequent fifteen months mostly unemployed, helped along only by temporary work from ESPN and HBO, while Lindner shopped him to stations. There were offers for Lauer to host infomercials, proposals for him to tape pilot episodes of game shows—but the two men had agreed that if Lauer ever wanted to host a show like *Today*, then, as Lauer put it in a 2007 interview, "There were certain things I couldn't do, there were certain paychecks I couldn't accept. We stuck with that strategy to the point of pain."

Lauer and his golden retriever Waldon had moved out of Manhattan and into a cheaper rental fifty miles north of the city. Rent was coming due when, desperate for cash, he answered a help-wanted ad from a tree-trimming company. Rationalizing the phone call, he thought, "I love the outdoors. I can operate a chain saw. I am young enough to climb trees." Out in the wilderness no one would see him, thus he might be able to return to television someday with his dignity intact.

The next call was from Rockefeller Center—and it wasn't

about trimming the Christmas tree on the plaza. It was from the office of Bill Bolster, the general manager of WNBC, the network's flagship station in New York City. Bolster's assistant asked Lauer, "Are you available tomorrow night?" The assistant had no idea, of course, that Lauer was flat broke and holed up in a cottage with his dog. "Of course," he answered.

Their dinner meeting was held at the 21 Club, the celebrated restaurant two blocks from Rockefeller Center. Bolster wanted Lauer to anchor *Today in New York*, the six-to-seven a.m. show on WNBC that preceded the nationwide *Today*. Lauer jumped at the opportunity. WNBC was the perfect place for him to build up his news credentials—the perfect practice for *Today*. Before long he was being noticed in two important places: the *Today* show control room and the NBC executive offices. Jack Welch, the CEO of GE, which owned the network at the time, "was a huge champion of Matt's," Andrew Lack recalled, as was Zucker, who noticed him early on at WNBC. The networks promote their morning shows by having "cross-talks" with big-city stations during the six a.m. hour, and Zucker noticed that when Lauer chatted with Couric or Gumbel in these teases, he had a comfort level that many local anchors lacked.

When NBC began to look for a new *Today* news anchor in 1993, Lack took a look at the tapes and at the live newscasts Lauer was cohosting. And he started checking off the boxes: Whip-smart. Experienced. Relatable. Humble. Self-deprecating. Lauer had it all. "You know, it's not hard to spot talent," Lack said humbly. "Whoever saw Mickey Mantle swing a bat first knew this guy could play baseball. Matt's a Mickey Mantle."

What was special about Lauer, he said, was an ability to comfortably talk to anyone about anything. "Matt could talk to a fire hydrant for three hours. And you need that," Lack said. "He'd actually be curious about fire hydrants. Why paint it red? Is that where the spout goes? Why? Is there a chain on the spout? Why do you have a chain?

"You can't teach that to people," Lack added. "You can teach craft—you've got thirteen seconds till break, look at this camera—but you can't teach curiosity."

Lauer started filling in as the *Today* show news anchor in 1993. He got the official nod the following year, joining Gumbel and Couric as a cast member and frequently filling in for them. The newly crowned *People*'s Sexiest Man Alive was excused from the WNBC morning show gig, but he continued to host that station's *Live at Five* until 1996—alongside, as it happened, his future *Today* show sidekick Al Roker, who at the time was the weatherman on WNBC.

As the heir apparent to Gumbel, Lauer stuck to the "certain paychecks I couldn't accept" strategy outlined by Lindner. He turned down a chance to host a new show called *Access Hollywood*, and, partly because doing so helped him preserve his journalistic integrity, was named the new cohost of *Today* when Gumbel decided to retire. Gumbel was clearly happy to turn over the chair to Lauer, which made his fans happy; in fact, it was the kind of transition every executive dreams about. The streak was entering its second year then, and Lauer only made the show stronger. His chemistry with Couric was legendary. "Do we get credit for recognizing it and producing it well? I hope so," said Zucker, their producer in the 1990s. "But the fact is, the two greatest stars in the history of morning television both walked into our door within years of each other in their mid-thirties. You know?"

In morning TV, some producers say, there are two types of hosts: actors and reactors. When Lauer became a cohost in 1997, Couric was the star: she was the actor, and he was the reactor to her. It was noticeable in small but important ways: who spoke first, who set up jokes, who started and ended each broadcast. Then, when Couric left for CBS, the roles changed. Lauer stepped up and became the actor, and Meredith Vieira was the reactor to him. They knew their roles and played them exceptionally well.

Lauer was skeptical that Curry could do the same. Months before Curry was promoted, while Vieira was leaning toward leaving *Today* and Lauer was weighing whether he should, too, he talked to his old friend Couric about an idea that would have dazzled the television industry—a syndicated daytime show that would reunite the *Today* legends. The idea of a one-hour daily chatfest held considerable appeal for both Lauer and Couric. Since such shows are typically taped in advance, it would allow him a much more normal home life. And they could probably make the move without taking a significant pay cut. Couric had already been talking to Zucker about a solo show that would fill the void that Oprah Winfrey was about to create by moving to cable television. Zucker told friends that Lauer called him in late 2010 (as Zucker was packing up his NBC office) and uttered a phrase that millions of Americans have no doubt dreamed of saying: "Will you create a show for me and Katie?"

Lauer and Couric also batted around the idea of another kind of reunion—as daily cohosts of the *Today* show. Lauer, according to one of his friends, was very interested in this possibility—and not just because he was anxious about the prospect of Curry sitting next to him. Despite the squabbles they'd sometimes had over A-list interviews and airtime when they worked together, "Katie and Matt knew they were better with the other one there," the friend said.

Couric and Lauer met up several times to talk about reuniting in some way. Her representatives imagined this scenario: Couric could come back to *Today* in the fall of 2011, take over for Vieira, and cohost with Lauer for two years. NBC, during that time, could very publicly groom two new hosts. Then Couric and Lauer could hand off the show to them and move to an afternoon time period as the cohosts of a talk show for NBC stations. Curry would be stiffed again, and would almost surely stalk off. But her departure might be overshadowed by an historic Couric-Lauer reunion. Couric admits she was mildly intrigued by the idea of returning to *Today*. "I feel like it would have been a fun thing to reunite and to show that you *can* go home again," she said. "But I also thought, there's a reason why I left the show." Ultimately, it was merely a great moment in mootness. Bell did ask whether she'd think about returning to *Today*, but no one at NBC ever actually extended an offer to her. ("I'm not sure if I would have considered it seriously," she said.) And because Lauer was contractually tied to his *Today* duties for nearly two more years, and Zucker and Couric were looking at a September 2012 start date for a syndicated show, the timing was wrong for their combined attempt to replace Oprah. A reunion in the daytime "wasn't really viable," said Zucker.

So Vieira left, Curry came in, and Lauer contemplated leaving for less awkward pastures. By the time the sixtieth anniversary show rolled around, everyone had started to say that Lauer was inching toward the exit. "I think our competitors started thinking that way," Capus said. "I think the people who cover us started thinking that way. It became an echo chamber. Everybody started talking to each other, 'Hey, Matt's leaving, Matt's leaving. What are they going to do, what are they going to do?'"

But Lauer himself wasn't as certain as everyone seemed to think he was. Yeah, he'd been on a strange sleep cycle for fifteen years. He'd been trailed by paparazzi from the *National Enquirer*, which had repeatedly printed rumors about his cheating on his wife. (For what it's worth, some executives at NBC told me they believed the rumors, including the one about a relationship with Natalie Morales. But no one believed the malicious claim that the *Enquirer* said was circulated by competitors about a "love child." A spokeswoman for Lauer and Morales denied the affair and called the allegations reckless and irresponsible. Maybe what's more important is that the executives didn't think Lauer's behavior, real or imagined, had hurt the show.) At work he'd uttered countless words put in his mouth by writers and producers who didn't share his news sensibilities. Who would sign up for more of that? Then again, he made more money in a week than most Americans made in a year. He had a four-day workweek, access to NBC's fleet of corporate jets, and a small army of staff to prep him for stories and persuade presidents to talk to him. His television program was one of the most popular in the country. Men fantasized about being him; women fantasized about sleeping with him (surely some of those men did, too). To an entire generation of aspiring television journalists, he represented the pinnacle, the peak of the profession. And, at age fifty-four, he had so many productive years ahead of him.

A deliberate person by nature, and also genuinely unsure of how he felt about moving on, Lauer said he wanted to postpone negotiations with the network until after the Summer Olympics, which would end in August, four and a half months before his contract expired. "He was saying, 'I'll wait until the end of the year and then see what's out there,'" said one of Lauer's friends.

Lauer was well within his rights to suggest such a thing. But Burke and Bell couldn't be that patient. They wanted Lauer locked up contractually by April 1, a date that Burke rather arbitrarily came up with. So in February Burke officially put Lauer in the loop about the plot to replace Curry with Savannah Guthrie. Not everyone agrees on the sequence of events here. Lauer's protectors say Burke never explicitly stated the connection between Lauer's renewing his contract and Curry's losing her cohost chair. They say he told Lauer that Curry would be gone regardless of his decision to stay or go. Lauer was against it, these people say, and he told them immediately that he thought it was a bad idea. "You're willing to risk losing both of your coanchors?" he asked, and was told yes.

But this sequence of events makes very little sense. Why would NBC take that risk?

Other people with knowledge of what went down say that Lauer's staying and Curry's leaving were explicitly connected by Burke. According to one of these people, Burke told Lauer, "We need to sign you so we can do Ann." This makes more sense. As a top NBC executive said to me after the fact, "Matt's decision guided everything else."

What is clear is that, despite reports to the contrary, Lauer never negotiated to have Curry's ouster guaranteed in writing. Lauer didn't want or need such a cutthroat clause because he was assured early in the process that she was a goner. Suddenly one of Lauer's biggest hesitations about sticking around—that he'd be sitting next to Curry for years to come—wasn't even worthy of a second thought. That's how this business works.

To further motivate him to make up his mind quickly, Burke offered Lauer a financial incentive—a signing bonus of several million dollars, according to one person with direct knowledge of it—if he reenlisted by April, and said NBC was immediately opening the so-called contract window that allowed him to talk to other prospective employers, rather than waiting until later in the year to open it.

One signal that Lauer had come around to NBC's expedited timeline was that he started those preliminary discussions as soon as NBC said he could. Lauer had a late breakfast at the Manhattan power spot the Regency with Richard Plepler, a copresident of HBO, where Gumbel had a monthly sports newsmagazine. He also had an early lunch with Jeff Fager, the chairman of CBS News, about a spot on *60 Minutes*. CBS wasn't prepared to offer Lauer even half as much money as NBC; as Fager later put it, "it was a pure play on pride." Still, Fager sensed that Lauer had thought about the possibility. "When any one of us has a contract up, you see it as an opportunity in life to make sure you're going in the right direction," he said.

Lauer's only really serious discussions were with the Walt Disney Company, the parent of ABC, which had become the home for Couric and Zucker's forthcoming daytime talk show. Disney had been putting out feelers to Lauer for years. Thus it hardly seemed notable when Ben Sherwood, who knew Lauer from his time at NBC, met him for a social lunch on the East Side of Manhattan shortly after stepping into the ABC News presidency at the end of 2010. But now Disney was in full pursuit mode. In early March 2012, a few weeks before Burke's proposed April deadline, a wide-ranging package was put on the table by ABC: Lauer could join Couric on her talk show, have a high-profile role at ABC News, and contribute to ESPN, the sports empire also controlled by Disney. Notably, the package did not include a role on *GMA*. ABC thought, rightly, that Lauer would not even consider such an act of betrayal. Besides, as a practical matter, he didn't want to wake up early anymore. At least that's what he told Disney.

Lauer had a fruitful meeting with Disney chief executive Robert Iger in New York, according to people with knowledge of the negotiations. Iger, one of these people said, was genuine and "touched all the right buttons." Lauer also sat down repeatedly with Anne Sweeney, the president of Disney/ABC Television Group. The same person who praised Iger said Sweeney "didn't seem to care as much about Matt coming to ABC." She wondered whether Lauer, or any news personality for that matter, was worth a twenty-million-dollar-plus annual salary while ABC was actively trying to reduce anchor and reporter salaries elsewhere. But others with knowledge of the negotiations disputed this. Either way, the prospect of reuniting with Couric—and with Zucker, the producer of the syndicated show—was evidently quite tempting for Lauer. ABC thought, for a little while at least, that it had snared NBC's star. "There were a number of days where it seemed to us that Matt was gonna come," Sherwood said later.

One reason the ABC folks might have gotten that impression was that Lauer's talks with NBC got off to such a poor start. Another person with knowledge of the negotiations pointed out that Lauer "was not happy with the management change there"—by which the person meant Comcast and Burke. None of this has ever been said on the record, and odds are it never will be: paychecks in Lauer's league come with the understanding that no ill will toward the company will come out. But it exists, right alongside immense gratitude for the opportunities the company affords him. Comcast "was blowing it in the early going," one of the people with knowledge of the negotiations said. "Not over money—there was money. But there was a coldness to it. A coldness to it."

NBC took the talks seriously; they were known internally as the "big picture" discussions, since the network was ready to offer him just about anything to stay. Want more stories on *Dateline*? Easy. Want a show on the Golf Channel? Done. But remember: Lauer had tried to warn his bosses about what a Curry-cohosted *Today* show could look like, and they'd gone and done it anyway. For that reason, among other obvious ones like money and curiosity, the door to ABC "was wide open. Wide open," said the person, who wisely noted, "David Letterman went to CBS for one reason only. NBC opened the garden gate and said, 'Bye.' That's the only reason David Letterman is on the CBS television network today. NBC opened the garden gate with Matt. They're fortunate to still have him."

Lauer had all the leverage in the world. NBC had no obvious successor, a clear failing on the part of the network executives—but also a testament to how few men out there are in Lauer's league. Ryan Seacrest is one of them, and when his name was floated in late 2011, he didn't do much to discourage the speculation; nor did Bell, who may have wanted the world to think that *Today* had options in case Lauer up and left. But let's be honest: Seacrest, who already had his own morning radio show, wasn't about to upend his life in Los Angeles to host *Today*, and NBC wasn't about to put him in that chair without grooming him for years. His talks with NBC were primarily about a fat new contract encompassing everything from E! to the Olympics. The eventual contract included a bit about his being a special correspondent on *Today*, propping the door open for a real seat in Studio 1A someday. But for the time being that seat was still Lauer's. Right around April Fools' Day he decided to stay at NBC, the network that had made him a superstar. Maybe he'd just used ABC to scare his bosses, or maybe he got scared by the prospect of leaving. Lauer, after all, is so predictable he's borderline boring: he once called himself "a bit of an OCD person" and, as evidence, said, "God forbid someone comes over and moves a coffee-table book; I move it back three inches to where it was."

The spurned executives at ABC wondered if one factor that figured into Lauer's decision was Couric's appearance as a cohost for a week on *GMA*, starting on Monday, April 2. Her guest stint—she was filling in for Robin Roberts, who was on vacation—had been heavily advertised for four days in advance and had forced *Today* into a defensive position, as demonstrated by the desperate booking of Sarah Palin as counterprogramming. Many people on the staff truly thought *Today* could lose for the first time in sixteen years, and Lauer could see the fear in their eyes. In the end Couric failed to move the Nielsen needle, but ABC's exercise in stunt-casting showed that as *GMA* mounted its calculated assault on NBC's winning streak (now at 851 weeks), the network was ready to show a little swagger.

NBC executives denied that the competition played a role in Lauer's decision, and he didn't mention Couric when, in a CNN interview on May 30, he discussed his decision to stay put. But he did describe feeling protective of and loyal to an organization that had made him rich and famous. "I think that I have fed off the company trough at NBC for a long time, and I had been the benefactor of great success there," he said. "Times are harder there right now. I think it's been well publicized. We are—the show is not where I want it to be right now. The ratings are not where I want them to be.

"I want to make it better," he continued. "I want to, you know, reinvigorate the show in some ways that perhaps we have, you know, let up on in the past couple of years. And so to leave now seemed like leaving when work needed to be done." He paused. "I think it would have been a lot easier to leave if we were soaring to new heights, but the competition is tougher. There are a lot of challenges out there and as a result, that just didn't feel like the right time to leave the people."

April 5 was visiting day at the Taft School, an exclusive boarding school in Connecticut where Burke's fourteen-year-old daughter was considering enrolling. Burke was in one of the classrooms, sitting in on one of the classes, when his BlackBerry buzzed. It was Lauer's agent, Lindner. The day before, April 4, Lauer had called Burke and told him he wanted to stay, and now Lindner needed to hash out the remaining details of the deal. Burke ducked outside and spent the better part of the next six hours on a park bench, cell phone to his ear, while his family members continued the tour. "Dad, you shouldn't have even come," his daughter told him afterward. But the deal got done. NBC re-upped its morning MVP.

Then Lauer phoned ABC. For Zucker, it was personal: he had lost the fight with his former network, though in retrospect it might not have been a fight at all. "He was never going to leave NBC," Zucker said a few months later.

At about six p.m. on the fifth, Capus called *The New York Times* to trumpet his news. "Matt is the franchise, and our franchise player has decided to keep leading our team," Capus said. Maybe he should have stopped there. But he continued, "Matt always said he would only continue if he could be all-in. The all-in factor was really key. This is a demanding job with a demanding schedule. For him it was a question of lifestyle. As his family is getting older he wants to be able to spend more time with them." As head-scratching statements go, that one was positively Curry-esque. How could staying on the job lead to more quality time with the kids? The answer: it couldn't, as Lauer's wife Annette knew. She was openly disappointed with her husband's decision. When I brought up the deal to her a few weeks later, she said, somewhat bitterly, "Two more years, and then he's mine."

Lauer's re-upping might have been the ultimate retaliatory stunt by the *Today* show at the end of *GMA*'s brazen Couric Week. But Lauer didn't want it to come across that way. He thought on-air hoopla about a huge new contract would be detrimental to his regular-guy image. On the April 6 *Today* show, opposite Couric's last day on *GMA*, Lauer's big announcement was barely teased at all. When it came up at seven fifteen, right after the morning's news headlines, Lauer started off sheepishly and self-consciously by poking fun at his receding hairline. "Truth be told, I was developing an idea for a new show, where viewers could tune in every morning and see someone they know lose a little more of his hair every single day right in front of their eyes." But "I thought, 'I don't have to do that, I could just stay here and do that!'" Then, knowing that the viewers like nothing more than harmony with their morning grits, he showed the world a serene face. He confirmed that he'd renewed and said, "This is my family. I love this job. I love working with you guys and all the people behind the scenes. I'm excited. Let's keep going."

Curry, who had confided to friends that she felt Lauer's shoulder would only get colder now that he had renewed, wrapped up the segment with one of her signature "Huh?"-inducing sign-offs. "We're stuck with you for a long time," she said. "So let's have some fun."

The contract renewal was a Brobdingnagian accomplishment for Burke, Capus, Bell, and NBC News as a whole. Lauer's future had been a frustrating question mark for the better part of two years. The executives felt that the renewal reaffirmed their commitment to real news reporting, in contrast to what they privately called "the crap on *GMA*." Capus felt he should have been hailed by the press as a fighter for quality and integrity. But reporters didn't want to talk much about Lauer, except to ask if it was true that his contract contained a "dump Curry" clause. They were onto something; changes were coming. Capus still believed he could stop or at least stall the second phase of Operation Bambi, the elimination of Curry—he was recommending that any change happen at the end of the year, no sooner. December was a logical time, right after the presidential election. But Bell and Burke believed in their Olympics timetable.

Along with the Curry chatter, the *Today* show spokeswoman Megan Kopf had something else to downplay: the price tag on Lauer's contract. Unlike other TV stars—his former cohost Couric comes to mind—Lauer never wanted anything about his salary known. But anonymous sources with knowledge of his deal did, and they put out a big round number: twenty-five million a year. Kopf swore the number was inaccurate, and at her urging Lauer later started using a quip that they hoped would put a damper on the money talk: "I have not heard anybody come up with the right amount."

On *Saturday Night Live* that week, Seth Meyers had a better one-liner: "I think the answer to 'Where in the World Is Matt Lauer?' might be 'Buried under strippers and blow.'"

Even if the number was, say, twenty-two million instead of twenty-five million, Lauer was still by far the richest man on morning television, in the history of morning television. Inside

ABC there were two reactions to the Lauer deal. One was a tepid little joke that implied, probably rightly, that NBC had to pay Lauer more given the strengthened state of *GMA* and the weakened state of *Today*: "We will await our commission." The other response took the form of a rhetorical question: How soon, everyone wanted to know, before Ann Curry is gone?

# CHAPTER 5

---

# Denial

ON FRIDAY THE THIRTEENTH of April, exactly a week after Lauer announced his contract renewal, Jim Bell stopped by Ann Curry's dressing room. There was, he said, something they needed to discuss. He alluded to a problem of some sort, but he didn't say what the problem was, or whether it was a trifling matter or something important. With Curry set to go on vacation to California for a week, Bell said—rather cruelly, Curry's supporters would later maintain, for it was a remark that seemed designed to unsettle the mind and remove the soothing effects of a vacation before they set in—"We need to talk as soon as you get back."

For all the millions that had been spent to secure Lauer's services and all the political maneuvering and press-leaking that had transpired since the first of the year, the most difficult part of Operation Bambi—the reverse seduction of Ann Curry—hadn't started in earnest yet. But it would soon enough.

By April, 2012 had already been a rough year for *Today*. There was the threat from *GMA* and the tension between Bell and Capus. And there was this: in late March the show accidentally but repeatedly broadcast audio clips of the 911 call that George Zimmerman made before shooting and killing seventeen-year-old Trayvon Martin in a Sanford, Florida, neighborhood. The way the clips were edited distorted Zimmerman's words grossly, giving them a strikingly racist cast. Since Zimmerman was Hispanic and Martin was African American, the shooting had sparked a national conversation about race, and by editing the tapes *Today* had unnecessarily inflamed it.

The circumstances of the error did not exactly heap glory on the *Today* show's journalistic standards and practices. The clip was first aired on March 20, in a report by Lilia Luciano, a then-twenty-seven-year-old Miami-based Hispanic correspondent who had been hired by NBC from Telemundo, its Spanish-language sister network, a year earlier, and who had no prior English-language reporting experience. She had been paired with a twentysomething producer whose experience with major news stories was also necessarily limited. In their report Zimmerman's words to the 911 operator were, "This guy looks like he's up to no good. He looks black." In fact, Zimmerman told the operator, "This guy looks like he's up to no good. Or he's on drugs or something. It's raining and he's just walking around, looking about." When the dispatcher asked, "OK, and this guy—is he white, black, or Hispanic?" Zimmerman then and only then said, "He looks black." Similar distortions aired in two other stories later in the month. Conservative Web sites picked up on the misquotation and accused NBC of bias and negligence. The network never even broadcast a correction or an apology.

Some of the criticism aimed at *Today* came from within. Journalists elsewhere at NBC News complained that the morning show was held to a lower standard than the rest of the division. "They are under such colossal pressure from *GMA* that all sorts of things pass muster there that wouldn't pass muster on *Nightly News* or *Dateline*," one veteran NBC correspondent said at the time.

Capus ordered an investigation into the 911 tape editing to find out who was at fault, but the findings were never made public. Amid pressure to deal with the mistakes swiftly and harshly,

Luciano was let go, the young producer was laid off, and several other producers were given disciplinary letters. The investigation was a further blow to the *Today* show staff's morale at a time when *GMA* had the ratings momentum and the fate of one cohost was an open question. While Capus was right to rigorously investigate the mistakes made with the Zimmerman tape, his actions were still seen by *Today* staffers as a way to poke around the show, embarrass Bell, and gain leverage over him. One longtime staffer said flatly, "This is Steve's way to hurt Jim."

Capus said that was not his motivation. But he could barely conceal his scorn for Bell at a town hall meeting he held in the *Today* show work space on Thursday the twelfth. Trying to provide a bit of the leadership that he believed Bell wasn't supplying, he spoke at length about the need for quality and accuracy in reporting. "We used to be *The New York Times*. Now we're the *Daily Mail*," Capus said, referring to the British tabloid that the morning shows treated as a tip sheet. He wanted that to change. He wanted fewer stories from TMZ and more from NBC's own reporters. He wanted the staff to cut back on sensationalistic crime stories—no more than one missing person story per day. (When ABC's James Goldston heard about this, he remarked to an associate, "Good—more missing people stories for me then!") Wrapping up his speech, Capus repeated the journalism maxim that it's better to be right than first. "I don't care if we're number two if we don't give up our principles," he said. The mere mention of falling to second place seemed to make many in the room uneasy.

Curry, by this point, would have to have been as dumb as a second-hour morning show segment not to have realized that something was up with her employment situation. Bell had been minimizing Curry and Lauer's time together on air, and had Guthrie fill in every time she was away. He had been trashing her in conversations with colleagues. And the leaks had already started.

On a March 13 episode of *TMZ Live*, the gossip kingdom's daily webcast, TMZ editor Harvey Levin reported that Lauer was on the verge of renewing his contract at NBC. "But," he added, "there's something else we know"—something that involved Curry. Twenty-five years before, Levin had worked alongside Curry for a time at KCBS, a Los Angeles TV station, and he said as much on the webcast. "I like Ann," he said. "Matt does not like Ann so much. I can tell you, it's well-known in NBC circles, in the building, that he just doesn't like her. He doesn't like working with her on the show, you know, whatever they say publicly about it, that's just the way it is." Levin didn't link the ideas of Lauer's staying and Curry's possibly leaving. But the on-screen graphic read, "ANN ON CHOPPING BLOCK."

Two weeks later Gawker ran this headline on its Web site: "Ann Curry Will Be Fired as Co-Host of the *Today Show* Because Everybody Hates Her." The accompanying report, written by the site's top editor, A. J. Daulerio, called it a "foregone conclusion" that "once NBC gives Matt Lauer his presumed mega-deal, Ann is as good as gone." Citing anonymous sources, he said those at the network called Curry "hopeless" and "atrocious" and added that Lauer was "fed up with watching Curry turn what was once NBC's most charismatic and engaging program into a joyless slog." The most cutting part of the piece was this passage, written in the snarkily postmodern Gawker style: "'Everybody knows she's gone,' said one source. 'Everybody knows she's gone,' said another. 'Everybody knows she's gone,' said another." The item, which came complete with a two-minute video of some of Curry's most embarrassing moments on *Today*—including mispronouncing Benjamin Netanyahu's name and starting a newscast by saying "Good morning, good morning everybody, in the news this morning, good morning"—scored two hundred thousand page views, making it one of the site's top stories of the month.

Where did these leaks come from? The answer is not known and may never be for certain, but Bell, according to a colleague, was at that time "really speaking out of school," criticizing Curry and praising Guthrie. He had even asked a young producer at *Today* to come up with a collection of clips documenting Curry's gaffes on the air. There was no apparent connection, however, between the blooper reel Bell commissioned and the Gawker video.

Kopf dismissed the talk about Curry's imminent reassignment as "100 percent gossip," unfit for print in respectable publications. Which of course it was not. While she issued specious denials, the ratings gap between the Big Two continued to shrink, causing even more stress. And right then, at the very moment NBC News PR needed all the help it could get—we're talking a fully pimped-out war room with crisis consultants and social media whiz kids and ample handfuls of Snickers and Kit Kats—Kopf's boss Lauren Kapp left for a job at the Huffington Post. Kapp was not only the best leak-plugger at NBC News, she was Capus's most trusted advisor and problem-solver. Kapp deserved a lot of the credit for the seamless handoffs from Couric to Vieira in 2006 and, even though this one might have been a mistake, from Vieira to Curry in 2011. But she wouldn't be around for the next one: Kopf would have to do it all herself.

On the twenty-third, with Bell's warning that "we need to talk" still on her mind, Curry returned to work and—ill-advisedly, some thought—brought up the ratings in an acceptance speech at the Matrix Awards, an annual ceremony for women in media. In front of hundreds in the grand ballroom of the Waldorf-Astoria Hotel she thanked "the exceptional men I get to work for today," then added, "I'm not sucking up, even though recent ratings events might dictate that I should." There was laughter and applause—but also some baffled looks. "What an awkward thing to say," remarked one male executive in the room. "But that's Ann Curry in a nutshell."

Curry may be mistake-prone, but she's no shrinking violet. The thrust of her speech that day was a critique of the boys' club that still ruled morning television and network news. "Considering that all my bosses—*all* my bosses"—she struck the podium with her left hand—"have been men, I have wondered what has happened to this hope for full equality in America," she said. "And I confess, I am weary of still living in a man's world. And I know I am not alone." There was applause again. "We are not done."

Curry said women in the media industry needed a renewed call to "know our worth" and to excel. "If we can close our eyes and just listen," she said, "we can almost hear the clamor of all these young, talented, smart young women coming up behind us. Cheering us on. Let their hopes and their dreams embolden us."

At *Today* it was generally agreed that the divide within *its* boys' club, that is, between Capus and Bell, undermined the show and distracted both executives from putting out a better product. Capus, as we've seen, technically had more power—Bell was supposed to report to him—but he was feeling pressure from the man *he* reported to, Burke, as well as from NBC's affiliates (both its owned-and-operated stations and those owned by other companies were suffering from the *Today* show's ratings slump), to "do something" before the start of the Olympics. The news division "had to satisfy the growing discontent," said a person who had read the e-mails and heard the calls from the affiliates.

To the extent that he was involved, Lauer was trying to have it both ways—giving Curry the proverbial cold shoulder but siding with Capus in the sense that he, Lauer, cautioned against making a sudden change against Curry's will. One confidant of both Lauer and Capus said they were advocating "a more nuanced, patient approach" than Bell was. Another said Lauer's message could be summed up in four words: "Give her more time." It wasn't because Lauer believed in Curry; to the contrary. Viewer research showed that having Curry to Lauer's left every morning was hurting him. (His Q Score, which was as high as nineteen in 2011, had fallen to fifteen. Curry's score had sagged, too.) But Lauer suspected that her hasty disappearance would hurt him further. "He was afraid of being blamed," one of his colleagues said forthrightly, as his best friend Gumbel had been blamed for the Pauley–Norville imbroglio. Gumbel's reputation arguably never recovered. So Lauer advised his bosses to be careful. "He *does* want Ann gone," a colleague of Lauer's said in April, "but he doesn't want to do it suddenly." Another colleague later recalled that Lauer said, "Let's not forget the lessons learned about other transitions."

While he and Capus advised caution, Bell took action. His Olympics clock was ticking. The week of the Matrix Awards luncheon, Bell took Curry to lunch at La Grenouille, one of his favorites, on Fifty-Second Street. Seated at what Zagat calls "the last (and best) of NYC's great classic French restaurants," they polished off two bottles of wine (Bell had the yeoman's share) and discussed The Problem, as he saw it, with the show: that Curry was "out of position." At some point fairly early in the meal he mentioned his solution: a new roving correspondent role for her, something better suited to her reportorial interests than *Today*. Bell reaffirmed his commitment to the kinds of overseas stories Curry had covered with such success in the past. To him, Bell said, trying to turn up the charm, Curry-as-roving-correspondent was not just a step toward better journalism, it was also a great way to brand *Today* as a serious show committed to important but oft-neglected stories. He may have even shared with Curry his pipe dream of trying to win for her the title of United Nations goodwill ambassador, a role she would share with Angelina Jolie, whom Curry had repeatedly interviewed about humanitarian issues.

It's worth noting here that many television journalists would have jumped at the once-in-a-career chance that was on the table. A pricey ticket, paid for by somebody else, to travel the country and the world! But the correspondent position was, of course, also a face-saving way for Curry to drop out of daily participation in an endeavor at which she was failing. As one person with ties to NBC put it, "They'll pretend Ann wants to go back to 'newsy news.'"

Although Curry was stunned by some of what she heard, the lavish lunch ended more or less amicably, with Bell proposing that she give some serious thought to the possibility he'd outlined. "I thought I'd gotten her halfway there," he later told colleagues.

As it turned out, he hadn't. Later, Bell's own colleagues would ridicule both his technique and his optimism. "At age fifty-four, she'd finally reached the top. This was never going to be Ann's idea," said one colleague who'd spent decades at NBC. Another colleague, one who viewed Curry with disdain, said "she had a huge sense of entitlement. She thought it was a Supreme Court appointment." Maybe—but to be fair, Couric and Vieira *had* held on to the chair as long as they'd wanted.

For all sorts of reasons, Curry was tough to reverse-seduce. Start with the fact that she had no agent. (After Alfred Geller died, she toyed with signing up with someone new but decided not to; she wanted to keep sending her commissions to his family.) Nor did she have a business manager or lawyer. This put Bell at a disadvantage: he had no one else to go to, no one else to bring into the conversation about her future. Looking back on Operation Bambi, NBC executives would conclude that her lack of representation had been a well-considered choice. Curry would look back and think her lack of representation had been a tactical failure, for it left her without a legal defender until it was too late.

Bell's belief that Curry was responsible for the ongoing ratings slippage was bolstered the week of their La Grenouille lunch. The week before, when Guthrie filled in for Curry, *Today* had had a strong week; when Curry came back from vacation, *GMA* had a strong week. While the weak numbers were objective fact, Curry would not cop to being their cause. She saw lame content—a daily diet of dubious fashion trends and equally dubious celebrity gossip—as the main explanation for the *Today* show's decline. As she told Capus, "Jim Bell has to fix this show."

Lauer did not disagree with her on this important point. In March, as he contemplated whether to stay or go, Lauer had confessed to a colleague that he felt the weight of the whole network on his shoulders—that in lieu of new ideas, NBC was relying on his talent and charisma. "There's more pressure on me now than there ever has been," he'd said. "They're relying on *Today* to prop up the whole network. If we fail..." He'd trailed off, leaving the consequences of failure unspoken. Lauer, like Curry and Capus, felt that the show needed a harder news bent. They both bemoaned their producers' use of TMZ and the British tabloid the *Daily Mail* for story ideas. But the stories the producers borrowed/stole about sensational murders and family feuds and shark attacks—one or two degrees shy of "trashy," the word they tagged *GMA* with—were the stories that tended to rate highest in the minute-by-minute ratings. They were staples of morning TV. Thus the *Today* family sometimes had its own feuds when Lauer called in to the office some afternoons and asked the senior producers what was in the next morning's "rundown," the second-by-second schedule of what will happen on the show. Lauer dismissed stories he didn't like (he particularly disliked the shark attack stories, staffers said) as "not relevant" to the audience at home. There are few places in midtown Manhattan more uncomfortable than the receiving end of that phone call.

Lauer knew that his involvement in story selection rankled some producers. But he wanted to resist pandering to the audience the way he thought *GMA* too often did. Whenever the ratings "tighten up, there is a little bit of a reaction to the other people—and I don't like it," Lauer told me in late April.

While Bell took issue with Lauer and Curry's views of how newsy a morning show should be—he was a strong believer in the traditional mix of serious and soft segments that had always been a hallmark of *Today*—he and his cohosts were united in their disdain for *GMA*. Bell called it a "freak show." Like Lauer, he frequently cautioned his staff not to get distracted by the competition, though that was much easier said than not done. He was proud of the quality of *Today*—the live shots from foreign countries, the better-living segments with financial experts, the kinds of stories he didn't see on *GMA*. He encouraged reporters to compare the content of the two shows and chastised those who didn't. "The competition in this case has chosen to do a very different show," Bell said later in the year. "If you watch them side by side you'll see. It's worked for them in the short term. But we're not going to do anything that's going to hurt our brand and the legacy of the *Today* show. We're going to stick to our knitting and be who we are."

Bell stuck to his belief that The Problem was not the time-tested formula—it was the way that formula was executed by Curry. But others began to worry that something bigger was broken. "It's not Ann," said one NBC executive at around this time. "Ann ain't great. But what about the show? *GMA* is quicker, faster, and smarter."

The *Today* show's predicament almost seemed straight out of a business school textbook. The brash advertising executive Donny Deutsch, a regular on the show's panel discussion "*Today*'s Professionals," told Bell that *Today* risked being a victim of its own success like General Motors, the automaker that had had nearly 60 percent market share in the 1960s, before Japanese automakers ravaged the business. "GM wasn't built to compete," Deutsch said. "Their whole premise was 'Don't break anything.' Then all of a sudden, when they really had to compete, it wasn't in their DNA. It's very hard for an enterprise that's been the dominant market leader to suddenly switch from 'leadership maintenance' mode to 'competitive counterpunch' mode."

Indeed, behind the scenes at *Today*, the tension seemed to increase daily, especially after Lauer renewed. Lauer was at odds with Bell, Bell's No. 2 Don Nash, and Noah Kotch, the seven a.m. producer who was known for his fixation on the daily ratings race. Kotch, despite his hard news background as Peter Jennings's head writer, programmed a disciplined menu of crime, sex, and celebrity scandal in the seven thirty half hour, which Lauer found particularly distasteful (but which morning viewers did not). Kotch's critics called him the "trash doctor." The atmosphere became so strained that Kotch started working from home in the mornings, not coming in until Lauer had left the office. Meanwhile Curry was saddled with more of the tabloid segments while Bell assigned Lauer the smarter segments to keep him happy-ish.

All the while, Operation Bambi was grinding on. Guthrie did her best to dodge the bountiful speculation about her future—and Curry's. Guthrie's usual tactic was to say, when asked about the personnel brouhaha, that she knew nothing—which in fact wasn't all that much of a stretch. Like everyone else, she had seen the Internet reports and heard the hallway whispers, but hadn't spoken a word about the subject to her NBC bosses. In fact, she'd gone a step further and instructed her agent not to pitch her for the job. She wanted to preserve her relationship with Morales, with whom she cohosted the nine a.m. hour.

Curry knew only a little bit more than Guthrie. She was processing the spiel about the roving correspondent's role that Bell had given her at their lunch—and the more she thought about it, the more she could see it for the easy letdown that it was. Sure, it could be touted as something prestigious like Christiane Amanpour's "foreign affairs anchor" position at ABC. But Amanpour, if you noticed, was barely ever seen on ABC. On television, airtime is oxygen, and leaving *Today* would be oxygen-depriving. It would be a demotion. Humiliated and angry, she decided she wasn't going anywhere without a fight. Two weeks after the lunch, on May 9, she sat down for a previously scheduled interview with *Ladies' Home Journal* and said something that would later scream to readers, "They forced me out": "I've been at *Today* for 15 years and I'd love to make it to 20."

For Curry it was the relatively little things—starting with Lauer's growing indifference, after a decade and a half of their working on the same set—that hurt the most, and, in the words of one staffer, "added up to an ominous feeling about her future at the show." Among the senior producers, Melissa Lonner was her sole defender as the others fell in line with Bell, whose actions were becoming increasingly heedless and, in the opinion of some, sophomoric. One day he called staffers into his office to chuckle at a verbal gaffe Curry had made during a cross-talk with a local station. More chuckling was heard when, for reasons that went unexplained, several boxes of Curry's belongings ended up in a coat closet—the sort of thing that would happen when a staffer left in a rush, or was unceremoniously booted off the premises.

A genuine meanness seemed to color the staff's attitude toward their troubled colleague, something that looked from certain angles like the giddiness brought on by a sense of doom. One staff member, offended by the behavior, said "a lot of time in the control room was spent making fun of Ann's outfit choices or just generally messing with her." On one memorable morning, Curry wore a bright-yellow dress that spawned snarky comparisons to Big Bird. The staffer, who called this day "extra harsh," said others in the control room Photoshopped a picture of Big Bird next to Curry and asked coworkers for a "Who wore it best?" comparison.

Given this behavior, it's not surprising that Curry asked an aide to put together a collection of her best field-reporting clips—what people at the show took to calling her "résumé tape."

A strange thing happened at around this time. Despite the dysfunctional nature of the *Today* family, the senior producers dusted off an old series called "*Today* Takes On," which looked very much like *GMA*'s ongoing attempts to demonstrate that its hosts were best buds. In "Takes On" segments the *Today* hosts would together do things like rowing with the Princeton University crew team and learning how to perform acrobatic feats at a Broadway show. During the latter episode, Curry, Lauer, Roker, and Morales were shown arm in arm, ready to leap off a platform for a finale-like moment. "Don't let go," Lauer said to Curry, looking nervous. "I'm not going to let go," Curry told him confidently. Viewers seemed to like the lighter-than-air segments. But if this exercise in chumminess sounds at odds with Operation Bambi, it wasn't really—at least if you listened to those well-placed observers who said that the point was to make the seemingly inevitable banishment of Curry look like a game of musical chairs played by dear friends.

Bell was willing to go to great and complicated lengths to make the Curry "transition" a smooth one. He knew that removing her would inevitably alienate some people who counted themselves her loyal fans. But he believed that if the show, as a result, took a temporary hit in the ratings, the decline would be (if the thing was handled with the appearance of sensitivity) minor, and *Today* would rebound during the Summer Olympics. Then Bell's bosses would be pleased, his job would be protected, and the morning show he loved would find its footing again. The Olympics loomed as both his salvation ("a once-every-two-year chance to introduce a new cast," said one executive) and an immovable deadline. But because Bell wanted Curry to buy into the change, and show the world through her own attitude and actions that she was making a choice for herself, he was willing to wait a week, and then another week, and then another, if that's what it took, to create the appearance of voluntary movement. In the meantime he told colleagues that Curry seemed unhappy at the show and eager to report more stories in the field. Everything Bell and his lieutenants did during this time was in the cause of "trying to get Ann to a place where she was comfortable with the move," said an NBC executive.

But it wasn't working. Rather than getting comfortable, Curry felt as if the walls were closing in. On May 15, while interviewing Betty White, who had stopped by the studio to promote her new hidden-camera show on NBC, Curry made a thinly veiled reference to her predicament. When White's other show, a sitcom on TV Land, came up, Curry exclaimed, "You've got two shows, you're ninety years old—honey, I mean, I barely am hanging on to one show!"

Many people believed Curry was in denial. Maybe—this is the more charitable point of view—she just didn't know who or what to believe. Lauer, for instance, had told her he didn't want her to leave. But he had also told her she needed to "protect" herself by hiring an agent. He was trying to help her, Lauer's allies said—he hated seeing her in this position. Bullshit, said *her* allies—he was just trying to protect *himself*.

Similarly, Capus had initially assured her that her seat on *Today* was safe. He still wanted nothing to change until the end of the year. But he had to start wooing Curry. A day before the Betty White interview, he told her to at least consider this roving correspondent idea. "They're trying to offer her something that will appeal to her," a staffer said after the meeting with Capus. "The sun, the moon, the stars—anything but sitting next to Matt every morning." Curry rebuffed the proposal once again. But by the end of May, a month after the lunch with Bell, she started confiding in friends about the situation. According to one of them, she hinted that the correspondent job might not be such a bad thing. But then why'd she tell *Ladies' Home Journal* on May 9 that she hoped to stay at *Today* for another five years? Some read sinister motives into the answer, but it could be viewed a different way: as proof that she truly thought she'd beat back Bell's attempts to push her out.

Curry decided not to talk to *The New York Times* TV critic Mike Hale, who was writing a column about her role on the show and had asked for an interview. But Lauer, knowing the piece was in the works *and* that Curry's removal was in the works, did agree to that aforementioned May 30 interview on CNN. His interviewer was a coworker and friend, Donny Deutsch, who was substituting for Piers Morgan, so Lauer knew he wouldn't be questioned about his concerns about Curry or his complaints about the show's sensational segments. But he would have a chance to publicly praise Curry in what would serve as a kind of advance obituary. She has "the biggest heart in broadcasting," Lauer said on the show, calling her "incredibly talented" and more concerned about other people "than anyone I've met." Without prompting from Deutsch, Lauer went on to say that he took responsibility for the show's recent ratings struggles. "When people start to write articles about what might be wrong with the *Today* show you know where you should point the finger, point it at me because I have been there the longest," he said. He added, "I truly feel that way, and that's why I stick around, because I think there's more I can do, I can do it better." Kopf, the *Today* spokeswoman who was trying to manage Hale's column, sent him the transcript of Lauer's interview, and he ended up including the finger-pointing quote.

Bell also praised Curry in an interview with Hale, calling her "one of the great journalists." Bell continued, "People nitpick certain details, but she is known and loved by our colleagues and our viewers, she's been doing this a very long time, she's had some moments that I don't think anyone else could have pulled off."

The TV screen told a much different tale. A few days after Lauer's interview on CNN, he flew to London for special coverage of Queen Elizabeth II's Diamond Jubilee. So did Roker and their old colleague Vieira, now a "special correspondent" for the network. But Curry didn't come along. She had Monday and Tuesday morning off; she was said to be picking up her teenage son from boarding school. Her absence was glaring—all the more so because the announcer said she'd be "live from Studio 1A" while Lauer was live at Buckingham Palace. Lauer had to correct the announcement. "Ann has the morning off," he said curtly.

Lauer and Vieira joked and teased each other all morning, reminding many viewers of their good old days—and rekindling rumors in the industry that NBC had approached Vieira about coming back to cohost, succeeding the woman who had succeeded her a year earlier. In fact, after they had casually taken Vieira's temperature by asking through her agent, Michael Glantz, if she would ever consider a comeback, and received a firm no, NBC executives dropped the matter of Vieira. They sensed she had several reasons for not wanting to return, among them a strong disinclination to be seen as hurting Curry. "There's no way she's going to help them with their Ann problem," said one of her friends.

Meanwhile, viewers of the highly rated jubilee coverage were left wondering: Where in the World Is Ann Curry? Kopf's in-box was a magnet for questions from reporters. "It's fucking unbeliev-able that she wasn't on," an NBC executive exclaimed that day, fed up with the mixed signals the network was sending about their still-sorta-new cohost.

Curry was back on *Today* on Wednesday, June 6. It was calm, sometimes even fun in the show's control room when I stopped by at the end of the week.

"All right, we're on," the jokester director Joe Michaels bel-lowed a minute into the show. "What do you want to do now?"

Snippets of conversation flew back and forth like code, almost indecipherable to an observer. "Talent heading in," someone said over a walkie-talkie. "Take Syria B-roll," a woman said from the back row during a news segment. "Just have her throw to Al," a man said to Michaels. Later, Roker and Michaels pretended to spar when Michaels showed two weather graphics out of order. Roker yelled through his microphone with a smile, "Do I have to come down there and staple the rundown to your forehead?" Michaels joked, "I'd like to start over. Can we start over?"

Come to think of it, their banter would make good TV.

Here, in the belly of the *Today* show beast, *GMA* was men-tioned only when I brought it up. CBS was never mentioned. But once in a while Lauer and Curry's concerns about content sprang to the surface, as when *Today* showed video of Ukrainian politi-cians punching each other in a brawl in parliament. As the video was shown over and over again during a news segment, Curry's mouth was agape in disgust. To protest the replay she started shak-ing her head no, knowing that the producers could see her in the control room. Later in the hour Curry interviewed a former Miss USA contestant, Sheena Monnin, who claimed the pageant was fixed. Monnin, booked on *Today* via a series of Facebook mes-sages, was a fan of Curry's; after the interview she told Curry, "I'll only do you." How many more Sheena Monnins were out there, watching *Today* every day just to see Curry?

Because Curry's imagined new role was going to be wide-ranging, beyond just the confines of the *Today* show, it fell to Capus to finish what Bell had begun at La Grenouille. Capus wanted to proceed slowly. But Burke, like Bell, still wanted to see the transition happen before the Summer Olympics. So in early June, with less than two months to go, Capus told Curry to go get a lawyer.

The lawyer Capus suggested to Curry was sixty-five-year-old Robert B. Barnett, a partner at the Washington firm Williams & Connolly. She agreed and signed him up. Barnett was uniquely situated because he did a dizzying number of different deals with all the major networks. He juggled corporate clients like Comcast (yep, the parent company of NBC), politicians like Bill Clinton and George W. Bush, and a stable of television stars like Brian Williams and Lesley Stahl. He routinely cut deals for splashy TV interviews tied to his clients' books. A genial man, at least until he invoked attorney-client privilege, he used the word *we* when speaking about the networks, as in "We produced a prime-time special." He was then in talks with all the networks about options for an exclusive interview with Amanda Knox, the American woman who was accused of murdering her roommate in Italy in 2007. So he was anything but naïve.

Curry might have viewed Barnett at first as a bulwark against her bosses' efforts, which were misguided in her mind, to rein her in. These secret wars happen all the time: a television star tells an agent or lawyer to "make it go away," whatever "it" is. Sometimes the agent or the lawyer succeeds. But in this case Barnett conferred with Curry's bosses and came back to her with bad news. "This is much more serious than you think," he told her, according to a person directly involved in the cohost change.

So the negotiations began. Curry's existing contract, worth nearly four million dollars a year, was coming due, and NBC was proposing that they rip it up and start over with a contract reflecting her new status as a roving correspondent. It's noteworthy that NBC didn't propose to just pay her off and be done with her—it truly wanted to keep her in the fold. The revised contract was worth about five million dollars a year for five years, according to two people with ties to NBC. It stipulated that Curry would be a national and international correspondent for NBC News. She'd have her own unit within the news division to produce her stories. She'd also anchor an unspecified number of prime-time specials. But she wouldn't anchor *Today*.

Curry wanted to believe the network was sincere, and not just trying to avoid a messy transition. "This is maybe for the better," she told one confidant, citing the chance to tell the stories of poor and disenfranchised people that were basically invisible on television. "I think she saw, on the merits of it, some advantages in leaving the cohost job and focusing on reporting," said her friend Nicholas Kristof. "At the same time," he added, "the way it was handled by NBC was just unforgivable. They humiliated her; they treated her in a way that I thought was just utterly insulting."

After a tense meeting on June 15, Curry cryptically posted to Twitter a quote attributed to Eleanor Roosevelt: "You must do the things you think you cannot do." Partly Curry felt she had indeed failed. But the other part of her felt she had been betrayed—not just by Bell, but by Lauer, too. Why would she want to stay at a network that treated her this way?

She also had to realistically consider what this new role would entail. Yes, she'd have her own unit of producers—but she wouldn't be tied to any specific show, so she'd have to fight for airtime on NBC's newscasts just like every other correspondent. "Frankly, foreign correspondent at a broadcast network is not even a full-time job these days," one longtime observer said, remarking on the scarcity of foreign-news coverage on the networks.

While Capus and Barnett secretly negotiated in Capus's office on the third floor of 30 Rockefeller Center the week of June 18, Curry kept showing up for work, though some mornings she looked rattled on the air. Staffers not privy to Operation Bambi could sense that something big was brewing—word was spreading about her hiring Barnett—though they didn't know what, exactly. Curry's friends could sense the same thing. One friend had been planning a blowout party to celebrate Curry's first full year as cohost, but those plans were scrapped.

The rumors came to a head on Wednesday, June 20, the same day that *The New York Times* published Mike Hale's review of Curry's first year as cohost. Hale zeroed in on Curry's difficulty "with the abrupt shifts in tone that are required of the morning show host" and her tendency to try too hard while chitchatting with Lauer and quizzing newsmakers. But those flaws, he wrote, were less important than this one: "As you watch the show, there's an inescapable sense that Curry is outside the group in a subtle but unmistakable way, like the stepsister Cinderella without a prince."

Eight hours later I wrote this on *The New York Times* Web site: "NBC executives are making a plan to replace Ann Curry on the 'Today' show, only a year after she became the co-host of the newly vulnerable morning television franchise." The secret was now out. The timing of the two stories was coincidental. I had asked Bell for a comment, and Capus and Curry, too, but no one had responded. Capus and Bell later blamed my story for torpedoing the negotiations. Curry later said the story prevented her from leaving *Today* gracefully. But neither she nor Capus nor Bell tried at all to stop or stall publication, as the subjects of stories often do.

Public knowledge of the negotiations may have helped both sides: it applied pressure to Curry and Barnett to accept the offer before the Olympics, but it also allowed Curry to rally her fans, now that they knew what NBC was doing. In the end, Curry felt she had little choice but to take the new contract. ABC wasn't calling to hire her. Neither was CBS. She wasn't going to make nearly as much money anywhere else. So she was stuck at NBC, doing what NBC wanted her to do.

Word spread around NBC at four p.m. on the twentieth that the story of Curry's imminent departure from *Today* was about to come out. A colleague called Lauer, who was at the gym, to give him a heads-up. "My hands are clean," Lauer responded.

About an hour later, Curry called in sick for the next morning's show. She feared she'd be overcome by emotions on air.

The story hit *The Times'* Web site at five fifteen. "NBC Prepares to Replace Ann Curry on *Today*," read the headline. A group of *Today* show staffers huddled around one person's computer—as if they didn't all have their own—and read it together. The story quoted a person who knew Curry who said she was leaving with great reluctance: "She got her dream job, and she doesn't want to let it go." Later in the day Bell told colleagues that Curry was the source of the story. But she was not.

With Curry out "sick," Hoda Kotb, who was on a day trip to Nashville and about to board a flight back to New York, was lined up to fill in for her. (People at NBC speculated that Kotb was chosen to shield Guthrie, Curry's usual fill-in, from criticism.) But as the evening wore on, Curry had a change of heart. After all, how would it look if she didn't show up for work in the morning? How would her fans react? She e-mailed a group of producers and said, "I'm coming in tomorrow"; the e-mail was forwarded to Bell, who replied with one confusing word, "Discussing."

Matters sorted themselves out during Kotb's flight to New York. When she landed, at about nine p.m., she found out that she was off the hook. Curry was going to host for at least one more morning.

☀ ☀ ☀

"ANN'S CANNED," read the front page of the *Daily News* the next morning. It wasn't quite true yet. But the vibe in Studio 1A on that Thursday was something other than business as usual. Before the broadcast, a security guard stood watch outside Curry's dressing room. His presence might have been connected to a security breach earlier in the week, when an unauthorized man had talked his way into the studio. But it was also true that Curry was being very careful about whom she saw and who saw her. When a producer, Sean Reis, came to brief Curry before the show, he was briefly admitted inside the dressing room, and saw that she was in tears.

At 6:28, Curry—unsmiling but no longer visibly upset—walked downstairs to the studio. She affixed a microphone to her blouse and took her seat at the anchor desk. She didn't speak.

Lauer came in a minute later and chatted with Don Nash. Then he took his seat at the desk. He didn't speak either. He didn't acknowledge her, and she didn't acknowledge him. They both just stared down at their scripts.

The time passed painfully slowly: 6:32...6:33...6:34...Curry brushed her hair out of her eyes. Lauer hunched over, as if carrying a heavy weight on his back. He sipped his coffee, wiped off his reading glasses, and waited to record the first tease for local stations. The most promotable story was Lauer's exclusive interview with the Connecticut mother whose children had all died in a Christmas Day fire. Lauer read the tease, looked down, looked back into the camera, bantered with the control room producers, and waited for his next cue. Ten minutes had passed now, and still he hadn't said a word to Curry or turned right to look at her.

If it was chilly in the studio, outside on the plaza it was already eighty degrees. The news ticker that encircled the studio said nothing about Curry's status, of course. And no one on the show said anything either, despite the fact that curious viewers were tuning in to see if Curry would appear for work. (Among those viewers were the producers of *GMA*, who guessed that *Today* would have Savannah Guthrie fill in. They were impressed that Curry showed up.) Curry maintained her composure, handling segments about the hot weather and the Jerry Sandusky trial as if it were any other day. But she did come up with one sly way to acknowledge the surreal situation. Four minutes into the show she wrote to her 1.2 million followers on Twitter, "Good morning." It was no big deal—except that Curry didn't usually post anything on Twitter during the show. "Good morning" was a wink to her fans—and they caught it, posting thousands of heartfelt replies. Her name was a trend on Twitter by the end of the first hour. "Save Ann Curry," some of the Twitter messages read. "Don't give up the fight," said others.

During the second hour, the *Today* control room made the mistake of showing the words "Here Today, Gone Tomorrow" below Curry's face as she interviewed Steve Carell, the star of a new movie called *Seeking a Friend for the End of the World*. The industry Web site TVNewser caught it, posted a picture of the graphic, and asked, "Really, 'Today' show?"

Why did Curry even show up for work that morning? Some at the network suggested she was trying to drum up public support: soldiering on, they said, was a way of garnering sympathy. "It sounds like she doesn't want to go quietly," one senior NBC staffer said after Thursday's show. Her detractors compared her to Conan O'Brien, who was briefly made the host of *The Tonight Show* in 2009. When his predecessor Jay Leno's attempt at a ten p.m. talk show failed, NBC proposed to move Leno to eleven thirty and O'Brien to 12:05 a.m. O'Brien resisted the plan and gained widespread support on social networking Web sites. O'Brien's resistance was public: he issued a press release about his predicament and made it the punch line to jokes on his last week hosting *Tonight*. Curry, in contrast, said little while NBC's mishandling of her became the punch line. When Curry appeared on

Thursday's show, an anchor at another network e-mailed Kristof and said this:

> Really fucking cruel how NBC is treating her.
> She does a lot of great and important work.

Kristof wrote back:

> She's irreplaceable. I'm hoping she lands with her spotlight intact.

The anchor followed up:

> One of the worst things about tv, the way executives destroy their own talent.
> Very telling detail in Bill Carter's book on late night—zucker suggesting best case scenario is leno works at 10, conan at 1130. Second best is one of them succeeds and the other is so damaged he cannot compete against NBC.

They may or may not have cared who was damaged in the long run, but Burke, Capus, and Bell were determined to come out of this difficult moment with all of their talent smiling. That was starting to look like an impossible mission. Before that fateful Thursday broadcast was over, Lauer, who after a lengthy holdout had only recently agreed to let NBC set him up with a Twitter account, was deluged with messages asking him if it was true that Curry was being forced out, or accusing him of getting her fired. Some commenters didn't bring up Curry at all; they simply informed Lauer that he was "obnoxious," "terrible," and "lame."

The gossip Web sites were no less active. While NBC was keeping mum about Curry's fate, TMZ and Radar Online were saying that Lauer had effectively stabbed her in the back. In their enthusiasm for pummeling Lauer, they also dredged up allegations about Lauer's extramarital affairs and reprinted the salary figure—twenty-five million—that he had so strenuously denied.

Capus, Bell, and Kopf all fumed as complaints about Lauer piled up. He was the future of the franchise. But he was also its possibly egg-flecked face. Prophetically, Andrew Wallenstein, of *Variety*, wrote on Friday morning that Lauer "stands to lose" in the wrenching transition to come:

> Put yourself in the sensible shoes of the soccer moms who are the foundation of the "Today" fan base, and Curry's departure could come off in a way that isn't too flattering for Lauer. The broad strokes of the media coverage to date appears as: "Today" is in trouble, Curry is the weak link, and Lauer believes she needs to go.
>
> And that narrative will only get worse on TV where Lauer risks looking caddish as he tosses aside his on-air partner and trades her in for what will probably be a younger, more conventionally beautiful-looking woman, if the reports of the ascendance of Savannah Guthrie and Natalie Morales are to be believed.
>
> Oh, the soccer moms are going to just *looove* that.
>
> On an almost primal level, the Lauer-Curry pairing feels uncomfortably close to a bad Lifetime movie. She devoted 15 years of her life to "Today" only to get kicked to the curb to make room for another female. And whether you like Curry or not, viewers have to be feeling for her given the beating she is taking in the press.

Thursday the twenty-first passed by without a deal, despite rumors that Friday would be her final day on the broadcast. Some executives at NBC grumbled that by not doing the inevitable and signing her contract, Curry was behaving unprofessionally, holding the show hostage to her emotions. "Some of them are ready to pull the plug," meaning fire her, claimed one person with ties to the negotiators on Friday. All weekend, all Kopf could do was deny that anything unhappy or untoward was about to go down. On Monday morning Lauer took his regularly scheduled day off and Willie Geist of *Morning Joe* filled in for him. Curry looked a little happier on air, and apparently off air, too: she and Geist chatted freely in the makeup room before the show, and the makeup artist remarked afterward, "That was the most she's talked in a week."

Backstage, Curry wouldn't speak to Bell; when she had a question about a segment, she contacted Nash. ("Your girlfriend's on the line," Bell quipped when Curry called Nash from the set, according to a colleague.) She was barely seen in the office after the show—"AWOL," said one producer. On Tuesday morning, with Lauer back in the chair next to her, TMZ claimed that Curry didn't want to stay at NBC. That wasn't true; neither was the report of her ten-million-dollar yearly salary, or the report that Guthrie's deal was already done. But the stories did further damage to the family that NBC had spent years and millions building up and up and up. "Even if you loathe Curry, you have to feel sympathy for her," observed Jon Friedman of MarketWatch. "NBC News used to be very good at handling major on-air change," noted David Zurawik of the *Baltimore Sun*. "The passing of the baton from Tom Brokaw to Brian Williams was textbook for how it should be done. But what NBC News president Steve Capus and his lieutenants are doing to Ann Curry as they let her twist in the wind at 'Today' is brutal."

Capus felt he was the one twisting in the wind. The apropos word for Curry's attitude might have been the one her mother had taught her, *gambaru*, meaning "Never ever, ever give up, even and especially when there is no chance of winning." But by Tuesday the twenty-sixth she had begun to accept her fate as a highly paid but probably underused NBC semi-star, and Guthrie had begun to talk to the network about reluctantly (under these circumstances) taking over.

Curry felt surprisingly little antipathy toward Guthrie. But she worried that her departure, if handled wrongly, would hurt *Today* even more than it already had been. "Ask them to call me something that's still related to the *Today* show," she said to Barnett ahead of a scheduled meeting with Capus. Barnett subsequently proposed "*Today* anchor at large," and Capus agreed. The last sticking point in Barnett's negotiations with the network was office space. This was a real prize in the close quarters of Rockefeller Center, and Curry wanted contiguous office space for her and her new unit of producers. On that matter, she got what she wanted.

☀ ☀ ☀

It was 6:33 a.m. when Lauer walked into Studio 1A on Wednesday the twenty-seventh. This was the last day he would have to pretend that nothing strange was happening at the *Today* show.

Curry was already at the anchor desk, preparing for teases for local stations—for the last time. Tomorrow she'd announce that she was stepping aside.

Lauer waited five minutes before sitting down. First he stood at the news desk while Curry read a tease; then he walked over to one of the floor-to-ceiling windows facing the plaza, where a few dozen people were standing already, waiting for their second of TV infamy. Protected by the tint of this window, Lauer was nearly invisible to the crowd.

What would this crowd think of him tomorrow?

Lauer and Curry didn't acknowledge each other when he sat down next to her. She reached for the morning's *The New York Times* and started reading the foreign section. A few minutes before airtime she said she felt self-conscious about her arms and tried on a black cardigan over her sleeveless pink dress. She asked the crew, but not Lauer, for their opinions; then she took off the cardigan and tugged at her dress to cover a bit more of her arms.

On the air, Lauer and Curry seemed to talk past each other. Some viewers, having read all about NBC's negotiations, were amazed that Curry was still there at all. "The Ann Curry hostage crisis continues," wrote one viewer on Twitter while watching Wednesday's show. "Ann Curry couldn't look sadder this morning," wrote another. "Is it just me or does Ann Curry look like she's going to cry?" asked a third. For NBC, the only good thing about the situation was that *Today* was still beating *GMA* in the overnight ratings, thanks in part to the public's curiosity about what would happen next.

On the evening of the twenty-seventh, Curry called from home and asked the supervising producer, "How are we doing this tomorrow?" Word spread among the staff that Curry's separation deal was done. Lauer called in, too, and asked how Curry's sign-off would be choreographed. No one really knew the answer. A source remembers that Lauer referred to the anticipated moment as "taking my cyanide pill."

The questions from the cohosts were passed along to Bell, who arrived at his third-floor office at about eight in the evening—uncharacteristic for a man who lived in the Connecticut suburbs and woke up at three most mornings. His lieutenants had slotted Curry's announcement for 7:45 a.m., the traditional time for *Today* show transitions. That's when Vieira had announced a year earlier that she was stepping down. Bell also considered 8:30 a.m., but later decided to shift the announcement to 8:50 a.m., apparently because Curry had said she was afraid she'd be too emotional to keep hosting afterward. "That was a huge warning sign that a bomb was going to explode," one producer said later.

Another warning sign had come earlier in the day, when Curry spent forty minutes on the phone with Susan Page, a veteran Washington reporter for *USA Today*. Barnett had connected the two women because Curry wanted an exit interview of sorts, a chance to right wrongs and tell her side of the story after staying silent on *Today* for a week. Curry told Page that the leaks had "hurt deeply" and that the claims of a ten-million-dollar salary were made up. "I can say that I'd love to earn that much," she said. She also singled out Hale's column in *The Times* for criticism: "I have never felt like a stepsister at the *Today Show* family, as some have described me," she said. "I've always felt close to the people here."

When the interview hit the Web shortly after midnight, it became clear to all that Curry was not going to pretend that this new role was her idea, nor was she going to pretend she was pleased. She said in the piece that she was "deeply sad" about being forced out. She said of her audience, "I don't want to leave them. I love them. And I will really miss them." And she said she didn't think she was given enough time to settle into the cohost chair. The Curry interview was the centerpiece of *USA Today*'s front page the next morning. The stark headline was a quote: "I know I am not to blame." (What Curry had said in full was "I know I am not to blame for the ratings worries. And my bosses have said to me there are many factors involved.")

She did accept some responsibility, though, for her less-than-satisfactory on-air interactions with Lauer. "You know, Matt and I have had great on-air chemistry for 14 years, been part of the No. 1 winning team for a history-making number of years. That said, I just finished my freshman year as co-host. In every single co-host's first year, there have been kinks to be worked out, and perhaps I deserve as much blame for that as anyone," she said.

Capus, in a separate interview with *USA Today*, called the correspondent job a better fit for Curry than the cohost job. But no one—not Curry, not Capus, not Bell, who wasn't interviewed by anyone—said explicitly why she was being forced out. No one took responsibility.

Curry and Lauer got through the first hour and fifty minutes of Curry's last show in a way that belied the fact that in the last ten minutes she was going to sign off *Today* forever. There was no highlight reel of her fifteen years on *Today*, no performance by one of her favorite artists, no dance party on the plaza—just a small blank space on the rundown for her to bid adieu. NBC executives later claimed that a proper send-off was unwarranted because Curry wasn't completely leaving the show, she was simply leaving the cohost chair. She'd still be the "anchor at large." But that excuse was laughable. Vieira, after all, stuck around NBC as a "special correspondent" and a contributor to *Today*—yet her jubilant farewell took up the better part of two hours. To Curry, the poor treatment was a message from her irresponsible bosses: "Get the fuck out."

Curry chose scarlet for her last day. She sat to the right of Lauer on the show's trademark couch. Morales sat to Lauer's left. Al Roker, Curry's closest friend among the cast members, sat in a chair opposite Lauer. When the show came back from a commercial break, she had to introduce herself. "Welcome back, everybody," she said. "It's 8:50. This is not easy to say, but today is going to be my last morning as a regular cohost of *Today*."

And then it happened. Her voice caught. She paused, tried to compose herself, and pointed at the camera that was televising a four-shot of the cast. The teleprompters in the cameras had a set of talking points that Curry had written and Capus had approved, including this one: "I will still be a part of the *Today* show family, but I'm going to have a new title and a new role." She read them, mentioned her "fancy new titles" and said "we're being given the chance to do the work that most of us got into journalism to do." But she also signaled to viewers that this was a demotion, not a promotion. "This is not as I expected to ever leave this couch after fifteen years," she said. Then, attempting a moment of humor, she added, "After all of these years, I don't even know if I can sleep in anymore. I'm not even sure I can, but I know that whatever time I wake up, I'll be missing you and I'll be believing in you."

Curry felt she had both an obligation and a right to tell the viewers all of this. "I'm not going to lie," she'd said to Capus a day earlier when they came up with the script. It sounded OK on paper, but man it sounded awful when read out loud. Morales sat, motionless, as Curry read her lines. Lauer, lips pursed, stared at something in the distance. Roker looked offstage sometimes, too, as if Curry's speech was too painful to watch. It was: viewers at home winced and some cried as she choked back tears. As she wrapped up, she said, "For all of you who saw me as a groundbreaker, I'm sorry I couldn't carry the ball over the finish line, but man," she said, pointing at the camera again, "I did try."

As Curry apologized for turning into a "sob sister," she wiped away tears with her hands. No one had thought to put tissues nearby. In the control room, Steve Burke cringed. His network was beaming this disaster to the whole country, and there was nothing he could do about it.

For the remaining two minutes, Curry's colleagues took turns praising her work over the years, further inviting viewers to wonder: why is she leaving, then? After she apologized again for crying, Lauer tried to ease the obvious tensions: "Can we just say, it's not goodbye, not by a long shot?" She looked down, frowned, and said, "Nah." She knew that this was goodbye, no matter the denials from NBC.

Curry squirmed when he tried to kiss her on the cheek, then practically jumped into Roker's arms for a hug as the show cut to a commercial break. Seconds later, Curry stood up and walked out of Studio 1A, and left the building immediately. She was still crying as she stepped into the town car waiting for her outside.

In and out of the TV industry, people who had witnessed the scene were stunned—not just by Curry's behavior, but by the clueless callousness that NBC had shown. One rival producer said the segment was "the equivalent of finishing up a pleasant, two-hour family dinner by saying, 'Oh, by the way, I forgot to mention: Mom and I are getting a divorce. While you were sleeping last night she packed up all of her stuff. There's a cab waiting outside to take her away right now. Say goodbye, kids...OK, now that we've done that, who wants dessert?!'"

"Ann's awkwardness proved the point—it proved why she needed to go," said a person close to NBC. But the way she'd proved it, Bell thought, was unforgivable. Lauer was furious, too. He felt that Curry had lobbed a hand grenade into Studio 1A on her way out, wounding him and others. Certainly the messages to @MLauer on Thursday were venomous, blaming him for making her cry. "You are a phony." "A bully." "You're the problem, not Ann." They were channeling the troublemakers over at *GMA*, who said Lauer looked as if he'd been caught sticking a knife in Curry's back.

"I'm never looking at Twitter again," Lauer told a colleague.

At lunchtime that day Bell took the *Today* show's top producers to Brasserie Ruhlmann, a Rockefeller Center restaurant that on some days seemed like a high-end NBC cafeteria. Bell, Nash, Noah Kotch, eight a.m. producer Debbie Kosofsky, and supervising producer Matt Carluccio sat outside—it was a beautiful June day. While Curry's sole defender among the senior producers, Melissa Lonner, watched from a nearby table, the group clinked wineglasses to celebrate Curry's departure. The *Today* show was wounded but alive. With the ascension of Savannah Guthrie, Operation Bambi would be complete, and the show's preeminence would surely be preserved.

# ACT 2

# GOOD MORNING

# CHAPTER 6

---

# Try Harder

LET US REWIND TIME and travel now about five midtown Manhattan blocks southwest, from the often tense and, figuratively speaking, bloodstained environs of Studio 1A to the cheerier corridors of *Good Morning America*. How different it feels to stroll through the Forest of Happy Hosts—*Look, there's George Stephanopoulos!*—and imbibe the atmosphere in a place that, like the New York Mets, Garfunkel, and Avis, was born to finish second. Consider that when *GMA*'s forerunner first struggled out of the womb on January 6, 1975, with hard-living, four-times-married ABC lifer Bill Beutel and Stephanie Edwards (whose claim to fame was a recurring role on the NBC series *The Girl with Something Extra*) as cohosts, and Peter Jennings relegated to the job of newsreader, no one really believed that it would topple the mighty *Today*, which was then, twenty-three years into its history, in the estimable hands of Barbara Walters and Jim Hartz. Indeed, for a while the ABC entry, which was called *A.M. America*, was getting the crap beat out of it in the ratings by CBS's *Captain Kangaroo*.

*A.M. America* was not, shall we say, the most ambitious endeavor ever attempted by ABC News. The unimaginative producers "booked the show by watching *Today* and then bringing all of *Today*'s guests in the next day," said the ABC producer George Merlis, exaggerating only slightly. The network suits had run the numbers and found that you could survive quite nicely, thank you, on the Nielsen leader's leavings. But its affiliates scattered across the country agitated for something more than mere surviv-al. Some threatened to switch affiliation to NBC or CBS if ABC didn't—pardon a second Avis reference here—"try harder."

Six months after *A.M. America* premiered, by which time Beutel had expressed a strong desire to return to local news, or for that matter go anywhere that was not the dinky *A.M. America* set, and Edwards had stormed off, still angry about a producer whispering in her ear, thirty seconds before the initial broadcast was to begin, that she should have worn something orange or pistachio green instead of the demure gray suit she had on, the legendary TV executive Fred Silverman, who had just arrived at ABC, went to work on fixing the show, going over a list of po-tential hosts that was longer even than this sentence. There must have been 150 or two hundred of them, according to ABC vice president Ed Vane, who had a Rolodex bulging with fully posable life-size Ken dolls he'd known in his capacity as the overseer of *The Dating Game*, *The Newlywed Game*, and the network's other afternoon game shows. Which one to install in their dreary little dream house?

Wisely—not a word you will see all that often in a book about television—they settled on possibly the most un–Wink Martindale–ish name on their list: David Hartman, a forty-year-old Air Force–officer–turned–folksy–actor who had played a ranch hand on the Western series *The Virginian*, then a doctor on *The Bold Ones: The New Doctors* and an English teacher on *Lucas Tanner*, all on NBC. Hartman, an ardent believer in the teaching power of television, saw those prime-time series as informational as well as entertaining; he pushed for *The New Doctors* to be as medically accurate as possible. In the early 1970s an executive at

NBC "asked if I'd be interested in switching over to working at NBC News," Hartman said. "There were logistical challenges we could not solve, but the seeds were being sown." Hartman was, despite his earnest streak, a brilliant and historically significant choice to helm a morning TV broadcast, given his blue eyes, boyish face, and paternal demeanor. What he lacked in melanin and other evidence of ethnicity, he more than made up for in the levelheaded-liberal vibe he emitted whenever he furrowed his brow or gawked his crooked smile. Indeed, NBC had noticed that he possessed the elusive, slightly puffy-eyed quality of wake-up-with-ness and had booked Hartman to cohost one episode of the *Today* show the following year. In a celebration of the United States bicentennial, *Today* was planning to relocate to a different state every Friday in 1976, and Hartman, that proud son of Pawtucket, was going to cohost from Rhode Island. And then came the phone call from ABC's Bob Shanks, who if you read histories of *The Tonight Show*, *20/20*, and the other enterprises he was involved in, seems always to have been the vice president in charge of significant phone calls. Hartman had to cancel on *Today*, but he had a good excuse: he'd be hosting the competition.

If *A.M. America* was an imitation of *Today*, the retooled and renamed *Good Morning America* was an alternative—more entertaining, more appealing, and maybe even, as the name implied, more American. When *GMA* had its premiere on November 3, 1975—and a cheerful Broadway actress named Nancy Dussault was brought in to be Hartman's perky but unsexy cohost—it was ABC's entertainment division that was in charge. Structurally this gave *GMA* more freedom to stray from news ethics and standards; practically, as TV critics were quick to point out, it allowed the show to go "softer" than the *Today* show, which was a product of NBC's news division. Hartman described *GMA* this way: it "had a different look and feel from a traditional news program," including a more conversational style (the writers would substi-

tute *a lot* for the more formal *many*, for instance) and a set that
was supposed to look like a dreamy suburban home (with a living
room, a den, a kitchen, and what appeared to be a leafy backyard).
Still, ABC News produced the newscasts that were shown within
*GMA* every half hour, and the anchor of the newscasts, Steve Bell,
joined Hartman for most of the show's hard news interviews, as
a sop to those who believed, in those pre–Ronald Reagan years,
that an actor should not try to examine and explain affairs of state.

Given Hartman's never having possessed a press badge, "the
journalists among us were anguished," said Merlis, who was the
first producer hired at *GMA*. "And the first week looked like it
would prove us right. David would ask questions that caused the
news guys to groan and wince." But what Merlis and others didn't
realize at the time was that Hartman was asking the questions
the viewers would have asked, not the questions TV newsmen
ask to show off how much they know. Before long it was generally acknowledged that whatever it was Hartman was doing was
working, and then, in short order, Merlis said, "the news guys
started asking those kinds of questions, too."

It was fine with *GMA*'s producers if the journalists in the building imitated Hartman a bit, but they didn't want their new show
to similarly flatter *Today*. *A.M. America* had done that by booking its sloppy seconds, and it had lasted less than a year. So there
was an ironclad rule that *GMA* could not book people who had
appeared on *Today* the day before. Thus an era of frenzied, cutthroat, and, as we shall see, occasionally unethical competition for
the most coveted guests was born.

ABC president Silverman—a pooh-bah of prime time who
had already brought *All in the Family* and *The Waltons* to the air-
waves, and at the time was working on *Charlie's Angels*—felt in
his golden gut that *GMA* should conform to the morning habits
of the audience—assuming you define the audience as a sea of
middle-class, middle-American, cereal-eating salary workers, and

not a bunch of cab drivers or hookers, dragging their asses home just as Hartman was saying "Well, here we are again!" To Silverman, predictability was the plan and the point. So weather was at exactly the same times every day. And so were the headlines and so were the Hollywood gossip segments. The format was modeled on the "wheel" formula of radio newscasts, made for a mom at home. Its exactness sometimes frustrated the hosts, but the producers believed the unvarying formula attracted radio listeners and converted them to television in the morning—exactly what Sigourney's NBC executive dad Pat Weaver had set out to do with *Today* in the 1950s.

*Today* hardly flinched when *GMA* premiered. It had what it thought were bigger problems. The NBC News president at the time, Richard Wald, thought cohost Jim Hartz wasn't up to the job; he told Hartz more than once to "sit up," and Hartz knew it wasn't just a reference to his posture. But Hartz also knew, as he told a reporter when he was forced out in 1976, that he could only be himself, "and if that wasn't good enough, there wasn't anything I could do about it. There's enough artificiality in this medium without altering the way you are." That sounds like something Ann Curry would say. Wald proposed—and Hartz reluctantly accepted—a roving correspondent role just like Curry's, with a fancy "traveling co-anchor" title. The publicists for NBC dodged questions about Hartz's new position, which vanished within a year.

Meanwhile *GMA*, strengthened by the addition of contributors like Joan Lunden and Geraldo Rivera, inched toward *Today* in the ratings. Was NBC, the network that had invented morning TV, worried? It certainly looked that way by the time Silverman, who changed channels more often than your sister's preschooler, became president of NBC in June 1978. He immediately shook up the *Today* show, said Paul Friedman, then the executive producer of *Today*: "He insisted that we program more segments at shorter length, as *GMA* was doing, and that we do more 'news you can use'—particularly medical and consumer news—and pop culture segments." In four words: be more like *GMA*.

*Today*'s main obstacle in this regard was that it couldn't clone Hartman. In 1979, as *GMA* closed the gap with *Today*, audience research commissioned by NBC showed that Hartman (then cohosting with Sandy Hill) was considered more relatable and approachable than Hartz's successor Tom Brokaw, who was perceived, fairly or not, as being eager to show off his journalistic chops at every opportunity. "The audience rated the two shows equally in terms of content and style, but was in love with David Hartman," Friedman said. "He was 'everyman,' and he was the difference."

NBC execs were so flustered that at lunch they often pushed away their clams casino half eaten and flubbed their lips in their martinis. At a meeting convened by Silverman to discuss the morning show war, Friedman mused that perhaps the money expended on all the research should instead have been spent to hire a hit man to kill Hartman. Silverman didn't laugh. But the joke exposed a question that haunted all the morning shows: what influenced viewers' choices more, the content of the shows or the chemistry of the cohosts? Most people thought chemistry triumphed, a view backed up by NBC's research and the ratings race. In January 1980 the once-unthinkable happened and *GMA* started to beat *Today* some mornings. A month later ABC televised the highly rated Lake Placid Winter Olympics (think Miracle on Ice), giving *GMA* another lift that lasted into the morning hours. As *GMA* pulled ahead decisively, reporters used words like *surrender* to describe NBC's underwhelming response. Decades of dominance by NBC, dating back to the dawn of television, when chimpanzees strode the morning landscape—those were no more.

This is when the gentlemanly competition among network executives who sat next to each other on the commuter trains from Connecticut and Westchester each morning, and drank and played cards with each other in those same smoke-filled cars each night, boiled over into mortal combat. The three best fights of 1980 were two Roberto Durán/Sugar Ray Leonard battles, and *Today* versus *GMA*. In the control rooms and on the sets, staffers from one show talked about the other guys like boxers describing an adversary. They took the rivalry personally. Hartman and his cohost Joan Lunden might have made a handsome living from their plenteous pleasantness, but "I view them as trying to take my mortgage away, stop me from eating. I view them as the enemy," Steve Friedman, the fast-talking, heavyset producer (no relation to Paul) who ran *Today* in the 1980s said in one of his buck-up-the-troops staff meetings. This wasn't hyperbole, he said decades later: "I thought they were trying to kill me and I tried to kill them."

Sometimes he did it with money. "Those were the days when you'd spend your way to win," Friedman said, referring to a tactic much easier to employ at a time when there were only a few television networks divvying up all of Madison Avenue's cash. Under Friedman, *Today* started traveling around the world—spending weeks in Russia, Italy, Argentina, Australia—and stopped recycling so much of the prior day's *NBC Nightly News*. "It became really the *Today* show, and not the *What Happened Yesterday* show," Friedman said.

An age-old law of morning TV states that you don't only help yourself to better ratings, you are also boosted by the sloth and incompetence of your rivals. Good fortune runs one way, then the other, seemingly in cycles. By the late 1970s *Today* was stale; *GMA* surged ahead. But by the mid-eighties *GMA* was the stale one, a condition blamed, fairly or not, on Hartman. Friedman, who called Hartman "potato face," assured his staff that their enemy's star would soon fade, and he was right. By 1986 *Today* had once again taken command in the ratings, and by 1987 Hartman had announced that he wanted to spend more time with his family.

But when you're talking morning television, there is always another twist to the tale. In this case it's a Gibson with a twist. Charles Gibson, the anchor who replaced Hartman, was a child of privilege (Sidwell Friends, Princeton) whom average Americans nevertheless liked, the way you might actually if grudgingly like a guy who pays you to blow the snow out of his long, winding, tree-lined driveway, or tune his Jaguar. As soon as he arrived at the show, the audience research and the ratings started changing in ways that got the *Today* folks worried, and with good reason, because even those who "watched" *Today* through a closed bathroom door could tell that, despite its top spot in the ratings, it was at that time more than a bit of a mess. That's why, in the summer of 1988, *Today* producer Marty Ryan asked Gumbel, then in his sixth year as host, to write a memo detailing what was wrong with their show and what they might do to keep *GMA* at bay. Gumbel responded with a scathing novella that criticized Ryan and almost everyone connected with the show (except Pauley, whom he was already known to dislike). Gene Shalit was always late with his movie reviews and did bad interviews, Gumbel opined. The talent department was hampered by "a lazy broad who uses bad judgment." Of weather-weeble Willard Scott the cohost said, "He holds the show hostage to his assortment of whims, wishes, birthdays and bad taste." We know all this because someone leaked Gumbel's put-downs to *Newsday* reporter Kevin Goldman, who published the highlights. Said *The New York Times*' Walter Goodman: "The commotion over the Gumbel memo offers the watchers of early-morning television a fresh perspective on the form.... Mr. Gumbel's criticism of one co-worker for dumb carryings on and of others for unoriginality gave him the appearance of a vaudeville piano player clucking his tongue over how the jugglers are distracting the customers from his Liszt concertos." NBC News president Michael Gartner condemned the leak but expressed little sympathy for Gumbel, who said he didn't feel there was "a proper expression of support from the executive side." To paraphrase Tolstoy, every unhappy family is unhappy in a way that repels morning TV viewers. The internal discord at *Today* drove many thousands over to *GMA*.

But the best was still to come for the ABC show, for now NBC took dead aim at the foot it had not yet shot itself in. In the summer of 1989, Dick Ebersol, who had been brought over from the sports division to solve the problems at *Today*, in part because he was a friend of Gumbel's, thought it would be a peachy idea to bring in Deborah Norville, the anchor of the early-morning newscast *NBC News at Sunrise*, to become the *Today* show's news anchor. He was wrong about that the way Liza Minnelli was wrong about David Gest, the way AOL was wrong about Time Warner. Norville was an obviously ambitious, obviously stunning and sexy young blonde whose very presence at the news anchor desk, near the traditional fake husband-and-wife combo of Gumbel and Pauley, was just as likely to annoy the mostly female viewers of *Today* as to enchant them.

But Ebersol, with his Minnelli-like wisdom, didn't put her at the news desk; he put her right next to Gumbel and Pauley in an arrangement that took on the air of a sheepish threesome the morning after. To *Today* show loyalists it screamed, "Man, wife, and mistress"; by the thousands they called and wrote to the network about the odd bigwig-fantasy-made-flesh, with most defending the lovely but soccer-mom-ish Pauley and eviscerating Norville as a home-wrecker. About seven weeks later Pauley, who was as unhappy with the arrangement as anyone else, announced that she was leaving the show. Making a nod to the bad press, she calmly told viewers, "It has hurt to see two of my friends, Bryant and Deborah, assigned roles in this that they did not play." But the obvious follow-up question—what roles *did* they play,

Pauley?—was never answered sufficiently by anyone in a position to know. (NBC would make this mistake again in 2012.)

Norville's debut as cohost, in January 1990, tipped the already weak show into second place for the first time since 1986. Within a few months Ebersol had issued a rare mea culpa for the furor—"I wanted to send a very clear signal that there was someone who would stand up and take responsibility," he told the *Los Angeles Times*—and returned to NBC Sports full-time. In short, it was a heartwarming moment for the once-again-first-place *GMA*, and no one could have faulted its staffers for celebrating— and yet their joy in retrospect seems sadly misplaced, their champagne popped under false pretenses. Yes, the departure of Norville thirteen months later—she left to have a baby and never came back—caused even more bad press. *Today's* ratings sank so low that NBC's own stations tried to wrestle the eight a.m. hour away from the network so they could air their own programming! "There is nobody in America who wants to see this show for two hours anymore, nobody," the stations chief bellowed. But he was wrong, just as *GMA* was wrong to chug champagne and let its guard down. For the departure of Norville also led to the ascension of Katie Couric, a misleadingly cheery-looking former cheerleader from Arlington, Virginia, who would kick their asses for many years to come.

# CHAPTER 7

# A Hole Dug Deep

FROM THE MID-SEVENTIES, when *GMA* was born, until the mid-nineties, the two main morning TV shows were like gaily colored merry-go-round horses moving side by side. Their crazy-eyed expressions remained frozen but their positions constantly changed. When one was high, the other was low. (CBS, in our metaphor, can be thought of as that flightless swan chair that nobody ever sits in.) Instead of being driven by a clockwork mechanism, though, *Today* and *GMA* rose and fell according to how well their hosts were demonstrating that ineffable thing called chemistry, or how misguided their producers were when it came to anticipating the audience's desires. Errors played as large a role as home runs in the grand scheme of things, and the upward stroke was always a prelude to the downward. Since fantastic amounts of advertising revenue, and many careers, hung in the balance, the suspense over the Nielsen numbers remained a nauseating constant, especially if like most people in TV you thought in terms of failure and punishment. For about twenty years it was bad to be down and not much better to be up, the one sure sign you'd be down again presently. And then one day one of the carousel steeds turned into Secretariat and galloped right off the ride.

There was no magic involved, though; in morning TV, except

for the mysterious coming and going of on-screen chemistry, there never is. No, what the *Today* show did to change the dynamics of the so-called morning wars, and start its unprecedented streak of victorious weeks, was and remains fairly obvious: its producers put Deborah Norville on permanent maternity leave, teamed Katie Couric with Bryant Gumbel, built a new street-level studio in midtown Manhattan, and set Jeff Zucker loose on the joint. But because, as any life coach worth her masters in Russian lit will tell you, you always learn more from losing than from winning, let us focus on what *GMA*, starting in the early nineties, got so gloriously wrong, for it was the size of the hole it dug that made the show's climb to daylight, sixteen years later, so amazing.

First a word about the way the game was played in those days. It was played, in one very important way, like chess. If you look at the morning show record from back in those less-diverse days you'll see there was a direct connection between Nielsen success and how well you managed your blondes. Protect the queen! Walters, Pauley, Norville, Couric, Diane Sawyer—these women all had a powerful impact, one way or the other, upon the ratings, and you had to handle them with care. *GMA* went platinum in 1980 when it promoted Joan Lunden, a California bottle-blonde born Joan Blunden, to the chair beside Hartman, replacing Sandy Hill, who let us just say does not today have her own Wikipedia page. Lunden got her big break on the show, as a last-minute substitute host, in *42nd Street* fashion, when both regulars came down with laryngitis one morning, and the audience loved her from her storybook start. When Gibson replaced Hartman in 1987, she made a seamless transition from one potato-faced partner to the next. Profiting from the Norville debacle at *Today*, the Gibson-Lunden team helped lead *GMA* back to the top in the ratings and helped keep it there for five years. They didn't sizzle, but they made you feel warm and safe. "Charlie used to say we were like an old married couple," Lunden said. "We could finish each other's sentences but we didn't have sex." Still, when *Today* countered with Couric in 1991, ABC could not prevail in that epic battle of the blondes. *Today* caught up to *GMA* at the end of 1994 and started trading off turns at number one. At the end of 1995 the seesawing stopped and the *Today* show streak began. The crazy talk about taking away the eight a.m. hour was silenced, thank God.

A lot of the credit for this went to *Today*, specifically Jeff Zucker, for latching on to the Trial of the Century of 1995, the O. J. Simpson murder trial. Zucker said he loved what the trial "said at every level about race and crime and status in society. So I used the trial to cover all those things, and I wrapped a bow around it and made people think we were doing the smartest coverage of the trial." Not just salacious—smart. *GMA* consciously decided not to dwell on the trial, and suffered mightily for it. But Lunden, it must be said, was not entirely innocent of blame. She had, over the course of the previous decade, committed the cardinal sin of getting older. *GMA* had aged, too, and so was perceived by some as having gone stale—especially when put up against the younger, fresher *Today*. "Viewers gulp down early-morning TV like a first cup of coffee," Frazier Moore of the Associated Press wrote in early 1997. "But while Today delivers the sought-after kick, Good Morning America is strictly decaf"—and, he couldn't resist adding, "a dull grind." Interviewed for the story, Alan Wurtzel, an ABC executive who oversaw *GMA*, seemed happy to slam his own show: ABC, he said, "stayed too long with a very, very successful program."

Morning, as a category, makes mere mortals of the best TV minds. Pat Weaver went with a chimp as a cohost of the 1950s *Today*, Ebersol chose Norville—and in the mid 1990s Roone Arledge, after long resisting the idea, at last agreed to take *GMA* off the hands of the entertainment division and absorb it into ABC News, of which he was then president, though he had not a clue about how to make it better, nor did he realize that, the way things would work out, financially speaking he was doing the news division a possibly lifesaving favor. "We could hardly do worse than Entertainment, I figured, and in the spirit of helping a beleaguered program, we went for it," Arledge, who simply didn't get morning TV, wrote in his 2004 memoir. The Walt Disney Company, which was then in the process of acquiring the network, didn't know what to do with *GMA* either. But Gibson and Lunden had been around the TV business long enough to know that they should get out of the way of the inevitable fix-it crews.

It took the network a while to find the seemingly perfect Lunden substitute: Lisa McRee—blonde, California-bred, pretty in a Lunden sort of way but born in 1961 as opposed to 1950. Lunden signed off on a Friday and McRee took over on a Monday in September 1997. No doubt some people who didn't follow TV news all that closely thought that Lunden had had a little work done over the weekend. The look was that similar—but man, the chemistry wasn't. "At the time, Lisa was thought to be the future for the franchise," said David Westin, Arledge's successor atop ABC News. But the show, already in second place, sagged further in the ratings, and something like panic started to set in. "After several months, it was clear on the air and behind the scenes that Charlie and Lisa were not a good fit," Westin said. Making matters worse, mutual disdain between the news and entertainment divisions had made the handover to ABC News much harder than it had to be. There was so much finger-pointing you could lose an eye walking from Gibson's office to Westin's.

Not knowing what to try next, the executives tried everything. "We went through three or four different show structures behind the scenes," recalled Tom Touchet, who joined the staff in 1995 and was later promoted to be a senior producer. Management, he said, "didn't have a vision for what the show should be. Therefore, almost every week, you'd have these wild swings." One week the staff would be told to pursue serious news stories; the next they'd be told to soften up the show with fun features. "I think viewers ended up with whiplash," Touchet said. "We lost the continuity of what made the show work, and we weren't building toward anything new."

Gibson was the next casualty. On the first day of May 1998, *GMA* said goodbye to him the same way it had to Lunden the prior fall—that is, sentimentally, with a lot of fanfare, beginning with a videotaped message from President Bill Clinton. At the end of the two-hour tribute show, Gibson thanked the audience for watching *GMA*, then looked off camera and said, "Lisa, Kevin, take care of it."

They didn't. Nothing was right, singly or in combination, about McRee and her new cohost Kevin Newman, a pleasant but bland Canadian who had been made the news anchor on *GMA* the prior fall. They hardly knew each other, and it showed—"It was a shotgun marriage," Newman said later. The audience didn't know them either—nor did it have any desire to watch them perch uncomfortably on their new, cold, hard, chrome-heavy set, for which ABC had spent three million dollars. By the end of the year *GMA* had dropped dangerously close to third place in the morning race. Looking back on the period, Newman said he sensed disaster from the moment Westin called and breathlessly offered him a job that even he knew he was unprepared for. He regretted ignoring his gut instinct, which was to say no to the high-paying, high-profile position. "Too much change in TV is never a good thing," he said.

He was right about that, but more change was to come. As viewers fled, Westin knew he had to do something. There was talk about scrapping the *GMA* format altogether and running an hour of news followed by an hour of *The View*, the new eleven a.m. talk show that was quickly turning into a hit. Gibson thought that was such a bad idea he went to Westin to protest it.

"You've got more than twenty years invested in this concept," Gibson said. "You've got the best-named program in the history of TV. This is a tried-and-true formula if you have the right people."

"Well," Westin said, "would you come back and host again?" .

The idea sounded as outlandish then as it does now. Thus Gibson declined, but when he heard whom he'd be paired with—Diane Sawyer, then in her tenth year of hosting ABC's *Primetime Live*—he started to reconsider. Many stars of ABC News had shunned *GMA* in the past, but Sawyer's presence, he predicted, would change that. As it turned out, Sawyer caused an attitudinal change over at *Today*, too. "I remember thinking, 'That's a big move' when they brought them on," said Don Nash, who was a West Coast producer for *Today* at the time. "Game on," Nash and his colleagues thought.

Newman and McRee, as you might have guessed, were re-placed faster than you can say *severance*. McRee returned to California, gained a lot of weight, then lost it, and now runs a weight-loss Web site. Newman returned to Canada, where he now hosts a newsmagazine. When *GMA* celebrated its thirty-fifth anniversary in 2010, "Lisa and I were nowhere to be found in its official history," he wrote in a magazine essay. "We never hap-pened."

Sawyer and Gibson (who at first said they'd host the show for only a few months—maybe to protect themselves in case the rat-ings went even further south) made for a dramatic and almost instantaneous improvement in both the quality of *GMA* and the quantity of its viewers. He calmed her down and she revved him up. "Charlie was the key," Sawyer said. "Charlie was the institu-tional memory for the audience. I was new energy for Charlie."

But others at the network believed that it was Sawyer who was the secret of *GMA*'s recovery, and credited new show producer Shelley Ross, one of the few women ever to make it to the upper reaches of morning TV, for bringing out the best in her. Sawyer and Ross were constantly searching for the special something (crime stories? inspirational interviews? overseas trips?) that would restore *GMA* to first place. They had endless amounts of energy. *Today* withstood the challenges and continued winning every single week. Years passed and as the streak was further cemented, it became the stuff of legend—completely unprecedented in the television industry. But the funny thing was, it didn't yet feel unbeatable. Especially after a forty-year-old producer named Ben Sherwood took over *GMA* in 2004, there were half hours and then days and then weeks to feel good about; there were causes for hope. In morning TV, you gotta give 'em hope.

Sherwood is one of those highbrows who is not afraid to go low and aim for the emotional labonza, to hit the groundlings where they live. He graduated Phi Beta Kappa from Harvard, then spent several years at Oxford as a Rhodes scholar before working his way up through the news divisions at NBC and ABC. He's written a best-selling novel that was made into a movie, and a substantial work of nonfiction brought out by the publisher of the book you hold in your hands. He probably likes classical music and stuff. But when he focused on *GMA* as its executive producer, practically the first thing he saw was a chance for the shameless promotion of *Desperate Housewives*, one of his network's cheesiest and most successful prime-time entries. Over the course of nine months, Gibson, an easily lathered fan of the nighttime soap, and Sawyer interviewed no fewer than five of the show's MILFy stars. The effect on the ratings—and on the equally besotted *GMA* staff—was nothing short of electrifying. After Gibson's hard-hitting chitchat with *Housewives* narrator Brenda Strong in February 2005, the cast and crew gave them a standing ovation.

"It's funny," Strong told the *New York Observer* afterward, "because I didn't really realize kind of the far-reaching impact that our show had until I went on and Charles actually said, 'You know, you guys don't understand—it's even trickling down to the news department. The entire network feels like it's gotten a fresh surge of optimism.'"

The *Observer* called the *GMA* hype-fest a "slightly sloppy, gushingly passionate intra-network hug," and some people at *Today* rolled their eyes at the utter crassness of ABC running virtual infomercials for its own prime-time programming. But the idea of jumping on the company bandwagon, and trading exclusive access for fawning coverage, was nothing new—NBC did it often, too, with the casts of *ER*, *Friends*, and the other hit series it had in the days before it was a nocturnal also-ran. "The thing is, they pioneered using the prime-time schedule to advantage in the morning," Sherwood said of NBC. "And, you know, we were lucky in 2004–2005 to have a couple of great shows come along and help us."

The *Housewives* tie-ins worked so well that in the second week of May 2005, many people at NBC—including Jim Bell, who had just been appointed the producer of *Today* in April, and Phil Griffin, who'd been appointed the executive in charge of the franchise—feared that ABC was going to break its nearly ten-year streak. "It was an atmosphere of triage. 'How do we stop the bleeding?'" said a producer who was there at the time. "All of our careers were kind of on the line," said another producer. "We knew that if we saved the show, we'd be in good standing there. And if we didn't, we'd be the guys who were on watch when it fell." Bell, Griffin, and a phalanx of publicists even met in a dingy conference room to talk about what to tell the press if *GMA* won.

That may sound silly, but their fear was real. Jeff Zucker, the soon-to-be NBC CEO, was so worried about the streak's being broken by *GMA* that week (rumor had it that ABC had already bought the champagne for a celebration) that he cut all the national commercials that were supposed to run after eight a.m. on Friday's broadcast of *Today*. Exploiting the fact that Nielsen, for complicated reasons, didn't rate the parts of shows without commercials, Zucker managed to inflate *Today's* total rating for Friday and for the full week.

The move cost the network hundreds of thousands, if not millions, of dollars in advertising revenue. It made no business sense—"it was an ego-driven thing," said a producer. In the end the commercial trick wasn't even necessary. *GMA* lost by forty thousand viewers for the week. Its best wasn't quite good enough.

But the episode illustrated just how obsessed NBC was with negating the *Desperate Housewives* effect and staving off *GMA*. At any cost, and by any means necessary. As bizarre as it may sound, some were so intent on keeping the ratings streak going that they prayed it would be broken, just so, while sinking back into despair and poking around for future employment, they could get some relief. But the streak did keep going, and the staff of *Today* spent all summer plotting how to defend itself when the drama returned in the fall. Here's how seriously they took the war: Griffin, who was addicted to *Housewives*, gave up his habit cold turkey. He just couldn't enjoy the soap opera on Wisteria Lane anymore, not with morning TV supremacy at stake.

Their counterparts at *GMA* were no less obsessed. Sherwood's wife Karen once calculated that her husband's "net sleep deficit" after spending two years and five months at the helm of the show was 1,400 hours. Sherwood was the sort of executive producer who thought, like a dogfighting World War II pilot, that victory would always go to the guy who could withstand the g-forces of sleeplessness the longest, and thus not pass out before his adversary did as they plunged around the wild blue yonder. Still, sleep deprivation, he conceded, "produced every imaginable personality defect" in morning show executives, staff members, and stars.

Sometimes he'd suffer short-term memory loss and mood swings and, maybe scariest of all, feel momentarily unambitious. "There is a reason that at Guantanamo Bay, one of the approved ways to break an al-Qaeda terrorist is to deprive them of sleep," he said. Throughout all his time in the morning TV business, he added, "I've rarely seen anybody who is able to keep it completely together 'cause everybody is functioning on a sleep deficit."

Sherwood, it was true, could get a little weird sometimes while running *GMA*. He talked of morning TV as a game of three-dimensional chess, which put off those around him who were especially sensitive to clichés. But his ability to think two or three moves ahead impressed others. "I developed a deep love of the program and the arena," Sherwood later said of his time at *GMA*. "I couldn't help it. It's a feast for people with curiosity about lots of different things. Everything fits under the morning TV tent."

Sherwood's ability—or even his desire—to play well with others has long been a controversial subject at the places he has worked. He has been called "polarizing" by people who are on his side, and worse things by others. While he was twenty-four and completing his studies in British imperial history and development economics at Oxford, he was savaged in a *Spy* magazine article titled "Résumé Mucho" by Andrew Sullivan, who called him "the ultimate in a long line of centerless résumé featherers." The article quoted classmates who said things like "Ben is one of the most hated people alive" and "It's bizarre. People actually make an effort to dislike him." Let's not forget, that's when Sherwood was getting sufficient sleep.

The article, which came about when Sullivan went looking for the person he called "the archetypal Rhodes scholar," dogged Sherwood all his professional life. "I don't think there is a person in the world who would want to have their college persona written about and described in a satire magazine," Sherwood told *The New York Times* in 2011. Sullivan included. "I have no opinion of my own" about Sherwood, Sullivan told me. "I was merely conveying the astonishing level of contempt leveled at him by his peers." In the same *Times* article Sherwood also said, "What I do know about that time, is that I was a guy with a lot to learn."

One thing he's learned: how to manage his own press. His story is one of constant self-reinvention. For a time in the early nineties he was a producer for Diane Sawyer's *Primetime* newsmagazine. Then, spurred by a near-death experience while covering the war in Sarajevo and by the death of his father soon after, he left ABC and wrote a novel, *Red Mercury*, under a pseudonym. He returned to television in 1997, but this time to NBC, where he was a producer for Tom Brokaw's *Nightly News*. There he reconnected with Zucker, a Harvard classmate also known for proactive press relations, who calls him Benjy. Sherwood wrote a novel called *The Man Who Ate the 747* while at NBC, then left the network. Brokaw said Sherwood quit in a huff because he wasn't promoted; Sherwood, politely disagreeing, said he left to write another novel, *The Death and Life of Charlie St. Cloud*, which in 2004 became a best-seller and was adapted into a 2009 film starring Zac Efron.

Sherwood, according to associates, felt unappreciated by NBC. His return to ABC in 2004 came as Diane Sawyer was casting about for someone, anyone, who could get her ahead of Couric in the overnights. Rounding forty, he seemed just as intense as his younger self, but somewhat more likable. "He was very good at forging relationships with underlings," said one such underling, who noticed that he cared about even the littlest details of the show, like the graphics along the bottom of the screen. He exuded confidence and competence, others said—traits that are sometimes in short supply in second-place newsrooms. But even he couldn't snap the streak. Bell and Griffin had brought *Today* back from the brink of second place, and their show was better than ever. Two thousand six was a year of transitions. Couric left *Today* for *CBS Evening News*, and Gibson left *GMA* for *World News*. Sherwood left, too: he moved back to his native Los Angeles, where his mother was battling cancer. While taking care of her, he enjoyed stay-at-home-dad-dom with his two young sons and knocked out a nonfiction book called *The Survivors Club*, about why some people survive crises while others perish. To Sherwood, and to the people who slept with one eye open so they could keep track of him, this period felt like a break but not a whole new direction: he would return someday to television, "the arena" that he loved, everyone felt.

# CHAPTER 8

---

# Unfinished Business

THERE WAS NO NEED for the producers of *Good Morning America* to conduct a nationwide talent search, or to stay up past their usual bedtime of nine thirty p.m. endlessly watching audition reels, if they wanted to find the one person most likely to put them in a position to topple *Today* from its promontory spot in the ratings. She was sitting right on their set, and, as *GMA*'s news anchor, building a relationship with the audience morning by morning. It wasn't, of course, instantly apparent that she had the potential to affect the show in a way that would, if she was handled correctly, result in the diversion of tens of millions of dollars in advertising revenue from NBC to ABC, and thereby save the skin of no small number of news division executives, but it was there for the superior minds who run such enterprises to see. She was a woman of great personal dignity, stately beauty, and, what's most important in her mysterious genre, a certain *je ne sais quoi* that you can't just order up by the ounce from human resources. Naturally, because morning TV still comes down to a group of elite men trying to guess the needs of a mass audience of mostly women, many of the powers that were at ABC wanted to fire her ass as soon as feasible.

Truth be told, Robin Roberts was something of a project

when she first popped up on *GMA* in 1995, a tall, athletic-looking ESPN anchor contributing sports stories, like interviews with Venus and Serena Williams and live reports from the Sydney Olympics. She didn't exactly impress the news purists on the staff; in the words of one, "she didn't have a journalistic bone in her body." But she gained experience and started filling in for Diane Sawyer and Charlie Gibson, foreshadowing her promotion to news anchor in 2002. Even then, said someone who was a senior producer at the time, "There were a lot of people in the building that wanted to give up on her, and certainly everyone acknowledged that her lackluster performance and lack of growth and range was a problem." But ABC's research showed that the audience liked and related to Roberts's soft-spoken style. And to be fair, there wasn't a lot of room for her to grow in between Sawyer and Gibson, two of the brightest stars on TV. Even when she was promoted to full-fledged cohost in 2005, she was overshadowed by the other two, and there was a distinct lack of ease.

And then Hurricane Katrina happened.

Roberts grew up in the Mississippi town of Pass Christian, a tiny peninsula that juts into the Gulf of Mexico. Her mother, Lucimarian, was a social worker and educator, and her father, Lawrence, who died in 2004, was a Tuskegee Airman who spent thirty-two years in the Army and Air Force. They had deep roots in the area—and Roberts considered herself a die-hard daughter of the Delta, having graduated cum laude from Southeastern Louisiana University with a degree in communications in 1983. When Katrina washed ashore, she didn't ask, she *told* her producers that she was going there to cover it personally. What she didn't tell them was that her first priority was not to get the story but to try to locate her mother, her older sister Dorothy, and other family members who had hunkered down for the hurricane in Biloxi, and whom, since the storm hit, she had been unable to contact.

Initially this conflict of intentions made things a bit dicey.

Roberts and an ABC News crew landed in Lafayette, Louisiana, on Monday evening, some eighteen hours after the hurricane made landfall, and drove through the windswept night toward her home state 150 miles away. She recalled that when the crew arrived in Gulfport, Mississippi, she told them, "You guys stop. Set up. I'm going to go and find my family. If I can get back in time for the live shot, I will. If not, I'm sorry."

From Gulfport she drove by herself another fifteen miles or so to Biloxi. A police officer with an oversize flashlight helped her navigate on foot through the blacked-out neighborhood where her mother and sister had ridden out the storm. When they knocked on the door, Dorothy shouted, "No TV!" She thought the flashlight was the light of a camera crew.

Roberts reached the home about an hour before air time. She had to turn around right away to get back to the satellite truck in time for her seven a.m. live shot. She recalled, "My family was very encouraging of me to go: 'Tell the story!'" She wasn't planning on telling viewers about the reunion. But Gibson, at the end of her live report, asked if she had been able to reach her family yet. Roberts instantly teared up; she struggled for words, but gave him a thumbs-up sign and said, "They're OK. They're all right." Their house? "Not so good."

The moment was transformative. "I hadn't cried on air like that," Roberts said. "I think just the raw emotion of it came out. And here I think, 'All right, that's it, I'm going to get fired.' You don't show emotion! You don't get personal like that." She was shocked, she said, by the support that poured in from ABC and from the audience, which showered her with loving letters and e-mails.

Roberts may have gone off to Louisiana a not-very-squeaky third wheel, but she came back a star. When Gibson left *GMA* in 2006 to anchor *World News*, she and Sawyer were left to handle the show on their own. The decision, made by Westin and by

Sherwood's successor, Jim Murphy, was based partly on the belief that the two women could hold their own and challenge *Today*, and partly on the fact that the executives felt they had no strong male candidates up their sleeve. Moving forward without a man was considered risky, the mock married couple having been the morning show model since the days of Dave Garroway and J. Fred Muggs. Everyone—NBC, CBS, CNN, Fox News, even NPR's newly remade *Morning Edition* on radio—had a mix of at least one man and one woman. But Sawyer and Roberts proved they could make it work. "It was in some ways a way to explore sisterhood—beyond race, beyond age, beyond background," Sawyer said. Roberts concurred. "The beauty of it was that we didn't make a big deal out of it being two women," she said. "And there weren't a lot of articles written about it being two women. Which I think is a real credit to the two of us and also to where we are as a society."

Viewers didn't reject the pair, who called themselves Thelma and Louise, but the gap between *GMA* and *Today* was as stubborn as ever. To the strivers at *GMA*, the competition seemed downright indestructible.

As morning show personalities, Roberts and Sawyer were a study in contrasts. Despite the warmth she projected on screen and her ability to connect with viewers through the camera, Roberts kept her private life private. But she did share with the audience something that most television personalities don't: her faith. A lifelong Presbyterian, Roberts was open about her belief in God and the power of prayer.

Although she worked hard enough, Roberts wasn't a workaholic, nor did she seem quite as neurotic about breaking the NBC streak as some of her colleagues—as, say, Sawyer, who was described by one of her best work-friends as "one of the hardest-working people on Earth," but also "an infinite well of need." Sawyer was famous for calling in to the *GMA* assignment desk at literally all hours. Tom Cibrowski, who rose in the *GMA* ranks before taking over the show in 2012, recalled how Sawyer figured into the first date he had with his future wife Julie in 2005. Heading out the door to a jazz bar on Manhattan's East Side, he told Sawyer, "I have a date tonight so I won't be available." Usually, he explained, she liked to talk once or twice a night. "OK, OK!" she told him.

An hour or so later, however, when Cibrowski sneaked a look at his phone in the men's room, there was a message from Sawyer. "Can you call me?"

The Katrina story wasn't the only adversity that Roberts would face in front of the camera. On July 31, 2007, she announced on the show that she had just been diagnosed with breast cancer. She had surgery a few days later, and on August 20 she returned to work and ran a roundtable discussion among cancer survivors. When her hair began falling out as a result of chemotherapy, she admitted she was wearing a wig, but then declined to talk about it anymore. As she said in a blog post, "I never want to distract you from the story I am covering." But her story was riveting, and as she continued to show up each day and do good work, viewers felt more closely connected to her, an important side benefit for a morning host.

Two years later Thelma and Louise went their separate ways. Sawyer was offered the anchor chair at *World News* that had just been vacated by the retiring Gibson, a posting she had secretly coveted even before her old cohost was put there in 2006. She was named Gibson's successor in September. *GMA* assembled a spectacular televised send-off for Sawyer, whose last day on the morning shift was December 12, 2009—coincidentally, the fourteenth anniversary of NBC's ratings streak.

By the time Sawyer told her TV audience that she would be leaving *GMA* at the end of the year, the wooing of George Stephanopoulos had already begun. The night before the announcement came out, when he was in a Washington, DC, pizza place called 2Amys, picking up dinner for his two daughters, ages four and seven (his wife, the actress and comedian Ali Wentworth, was out of town) the White House–aide–turned–ABC–political–all–star got a call from ABC News president David Westin.

"Shortly, Charlie's going to announce that he's leaving. I wanted you to know," Westin told him. "And we want to talk to you about what's next."

In that brief call, Westin didn't mention *GMA*. Nor did he bring up the show in their follow-up talks, which initially centered on making Stephanopoulos the permanent substitute for Sawyer on *World News*, since it was no secret that Stephanopoulos, then the host of the Sunday morning political interview show *This Week*, had his eye on the nightly anchor chair. It was only after a few phone calls, when they met face-to-face for the first time about the changes, that Westin asked Stephanopoulos to think about *GMA*. The news president had a short list of candidates that included the current *GMA* news anchor Chris Cuomo, weekend *GMA* anchor Bill Weir, and weekend *World News* anchor David Muir, but Stephanopoulos was his first choice by a wide margin. "George stood out as the clear choice because he was the strongest anchor," Westin said. "He brought his special expertise in politics and public policy issues, as well as great range and warmth."

Perhaps one reason Westin hesitated so long before mentioning the cohost job at *GMA* is that he didn't think Stephanopoulos would believe him. In many ways it seemed like an outrageously poor fit, the former spokesman for President Bill Clinton chitchatting with a former ESPN reporter and matching wits with a weather guy about what they'd watched on TV the previous evening. Somehow it was hard to imagine the son of a Greek Orthodox priest, a brilliant student of government who had gone on to become the salutatorian of his graduating class at Columbia, describing lawsuits filed over injurious lap dances, interviewing Kim Kardashian, and telling America how to water-proof its sneakers.

Wentworth recalled the first conversation she had with her husband after Westin dropped his little bombshell.

"I think they might want me to do *Good Morning America*," he said.

"Well, you're not going to do it, are you?"

"No."

It wasn't just the ultra-mellow tone of early-morning television that Stephanopoulos, more accustomed to political matchups, had to consider—or the fact that he didn't seem to resonate in the same key as Roberts, or even that at five feet and ten inches she was four inches taller than he. There were also practical considerations pertaining to him and his family. He and Wentworth had just bought a handsome new house in Washington's Georgetown neighborhood and they didn't want to uproot their daughters. During the fall of 2009, Stephanopoulos went to Westin several times and said, "I don't think this is right."

Westin heard him out, but according to Wentworth, the entreaties from ABC "became less of 'Would you,' and more 'You will.'" Looking back on the discussions, Stephanopoulos says he was persuaded by the sheer reach of *GMA*—so many viewers, so much airtime—and "by the chance to help create something new there." The money also influenced his thinking, as it always does. (Stephanopoulos is believed to make more than five million dollars a year.) There were other selling points, too. The move to New York made him a bigger player in breaking news coverage. And, he said, "it was not lost on me that many, many anchors of evening programs cut their teeth on the morning programs." All that said, when he signed up he was still worried about feeling like a cod liver oil pill in a jar of jelly beans.

Jim Murphy, the *GMA* show-runner, was not opposed to the pairing per se, but he did balk at giving Stephanopoulos and Roberts equal billing and equal weight. He argued to Westin that the show should either be built around Stephanopoulos, the super-studious hard-news nerd with two children, *or* be built around Roberts, the laid-back jock with no children—but warned that they must make a choice. Westin admitted there were "substantial doubts" about the pairing, both inside ABC and out. But, he said, "I was confident that they would come together as a team because they share a fundamental decency and respect for others. Each would appreciate what the other one brought to the program."

The odd couple actually held their own. In their first quarter together, that is from January to March 2010, *GMA* was 1.24 million viewers behind *Today*; in their fourth quarter, October to December 2010, *GMA* was 930,000 behind in the two shows' combined pool of eleven million viewers. Progress! "In a world where most shows were losing audience, we weren't—we were closing the gap, at least a little bit," Stephanopoulos said.

Former *GMA* executive producer Ben Sherwood, watching from home in Los Angeles, wasn't privy to all the numbers (though his friends still at the network kept him pretty up-to-date). But as a graduate student of the genre, he could see NBC feeling the pressure, and, despite his competitive feelings, he loved to watch the pros at the *Today* show bear down under the threat. He thought their taking the streak so seriously, as seriously as he had once tried to end it, showed class, that there was "an honor to the arena, to the game, to the war, whatever you wanted to call it."

To put together hundreds of weeks of consecutive wins, you have to believe in yourself, Sherwood said, and never let up. "They won on July fourth week. They won on Christmas week. They won every week. And they would not compromise," he said. "They would put Matt there on July fourth week. They would put Meredith there on Christmas week. They put their frontline team there because the streak mattered. Because they could not let it stop."

Like any other civilian, Sherwood read of David Westin's departure from ABC News through the media. Westin resigned in September 2010, a few months after finishing a massive wave of layoffs mandated by Disney. (Nearly four hundred of the news division's 1,500 people were let go.) Anne Sweeney, the president of the Disney/ABC Television Group, was just beginning her search for Westin's replacement when Sherwood called her. On the hottest day in Los Angeles since record-keeping began in 1877—the thermometer in his Subaru Forester read 114 degrees—Sherwood came in for a talk at ABC's headquarters in Burbank. "I met with Anne at the recommendation of some people who thought that I, not in the business anymore, could offer some thoughts to her about the news division," Sherwood said.

His conversation with Sweeney was wide-ranging. They talked about *GMA*, about *World News*, about the ABC News iPad app, about the qualities the next news division president should have. But they did not talk about Sherwood as president. "I was not a candidate," he said.

But less than two months later, he asked to become a candidate, assuming Sweeney was still looking for one. She was, and she brought him in for a three-hour interview. Sherwood emerged the front-runner for the job, so Sweeney invited him and her boss Bob Iger to dinner. The subject of *GMA*, the news division's most profitable program, came up practically before the waiter could take their orders. Sherwood didn't promise Iger and Sweeney to make *GMA* number one in a specific amount of time. But he did say that if he got the news president's job the morning show would be a very high priority for him. *Very* high. That shouldn't have surprised anybody within earshot. After all, Sherwood had unfinished business in the mornings—he had previously brought *GMA* to within forty thousand viewers of *Today*, but hadn't broken the streak.

"I thought there were opportunities to make the show grow," Sherwood said later. "And I told them that I thought we would ultimately be victorious."

Sherwood recalled that Iger wanted him to get specific: "It's hard to find new talent. Who would you hire?"

Sherwood happened to have an answer ready. "He already works for you—at ESPN."

# CHAPTER 9

# Hacky Sack

SITTING AT HOME IN LA, finishing his book about survivors, listening to his family and friends talk about what they liked to watch on TV and what they didn't, and surveying the landscape with an eye toward getting back into the game, Sherwood had come to the conclusion that the thirty-eight-year-old ESPN anchor Josh Elliott was not just a good talker and a juicy slab of beefsteak but indeed the future of morning television. And this he said, more or less, to Iger and Sweeney at dinner. The bosses must have liked what they heard, because come the first week of December, Sherwood was named the new president of ABC News. Now all Sherwood had to do was convince Elliott to give up cable sports for network morning TV. Considering how ambitious Elliott was known to be, and the fact that he had long been fixated on *GMA* in particular as a venue for his talents, this would prove about as difficult as convincing Matt Lauer to take a day off golfing with Bryant Gumbel, or getting Charlie Rose to say yes to just a splash more Châteauneuf-du-Pape.

Sherwood wanted Elliott not just for all the tall, dark handsomeness he would bring to the show, but as an ingredient that would alter the chemistry in and around the studio. Roberts and Stephanopoulos managed to be dissimilar without being complementary—you might say they were like pieces from different puzzles—and although the ratings gap wasn't getting any worse on their watch (they'd gotten it under a million!) it wasn't going to go away altogether. In fact, when Sherwood arrived, some people on the long-suffering *GMA* staff wondered whether he would just fire the odd couple and start over from scratch. Given the show's fifteen-year losing streak, and Sherwood's passion for winning, anything seemed possible.

Let's start with Stephanopoulos. He freely admitted to friends that he didn't enjoy the softer parts of *GMA*, in particular the eight a.m. hour of reality show recaps, parenting tips, and celebrity interviews. Still, he took the job as seriously as any mission he'd ever undertaken. In production meetings he'd sometimes ask, "Why are we doing this?" He knew the segments weren't meant for him, they were meant for stay-at-home moms and, although the network craved women in their thirties and forties, grandmoms. Most men tuned out by seven thirty, he discovered through ABC's research; most college-educated viewers tuned out by eight. But he still wanted to know *why* the stories were relevant to the moms and grandmoms in the audience. "What I respect," he said, "is when people can explain to me why it's important or why it's of interest to our audience. I can't always be persuaded, but I'm open to persuasion."

When Stephanopoulos moved to New York for *GMA*, he and Wentworth bought an apartment on Manhattan's Upper East Side with his early-morning schedule in mind. They wanted one in which what would be his closet, and the bathroom, weren't attached to the master bedroom. That way, in theory at least, he could get up very early and get dressed without disturbing his wife. As soon as he started doing the show, Stephanopoulos established a daily pattern. He would get up, without help from an alarm clock, at 2:35 each working day, an hour earlier than his cohosts on *GMA*. (If he had any qualms about working harder than the rest, he kept them to himself.) Then he would slip out of his rather fabulous Italian neoclassical bed, trying not to disturb his wife of ten years, tiptoe past the bedrooms where his daughters slept, and go into the living room to check his e-mail and certain news sites, to see if anything significant had happened in the world since his nine p.m. bedtime. With that done, he would sit cross-legged and meditate for about ten minutes. (Meditation had been part of Stephanopoulos's regimen ever since he joined *GMA*. He said it helps center him and gives him energy to get through the day.) In the kitchen he would fire up a kettle and load a French press with coffee. The resulting brew, said his wife, "has the consistency of chocolate pudding." Then he'd swing back into the bedroom to kiss her goodbye, oftentimes waking her up despite his best efforts—the curse of the morning TV spouse. It was a sweet and loving ritual that ended with his arriving in a pop-culture fun house that he didn't totally understand, and didn't want to.

Roberts shared his disinterest. The former ESPN host and self-professed jock outwardly had little in common with the moms who made up *GMA*'s base. She "grudgingly participated" in the studious goofiness of the eight a.m. hour, one of her colleagues said, "but it's not really what she does or who she is."

But fluff-adverseness was about all Stephanopoulos and Roberts had in common. When the ABC News president looked at Elliott he saw the mortar that could make those bricks stick together. A chiseled six-foot-three-inch California boy with a smile that, to hear the besotted Sherwood tell it, is equally endearing to women, men, children, and small fur-bearing animals, he relates to the camera in an inoffensively swaggering way that makes you wonder if he has a tattoo that says, "Born to Throw It to the Weather Guy." And yet as Elliott, who doesn't mind talking about himself, will tell you, as a child he dreamed of being a writer, and he says he still thinks of himself as "an ink-stained wretch."

Elliott majored in English literature at the University of California at Santa Barbara and covered sports for its newspaper, the *Daily Nexus*. After earning a master's in journalism at Columbia, he took a job at *Sports Illustrated*, where he struck one perhaps envious colleague as "the kind of print journalist who wants to get out of print and get into something that gets you more money and more women as quickly as possible."

Around 2002, Elliott hired a TV agent, Sandy Montag, who introduced him to the ESPN empire by way of a panelist gig on the daily sports roundtable show *Around the Horn*. Montag thought he saw marketability, and asked, "If you ever wanted to do any more television, what would it be?"

"I don't know, anchor *Good Morning America*?" Elliott said. He thought the idea not so absurd since he had seen Roberts make the crossover from sports to news anchor. But the *GMA* job was one of the most coveted in the industry by the people who had the kind of hair Elliott had, and Montag just laughed.

Elliott's dreams seemed less humorous in mid-2008, when he became a coanchor of ESPN's signature newscast, *SportsCenter*, between the hours of nine a.m. and noon—the closest thing the network had to a morning show. Thanks to the Disney connection he even got to fill in on *GMA* once, on a weekend in early 2010, and he enjoyed the experience, but months went by and he never heard from anyone at the show about filling in again.

Elliott and his *SportsCenter* cohost Hannah Storm rang in 2011 in Pasadena, California, where they were leading ABC's coverage of the Rose Bowl. After the telecast they shared a ride to the airport and the pair, who had worked together two and a half years at that point, started talking about their futures in television.

"What would you want to do?" Storm asked him.

"I don't know," he responded. "Maybe I'd want to do *Good Morning America.*" What he hadn't told Storm—or anyone really—was that he'd met with the head of talent recruitment for ABC News, Amy Entelis, a few weeks before.

"Do you know anything about this new guy, Ben Sherwood?" Elliott asked Storm. She said she had met Sherwood socially a couple of times and that he seemed quite smart. Elliott, who had done a little research on the new guy, seemed to think so, too: the man was "writing books and they're making them into movies," he said.

At the airport, Elliott, who sometimes describes himself as a foodie, grabbed a copy of *GQ* because the cover promoted the magazine's list of the best new restaurants in America. Flipping through to the feature, he saw that the New York pick was Lincoln, a contemporary Italian spot that had opened near ABC a few months earlier. He made what he called a "note to self" to check out the restaurant soon.

Seated on the flight, Elliott saw that one of the movie choices was *Charlie St. Cloud,* which he remembered as the film made from Sherwood's novel. He also recalled that at his lunch with Entelis she had said, "Ben might want to have a drink with you someday"—and thought he should get up to speed with Sherwood's work. So he watched the movie and then, like any enterprising journalist, logged on to the in-flight Wi-Fi and dug up the Wikipedia page listing what was different about the book version. This, he figured, would allow him to bring up the subject of how Hollywood plays fast and loose with your work.

It was a good thing that he did this, because as soon as he got back to his home in Connecticut, at around midnight...well, it's best explained in his own words.

"I log on my e-mail and the first e-mail, sent at 11:05 that night, is from Amy Entelis. 'Can you meet Ben Sherwood for dinner?' It was sort of mind-boggling. So I write back, 'Hey, absolutely.' And she's like, 'I'm copying Ben so you two can talk.' So he sends me an e-mail, 'Looking forward to it. My son's not going to believe that I'm actually having dinner with you. How's Lincoln?' And I was like, 'There's no fucking way this is happening.'"

Sherwood and Elliott's dinner at Lincoln was scheduled for seven thirty p.m. on January 4, 2011, a snowy night in New York City. Elliott was planning to meet up with some friends at eight thirty. "He must be so busy," Elliott recalled thinking. "I took a straw poll of people who might know, and they said, 'You're lucky if you get forty-five minutes.'"

Sherwood was right on time. When a hostess sat them at a table at the center of the restaurant, Sherwood asked for a booth instead, so they could have a little privacy. Maybe, thought Elliott, this was going to last more than forty-five minutes after all.

"You're probably wondering why, on the third day of my tenure at ABC News, I want to have dinner with an anchor from ESPN," Sherwood said.

"Actually, yes I was," Elliott said, laughing.

Sherwood responded with a story about his then-six-year-old son.

Will Sherwood had started to show an interest in professional sports when he was four years old, the news chief said. So his parents turned on *SportsCenter* for him at six in the morning, before nursery school. This happened to be the time when Elliott and Storm were cohosting live on the East Coast. Sherwood wasn't watching—he was spending his early mornings writing *The Survivors Club* in another corner of the house. But he noticed that Will started periodically spouting off random facts about baseball players like Melky Cabrera and CC Sabathia and Manny Ramirez.

"How'd you know that Manny Ramirez grew up in Washington Heights in the shadows of Yankee Stadium?" his father asked.

"Josh told me," Will answered.

"Who's Josh?"

"He's the guy on ESPN."

After a while Sherwood began to watch *SportsCenter*, too. Will, he noticed, "was completely captivated by Josh." So was Sherwood's wife Karen.

As Sherwood told this story at dinner, Elliott thought to himself, "Just take a snapshot." Through the snow-speckled windows of the restaurant he could see Juilliard, the school for musicians, actors, and dancers, some of whom went on to be world-renowned, and others to be forgotten. "Just take a snapshot," he thought, "because this is not going to happen. Nothing will come of this, so just enjoy this moment." But as dinner proceeded far past the forty-five-minute mark, and the two men talked in detail about the chemistry and the connective tissue that make great television shows, it was harder and harder for Elliott not to get his hopes up.

When dinner finally ended at ten thirty, Sherwood asked, "I know this sounds odd, but can we take a picture and send it to Will? He'd think it's great."

Of course, said Elliott, who adored kids and had a two-year-old daughter, Sarina, at home. The restaurant maître d' took a cell phone photo of the two of them and Sherwood sent it to his wife, then called her. It was seven thirty in LA, where Will was about to go to sleep.

"Did he get it? . . . Oh, that's great, that's good."

Then Karen wondered: would Elliott say hello to Will?

"Sure, I totally will," Elliott said, reaching for the phone. "Hey, buddy!" Elliott and Will dove right into talk about the Dodgers and the Lakers. Knowing the Sherwood family was probably moving to New York soon, Elliott joked, "Do not let them turn you into a Yankees fan, OK? Do not let them turn you into a Knicks fan."

Then, as Elliott recalled it later, he turned serious for a second.

141

"You know what, Will? I just want to tell you this. And I know you're not going to understand it. It's not going to make any sense at all. But, you know, I just want to thank you for maybe changing my life."

There was a pause on the other end of the phone. And then Will responded, "You're welcome." Elliott started laughing.

Sherwood said of the phone conversation, "It took my breath away."

No job was discussed that night. But in short order Elliott had dinner with James Goldston, the *Nightline* producer who was about to replace Jim Murphy as the executive producer of *GMA*. Then Elliott, Goldston, and Sherwood all had dinner together—back at Lincoln—and talked in detail about where they saw *GMA* going.

When Sherwood first talked to him about taking over *GMA* in January 2010, Goldston, who had been the producer of *Nightline* for five years, was not interested; he had his sights set higher, on a VP job with oversight of all the news division's shows—essentially second in command to Sherwood. Sherwood had the same thought, but first he needed Goldston in the trenches, so to speak, to retool *GMA* with an eye toward putting it back in first place. "James had to be convinced," Sherwood said, chuckling.

Goldston's heavy British accent was a kind of warning to anyone at ABC who might bring up "the way we've always done it." He wasn't very interested in that, especially if what ABC had always done wasn't winning the time slot. Goldston, a former BBC and ITV producer, had many credits to his name, including Iraq war coverage, but the one mentioned most often was *Living with Michael Jackson*, an unsettling documentary that detailed the pop star's habit of sharing his bed with children. Originally produced for ITV, it drew twenty-seven million viewers when shown on ABC in 2003. Two years later Goldston was tapped to remake *Nightline* as Ted Koppel was retiring. Goldston, depending on your vantage point, either guided *Nightline* into the new century or presided over its decline. One thing was for sure: it had a bigger share of network television eyeballs when he was done.

As Goldston hashed out what changes might need to be made to *GMA*, he did not see the goal as the cloning of *Today*, which had been a basic premise of the competition for many of the previous thirty-six years. He's "a brilliant showman," said Victor Neufeld, a former executive producer of *20/20* who credited Goldston with having "little regard to the stale formulas that preceded him." Goldston wanted to create a looser kind of morning show, one that was, above all else, entertaining and inviting to the audience. That didn't mean ignoring major news stories that viewers *needed* to know about, but it meant emphasizing the stories that viewers *wanted* to know about—the toy recalls, the messy celebrity divorces, the girls gone missing—especially on the days, and there were many, when this or that disaster didn't dominate the headlines. "The aim was relevance in everything we did," he said.

Meanwhile, Sherwood wanted to get the chemistry just right. Rather than removing one or both of the stars, as some staffers had speculated he would, he was adding supporting actors—creating an ensemble that looked more like *The View* than like a traditional two-person morning show.

The other addition, Lara Spencer, was already close to signing with ABC. Sherwood's predecessor David Westin had wanted Spencer, a mother of two (her husband, David Haffenreffer, is a real estate broker and former television anchor), to be "the social butterfly and the 'mom' of the show," according to a *GMA* producer. But don't be fooled by Spencer's maternal air. She was a fiercely competitive diver at Penn State, where a professor suggested she try out sports reporting. Soon she was filing stories for the school's TV station and applying to be an NBC page. She'd been all over the map since: she'd covered the crash of TWA

Flight 800 for WABC, the ABC station in New York; hosted *Antiques Roadshow* on PBS (she cold-called the producers to get the gig); and created a short-lived game show with Cedric the Entertainer for NBC. Spencer had been a correspondent for *GMA* in the early 2000s, specializing in entertainment and family stories, but she was persuaded to leave in 2005 to host *The Insider*, a tabloid-y news show that was spun off from *Entertainment Tonight*. Now she wanted to come home. Picking up the discussion where Westin had left off, Sherwood met with Spencer on New Year's Eve, days before he dined with Elliott. He envisioned her as the lifestyle anchor, a new title at the new *GMA*. She'd come on during the eight a.m. hour for segments about parenting, health, fitness, and entertainment—all the sorts of stories that Roberts and Stephanopoulos weren't eager to cover. "The moment Ben Sherwood arrived [at ABC News], you could feel the momentum," Spencer said. "I wanted in. I wanted in."

So did Elliott. He was in the backyard of his home in Connecticut, kicking the soccer ball around with his daughter Sarina (his marriage ended in divorce in 2010) when Sherwood called in March to formally offer him the job. "He offered it," Elliott said, "and I looked up in the sky, and then I said to him, 'You know what? I appreciate what you're doing in offering me this. There's really no other way for it to end well other than that they'll think you are the smartest man in television. Because it's the only way it works out.' Or it could have ended miserably. It was a roll of the dice."

In an interview later, Sherwood said that he wasn't worried about Elliott's hiring working out, because of something his future news anchor had said during their first dinner together. Elliott had told him that he used to study improv. And the lesson Elliott came away with, he said, was "Never let it drop."

"The skill required to keep an improv going is considerable," said Sherwood, whose brother-in-law Steve teaches companies how to apply improvisational techniques to the workplace. "And Josh's love of keeping it going, not letting it drop, stood out to me. The hosts of the *Today* show, in its heyday, were excellent at the television equivalent of Hacky Sack. They could kick the Hacky Sack around and it never dropped. And they could do incredible tricks. And just when you thought it was gonna drop, bang, Katie would pop it up in the air or Matt would catch it on his shoulders or Al would bump it over to Ann and Ann would somehow get it back in the air. At *GMA*, we did not have that. We had a lot of things, but we did not have that improv."

Could these new players change that? Elliott and Spencer both started in May 2011, but Spencer got off to a rocky start. She'd gone from being the sole host of a half-hour show to being the fifth host of a two-hour show. And no one seemed to know what her newly made-up "lifestyle anchor" role entailed. "To be a part of this ensemble with these incredibly talented people and to not know exactly what my role was, was intimidating," she said. "And I hadn't felt intimidated in a long time. I wondered, How is this going to work?"

Sherwood sensed she was adrift when they met in June in his fifth-floor office. He likes to adapt his analogies to the person he's conversing with, so with Spencer, a former competitive diver, he thought sports. Not having aquatic analogies at his fingertips, he resorted to basketball. "Look, Spencer," he said to her, "I want you to think of yourself as Lamar Odom."

At the time Spencer and Sherwood had just moved back to New York from LA, and Odom was the sixth man on the LA Lakers—the recent recipient, in fact, of the NBA's Sixth Man of the Year Award. He was the guy who, coming off the bench first among the nonstarters, helped the Lakers to a division championship four years in a row. "In those days," Sherwood said later, "when Lamar had a good night, the Lakers won. When Lamar didn't have a good night, the Lakers didn't win."

Sherwood said he wanted Spencer to think of herself as *GMA*'s sixth man. "You know what?" he said. "Every single game, Coach Phil [Jackson] knows he can count on Lamar to score twelve to fourteen points. And that's what I need you to do. If you start swooshing and getting me those twelve to fourteen points then I'm going to give you the opportunity to score sixteen points."

The hardest part of many jobs is having to talk to the boss. Still, Spencer said the Odom analogy calmed her down. It was "a really easy way for me to digest it," she said. "I'm not kidding you, every single day I was like, 'I got to get my points.' And I pretty much think that from that day forward that I got my points every game." She even started signing her e-mails to Sherwood as "#7," Odom's number on the Lakers.

At around the same time *GMA* added a new segment for Spencer, the "Pop News Heat Index," that brought a bit of her old show, *The Insider*, to *GMA*. A creation of Goldston's, "Pop News" followed Elliott's news headlines segment at eight a.m. and provided a dedicated place for the showbizzy and gossipy headlines that viewers craved. In fact, *GMA* sometimes saw a spike in its minute-by-minute ratings when the segment came on. ("It's the one segment everyone watches, and no one admits to watching," one staffer said.)

Spencer and one of the show's writers e-mailed each other at all hours with conversation starters for the segment. The constant goal: to avoid Goldston's dismissing this or that story as "boooooring," a word he wielded like a weapon. "It fills a need on the show," Spencer said of "Pop News." "People want the headlines in the world of Hollywood and fashion and all things 'pop.' And it gave me a defined role." (Maybe NBC should share in the credit. A few days before "Pop News" premiered in mid-June 2011, *Today* unveiled an almost identical pop-culture wrap-up called "What's Trending Today." Likewise, later in the year *GMA* introduced a bargain-hunting segment called "Deals and Steals" that sure sounded inspired by the *Today* show's "Steals and Deals.")

Josh Elliott's job already had a definition—news anchors read the news—and he got off to a strong start by reporting on man-on-the-street reactions to the assassination of Osama bin Laden, which had taken place the night before his first show. Still, Goldston added another segment for him as well, "Play of the Day," to make him a fuller member of the cast. Elliott, joined by his cohosts, introduced a funny or outrageous viral video—a hero pig saving a baby goat, a dancing ping-pong player, an emu wandering down a highway—and laughed about it with his TV pals. It was a quick segment, sometimes just twenty seconds long, but it was scheduled at the same time every morning and became a bridge between the news rundown at seven a.m. and the more freewheeling portion of the show at eight a.m.

"Each one of these things had a very specific purpose," Goldston said. "It was to signal a new approach to the audience, and it was also to kind of cement Lara and Josh in their roles." All of the hosts, he said, "locked in to it incredibly fast. Within four or five weeks you could see it on air. Then of course the audience—well, that process takes much, much longer."

But something was happening out there in TV land. On the Wednesday morning in June 2011 that *Today* said farewell to Meredith Vieira, *GMA* lost by 1.2 million viewers. That was to be expected—smooth transitions are rewarded with temporary spikes in the ratings. By mid-June, however, the gap returned to about six hundred thousand viewers, right back where it had been before Vieira left. And after the Fourth of July it contracted even more, dipping below the psychologically significant five-hundred-thousand-viewer mark.

There was in truth a little trickery behind *GMA*'s momentum. Taking a page from the playbook of the *Today* show—which had been known to cut out all national commercials after eight a.m. to inflate the ratings on close days—*GMA* one morning in May started to move its last national commercial up by several minutes, thereby making the rated portion of the show a few minutes shorter. The dodge boosted the ratings a bit, giving *GMA* some psychological momentum (you gotta give 'em hope) while at the same time *Today* suffered from what would later be diagnosed as a slow fade. *GMA* ended the month of July—the first full month since "Play of the Day" and "Pop News" were added to the rundown—with 497,000 fewer viewers than *Today*. It was the closest *GMA* had come to number one in six years. It was also Ann Curry's first full month next to Lauer on *Today*.

# CHAPTER 10

## *Morning Joe*

WAS 2011 THE MOST INTERESTING YEAR YET in the history of the so-called morning wars? Quite likely. Think about it: you had at *GMA* a master alchemist mixing together a uniquely televisable team of personalities assembled not just to keep the show going as best they could, but to take back the top spot in the ratings after sixteen years. Simultaneously you had the *Today* show seemingly trying to help *GMA* toward its audacious goal by first propping up and then plotting to tear down Ann Curry as if she were a statue of Saddam Hussein. When the a.m. TV titans do battle, as we've seen, it usually comes to one show beating up on a show that is concurrently beating up itself. Go figure. The morning wars are weird that way.

But what of the non-titans, the more focused or indie-style a.m. entries designed for edgier or more eccentric tastes? How did they affect the larger scene as *GMA* rose up and *Today* did its slow fade? There are a lot of peculiar little programs these days, a dozen in all, many of them harboring dreams of becoming like *Morning Joe*, the cultlike MSNBC show that almost everyone in the industry speaks of with reverence. "You're the most talked-about show that no one watches," *Today* boss Jim Bell once said to his *Morning Joe* counterpart Chris Licht. To which

Licht responded, "You're the most watched show that no one talks about." If *Morning Joe* were a guitar player, it would be James Burton.

As anyone reading this book probably knows, *Morning Joe* is a three-hour-long political talk show cohosted by Joe Scarborough, a former Republican congressman from the Florida panhandle, and Mika Brzezinski, a journalist and the daughter of former National Security Advisor Zbigniew Brzezinski. Conceived by Scarborough in 2007, *Joe* is arguably the most innovative thing to happen to morning television since *Today* opened its street-level studio in 1994. The freewheeling show, which also features a cast of regular characters like Mike Barnicle and Mark Halperin, strips away some of the conventions of morning TV—like scripted and rehearsed "banter"—and gives guests far more airtime than the network shows normally allot.

"We don't play 'TV,'" Scarborough said.

They don't always play nice, either. Said Brzezinski, "If someone like [actor and former *People* Sexiest Man Alive] Bradley Cooper comes on the set, I'm going to tell him that his movie is the worst movie I have ever seen and I walked out of it. Then Joe's going to be like, 'You don't say that,' but it's the truth and that's how I feel and that's exactly who I am."

"And if I'm tired," Scarborough said, "do you know what I do? I slouch. And you know what? If Mika's on Ambien from the night before, she says, 'Sorry, I'm on Ambien from the night before.'"

The physical production of the show helps foster this feeling of spontaneity. The three main cameras are robotic and rarely move around, which makes the set on the third floor of 30 Rock feel a little bit less like a cold television studio and more like a meet-up of highly caffeinated political pals. Indeed, when Brzezinski senses that guests are nervous she will lean across the table before the camera goes on and say, "We're your friends, we're around the breakfast table. Let's just have a conversation."

And then she tells them how badly their movie sucks.

Before *Morning Joe*, Brzezinski (who's married to television reporter Jim Hoffer) was underemployed, to put it delicately. She had spent most of the prior ten years as a correspondent and substitute anchor for CBS News. But on her thirty-ninth birthday, in 2006, she was fired. She struggled to find another job, and when she finally did seven months later, it was on the bottom rung of the TV ladder, reading brief news updates between programs on MSNBC. She was freelance, meaning she had no contract and no health benefits from the channel. She spent her fortieth birthday on the overnight shift there, feeling as if things couldn't get worse.

And then they did. Scarborough, in early 2007, unwittingly took away a bit of Brzezinski's airtime. He was the host of *Scarborough Country*, the channel's nine p.m. talk show. "There used to be a minute-long news update," he recalled. "I cut it down to thirty seconds and I had no idea I was cutting Mika's job in half." ("Nor did I," she said, "because I didn't care.")

Scarborough was a conservative—a poor man's Bill O'Reilly, some said—on a channel that was moving toward an all-liberal lineup in prime time, and on a show that was like a paint-by-numbers parody of cable TV. "I was looking for a way to get out of cable news prime time," he said. Added Licht, his producer at the time, "I think we all knew our days were numbered."

But where else could they go? Certainly not to the mornings. For MSNBC's first eleven years, a simulcast of the Don Imus radio show had taken up the six-to-nine a.m. time slot. Cheap and nonthreatening to the company's main morning product, the *Today* show, *Imus in the Morning* was convenient filler for MSNBC—until Imus said on April 4, 2007, that he thought the players on the Rutgers University women's basketball team looked like "rough girls" and "nappy-headed hoes." One week later, on April 11, the simulcast was canceled. The executive in charge of MSNBC, Phil Griffin, and the channel's general manager, Dan Abrams, suddenly had a three-hour void in their weekday schedule. And Scarborough suddenly had a way out of *Scarborough Country*. When Scarborough, sitting on his couch in Pensacola, heard that Imus was out, he called Licht.

"I want to make a play for the morning show," he said.

"Why the fuck would you want to do that?"

Licht was wary because he knew the hours would be hard, and because the Imus time slot that he'd be inheriting was even lower-rated than *Scarborough Country*. (Scarborough's wife, Susan, and his parents were just as skeptical.) But the producer said he'd help if he could. On his home computer Scarborough mocked up a one-page pitch and a promotional poster for his imagined morning show. "The past week has been difficult for the entire NBC family," the pitch began, "but the morning opening also gives MSNBC the opportunity to create the morning newscast of the future." And, he added, a chance for MSNBC to beat CNN. The poster showed Scarborough's face and possible cast members, including Willie Geist, who had contributed stories to *Scarborough Country*, and Ana Marie Cox, who had founded the DC blog Wonkette and been a regular on Imus. It had a clip-art picture of a coffee mug with the words "Morning Joe" on it. Scarborough e-mailed the poster to Licht on Saturday, April 14, and said he wanted to get it to management "first thing Monday morning." Then he uploaded the poster to a FedEx Kinko's in midtown Manhattan so it could be delivered in person.

What was missing was Mika. The day before his tryout on May 9, while walking down the hallway at MSNBC's old Secaucus, New Jersey, headquarters, Scarborough ran into Brzezinski, whom he'd seen on the air but never met. She'd made an impression on him by ending some news updates with the line "Now back to *SCARBOROUGH Country*," exaggerating his name for comic effect. "Nice to meet you and by the way," he said, "I want you to know, I know you're making fun of my show."

Brzezinski, without blinking, responded, "How can I make fun of a show that I've never even seen?"

Scarborough liked her sassy style. "I immediately thought I had found my cohost!" he said. He told Griffin he wanted to have her beside him when he auditioned the next morning. "This," Griffin said later, "was the first time in history that a solo host of a program wanted a cohost." He gave Scarborough credit for recognizing that Brzezinski made him better: "He said, 'I need her.' That shows a self-awareness on his part that a lot of people on television don't have."

By this time Griffin had already tried out a battery of other hosts. "Phil had always liked Joe," Abrams said, but "didn't think Joe was the right choice for the morning slot." But no one else felt right, either. "He became, in effect, the only choice," Abrams said. And an excellent one. When he finally got his turn, Scarborough exuded confidence. "Maybe it was arrogance," Licht said, "but I don't think Joe ever entertained the fact that he wouldn't get the job."

Jeff Zucker, the NBC CEO, was impressed by Scarborough early on. ("On their third day," Griffin recalled, "I called Zucker, and he said it before I could: 'Joe's good.'") But executives like to feel they've earned their suits, and some at MSNBC and its parent, NBC News, wanted another woman paired with Scarborough, although, in the tradition of TV bigwigs, they didn't have specific suggestions of who that woman might be. "I was taken off a few times," Brzezinski said. "They kept trying other female hosts and there just wasn't chemistry," Scarborough added.

While the NBC brass toyed with her, Brzezinski gave *Morning Joe* its first bit of buzz. Shortly after six on a Tuesday morning in late June, she was handed a script for the news segment of the show. The top story, as selected by the writer, was Paris Hilton's release from jail—she'd been arrested for...wait, it doesn't matter—a few hours earlier. "I was supposed to sell the Paris story as interesting," Brzezinski wrote in her memoir *All Things at Once*. "To me, though, it was emblematic of everything that was wrong with television news."

Sticking to her principles, Brzezinski refused to read the script, and said it right on the air. "I hate this story and I don't think it should be our lead," she said. Scarborough, Geist, and the producers took this spontaneous moment and ran with it, making it a leitmotif of the three-hour broadcast. An hour in, at seven a.m., she pretended to light the script on fire; at eight she fed it into a paper shredder on the set.

The protest, noticed by TVNewser and hyped by MSNBC's Web site, garnered millions of views on the Web. "I am spinning...getting hundreds of emails," Brzezinski wrote in an e-mail to me two days later. The incident put the show on the map. "We knew what our voice was, and now others did too," Brzezinski said.

*Morning Joe* borrowed from *Imus* a willingness to talk about serious topics like budget resolutions and the obesity crisis, sometimes for up to half an hour at a time. The show also came together with a clubby sensibility that made viewers think they were listening in on a meeting of media elites. But it was not entirely an old boys' club as long as Brzezinski was around. The chemistry was so good that Licht even started showing up on screen, by virtue of a tiny camera installed in the control room. The move made sense because the three quickly became part of each other's off-camera lives: Licht even provided wake-up calls for Scarborough, who because of his ability to tune out alarm clocks has nearly missed the show's opening on several occasions, his closest call being a 5:56 a.m. arrival for a six a.m. live start. (Yes, it does sound impossible. But he swears he pulled it off somehow.)

In September 2007 *Morning Joe* was made a permanent part of the MSNBC lineup. While Scarborough and Geist were given contracts that specified they'd be cohosts, Brzezinski wasn't. She was given a generic MSNBC contract that put her several steps below the men. At the time, however, she didn't speak up. At least she had dental, she thought.

With the 2008 presidential campaign just then gathering steam, *Morning Joe* seemed to have been born with a purpose. Brzezinski worked overtime to book guests, including leading Democratic candidates Barack Obama and Hillary Rodham Clinton. Scarborough recalled, "She got everybody in the Democratic establishment, and a lot of people in the Republican establishment that would come on her show but not mine." On days when Clinton was running the morning show gauntlet, she loved to make MSNBC her first stop. "Joe would get her laughing," Brzezinski recalled. "By the time he was done, she was giddy and she was loose and she was ready to go."

Politicians and pundits also warmed to the show because of the sheer amount of airtime they were given. Tim Russert, NBC's Washington bureau chief, would finish up a three-minute hit on *Today*, then have nine or twelve minutes on *Morning Joe*. Through a monitor in the control room, Licht said he could see Russert visibly loosen up when it was time for *Joe*. "He loved doing the show because it was a conversation," Licht said, a gab-fest with jokes, with tangents, digressions—and especially shout-outs for Russert's beloved Buffalo Bills.

Scarborough lobbied Griffin for the money to take the show on the road to Iowa for the January caucuses, helping it to be identified early on as "event" television, something that people in political circles had to watch. And they did watch, as Scarborough knew from the angry e-mails he got from campaign aides who disagreed with something he'd said. Hard-core politicos don't occur in nature in sufficient quantities to make a serious Nielsen dent, but the show was reaching what TV execs call the "right" people: campaign aides, business leaders, advertisers, heads of rival networks. In some ways Scarborough, Geist, and Brzezinski broke down the wall between media and subject. In 2010, when Licht suffered a near-fatal brain hemorrhage, his *Morning Joe* colleagues called Vice President Joe Biden, who'd had two aneurysms in 1988. Biden, in turn, sought out a world-renowned neurosurgeon and asked him to see Licht. Weeks later, Licht thanked Biden for saving his life.

But the *Morning Joe* buds were for a long time not equal in the eyes of MSNBC. For the first two years Brzezinski was being paid one-fourteenth as much as Scarborough, her cohost. We're talking something under two hundred thousand dollars versus two million plus, here. The word that comes to mind is *preposterous*.

Scarborough, aware of the gross disparity, went to human resources and had a very large bonus check (she wouldn't say exactly how large) placed in her account through a direct deposit. "I found out about it when I checked my bank balance and expected it to be negative, and instead there was more money in it than I've ever had in my life," Brzezinski said. She was furious—but he fought back, telling her, "This is not about you, this is about business, and I'm making a business decision." That, she said, is when she decided that she would leave MSNBC unless Griffin, the network president, gave her a new and substantially upgraded contract. Griffin did. (And she kept the bonus.)

In 2010, during the midterm election campaign, *Morning Joe* did something that *Imus in the Morning* had never come close to doing for MSNBC: it beat CNN in the ratings. The show ended the first quarter with, on average, one thousand more viewers than CNN's shrinking *American Morning*. MSNBC bought a self-congratulatory ad in *The Times*, which annoyed the competition: when Licht bumped into a CNN vice president in Washington a few days later, the person told Licht, "Don't get used to running those ads." But MSNBC's advantage over CNN only grew, and by the end of 2011 *American Morning* had been canceled. The replacement show, *Starting Point*, which featured Soledad O'Brien and a roundtable of panelists, was roundly criticized for being a rip-off of *Morning Joe*, and CNN's morning ratings continued to sink. (O'Brien privately and rightly blamed CNN for not marketing the show.)

The ripples sent out by Scarborough, Brzezinski, and Geist reached the wider world beyond cable: there were grumblings on the *Today* set that whatever viewers MSNBC was gaining in the morning were coming at the expense of the uber-network's flagship show. Lauer was known to fume once in a while when people talked about a guest on *Morning Joe* as if that same person hadn't also just been interviewed by him. ABC had its eye on the show, too: when it was casting Diane Sawyer's replacement in 2009, some at Disney pushed for *GMA* to be "more like *Morning Joe*"—which is one of the reasons George Stephanopoulos was brought on.

No industry entity was more covetous of the cultlike MSNBC show than CBS—or as it should be more properly known in discussions of morning television, "poor CBS." What used to be called the Tiffany network had been flailing and failing in the a.m. since it introduced *The Morning Show* in 1954. Walter Cronkite was the original host, followed by Jack Paar and Dick Van Dyke, among others. *Good Morning!* with Will Rogers Jr. was the 1957 replacement, followed fourteen months later by a different *Morning Show* at seven a.m. with Jimmy Dean. By then *Captain Kangaroo* had settled into the eight a.m. hour. The public sausage-making was not pretty. In his book *Who Killed CBS?* Peter Boyer recounted how the network's longtime chairman William S. Paley would watch the morning broadcast while his valet served him breakfast in bed—then call the president of CBS News, Dick Salant, with specific complaints and changes.

The changes just kept coming: a very long series of noble experiments, halfhearted attempts, and outright embarrassments lasting fifty-odd years and starring (to name a few) Mike Wallace, Harry Reasoner, Sally Quinn and Hughes Rudd ("the beauty and the grouch"), Bob Schieffer, Diane Sawyer, Bill Kurtis, Meredith Vieira, Phyllis George, Maria Shriver, Forrest Sawyer, Bryant Gumbel, Julie Chen, Harry Smith, Paula Zahn, Hannah Storm, and Maggie Rodriguez. Rumor had it that every day at nine a.m. Paley's valet went into his crypt and rolled him over. The pioneer broadcaster, who died in 1990, certainly would not have liked what America was seeing. Consistency, generally agreed to be the single most important ingredient in morning TV, was present only in the form of its opposite. "We've been changing people like shirts!" said Phil Jones, head of the advisory board of CBS affiliates, in 1986. It was just as true in 1966, when the show was called *The CBS Morning News*, and in 2006, when it was called *The Early Show*.

"Morning needs patience," said Zev Shalev, who came in as the executive producer of *The Early Show* in 2008. "You're building an intimate relationship with the audience, asking them to tune in and give you two hours of their life each morning. They are looking for a long-term relationship."

There was a lot Shalev couldn't do—like ensure that his bosses would give him enough time to nurture a new cast. But he could replace the couch, which, come to think of it, is a pretty important part of the morning show formula, its presence implying that the cast is sitting in the same living room as the viewer. It wasn't easy, Shalev said, to find the right couch, in terms of softness and sight lines—"it's like Goldilocks, it has to be just right"—and he ultimately had to have one custom-built. And a nice couch it was. It was still there when he left eighteen months later.

* * *

Another *Early Show* producer came and went. And in 2011 it was time to try yet again. In February the CBS CEO Leslie Moonves put two new executives in charge of his news division: Jeff Fager, the producer of *60 Minutes*, as chairman, and David Rhodes, a former VP at Bloomberg and Fox News, as president. Fager wanted to remake the whole news division in the image of *60 Minutes*, a concept that had the full support of Moonves. Of course, much of what passes for news on morning television— fashion tips, trivia contests, literal bake-offs—is the antithesis of the one-hour-a-week newsmagazine. So *The Early Show* came under scrutiny right away. "I can tell you one thing, we were surprised as hell when they were doing karaoke in the middle of the eight thirty hour," Fager said, still able to picture the day a year later.

Fager and Rhodes decided that the problem had not been their personnel per se, or their furniture, but the fact that CBS had been so darned locked in to imitating the great *Today*.

"NBC's done a successful morning program for a very long time that has a particular format, and the audience has a particular expectation of what they're going to get," Rhodes said. "What we'd done for a very long time is put on different iterations of that—of the program they've put on. So they had a boy and a girl, we had a boy and a girl. They had a funny weatherperson, we had a funny weatherperson who wasn't quite as funny and wasn't quite as recognizable. They had a person at the news desk who read the headlines so we had a person who sat at a news desk and read the headlines. Everything was a pale imitation of what they have done very successfully for a long time.

"There's a morning orthodoxy," he continued, "that says, 'It's 8:19. We're sautéing onions.' We asked, 'Why are we sautéing onions?' They said, 'Because it's 8:19. That's what you do.'"

Here Rhodes paused for dramatic effect before adding, "But we're not good at cooking!"

Other great minds at other networks have come around to this same conclusion, about the futility of trying to win by out-*Today*-ing *Today*, but in TV the feeling is you're not alive if you're not imitating someone, so the CBS folks went with aping the anti-apers. Moonves had a very specific vision of what he wanted to do instead of slavishly imitating the industry leader. He wanted to fill his troubled two-hour time slot with *Morning Joe*.

Months earlier, in late 2010, a mutual friend of Moonves and Scarborough had reached out to Scarborough and Brzezinski to feel them out about a possible leap to CBS. The pair, as it turned out, were willing to listen. They had felt disrespected by MSNBC since the days in 2008 when they'd had to scrounge up the funds for a live show from Iowa. They'd wanted more airtime on the mother network, NBC, but had been rebuffed by NBC News president Steve Capus, who resented Scarborough's on-air and Twitter feuds with his fellow MSNBC host Keith Olbermann. Scarborough bluntly told associates that Capus "hated" him. (Capus said he didn't.)

Scarborough and Brzezinski had expressed their desire to leave MSNBC for bigger things as early as 2010. Jeff Zucker, still NBC's CEO at the time, had been willing to let them go if they agreed to stay off the air for six months. (When Olbermann left MSNBC a short time later, he accepted the same six-month non-compete clause.) Nothing had come of their dissatisfaction then, but they'd begun thinking seriously about leaving again when Fager and Rhodes took over CBS News. Scarborough and Brzezinski were particularly intrigued by Fager's talk about "moving *60 Minutes* to the morning."

Scarborough and Brzezinski were under contract to NBC, but their producer Chris Licht had more leeway. His contract was coming due, and after nearly four years of *Morning Joe* he wanted a change. On February 16, a week before Rhodes's promotion to president was announced, Licht came over to the *60 Minutes* office on West Fifty-Seventh Street, where Rhodes was borrowing the office of Anderson Cooper, a part-time correspondent for the newsmagazine. (Rhodes's own office across the street hadn't been renovated yet.) They talked about their shared belief in good reporting and stimulating on-air discussions of the sort that happened regularly on *Morning Joe*. Licht later characterized the meeting this way: "We're starting a revolution here and we want you to be part of it." He came away energized and thinking, for the first time, that he actually might want to work the morning shift at CBS. Licht went from CBS to a ballroom on the East Side, where Scarborough and Brzezinski were giving a speech at an AmeriCares fund-raiser. "I remember telling them that I was kind of blown away" by the discussion at CBS, Licht said, "and we all just sat there in silence."

While Licht entered into negotiations with CBS, Scarborough and Brzezinski talked again to NBC about possibly getting out of their contracts, which ran through 2012. Griffin, the MSNBC president, didn't think the pair would actually leave, but he was willing to let them look elsewhere. He told friends later that he had been bluffing, giving them the illusion of choice. Griffin's boss, Capus, said in a series of sometimes tense phone calls and sit-down meetings with the *Morning Joe* hosts that he wouldn't allow them to go to ABC (he saw that as an "affront" to the *Today* show) but that he would free them to negotiate with other networks, like CBS. One meeting between Capus and Brzezinski turned especially heated.

"Steve, listen," Brzezinski said. "You don't like us. You're not going to use us on the network. So let us go."

Capus—living up to his "Rage" nickname—screamed his response. "Why the fuck would I let two people go that don't even respect me?" He pointed and asked, "Do you respect me?" A heavy silence hung over the room. He leaned in and asked again, "Do you respect me, goddammit?"

Brzezinski sat across the table silently, trying to figure out what to say. After about five seconds, she had an answer.

"I respect the fact that you're in a very difficult position."

Scarborough and Brzezinski were in London for the Royal Wedding in April 2011 when they heard that the paperwork had come through, giving them permission to talk with CBS. Some in the industry thought they would stay on MSNBC through the end of the summer and then move on to CBS early in 2012. It was so serious that Griffin asked several colleagues for advice about how to replace *Morning Joe* in case the pair called his bluff and actually left. The best contender in-house, he thought, was Lawrence O'Donnell, MSNBC's ten p.m. host—O'Donnell had the authority, the sense of humor, the ability to shift from serious to silly and vice versa. No amount of flattery or money, though, would have convinced O'Donnell to work those hours.

Licht, meanwhile, was out the door and on board with CBS. "We wanted Chris for Chris," Fager said, meaning not because he might bring Scarborough and Brzezinski with him.

Then everything changed. On May 3, Mediaite, a media news Web site, got wind of the possible *Morning Joe* move. The *New York Post* followed up the next morning with a story titled "CBS Woos 'Joe.'" That stopped the talks. Several people involved say that friends of Steve Burke, the new NBC CEO, called and asked him, incredulously, "You're going to let these people go?" and that Burke in turn called Capus and told him to somehow make Scarborough and Brzezinski happy at NBC. There was briefly even talk about having them host the Sunday edition of *Weekend Today*, leading in to *Meet the Press*.

While they were trying to decide what to do, Scarborough and Brzezinski visited her father, Zbigniew—a *Morning Joe* regular—at his home in the Washington suburb of McLean, Virginia, for some career counseling. Should they stay or go?

"Let me ask you this question," the elder Brzezinski said. "Can you interview me for fifteen minutes on the CBS show?"

"No," they answered in unison. Despite all the talk about a *60 Minutes* sensibility coming to the morning show, they would not have anything near that kind of latitude. CBS was still network television, after all.

"Then don't go," Zbigniew said with a shrug. "The thing that makes your show special is that you can do what nobody else can do. Don't give that up."

Money also played a big part in their decision to stay. Scarborough walked away with a new contract believed to be worth four million dollars a year, while Brzezinski got half that. For that payout, NBC got not just the right to keep *Morning Joe* on MSNBC, but also the pleasure of watching CBS scramble to come up with a new morning format pretty much from scratch. That spectacle had the potential to be more engaging, to people in the industry at least, than anything the perennial morning loser would put on the air in 2012.

# CHAPTER 11

---

# May the Best Booker Win

IT WAS AROUND MIDNIGHT on a September night in 2011 when Charlie Rose sang Homer-like, through wine-darkened teeth, about vanquishing the *Today* show in the Nielsen ratings. He asked me, "Do you think I can beat Matt Lauer?" (I dodged the question by saying, "Well, you certainly have the hair for it.") Rose was lounging, among a half dozen friends, in a cozy corner of Le Cirque, across a courtyard from the headquarters of his friend Michael Bloomberg's media company on the East Side of Manhattan. Earlier that evening Bloomberg (the company) had thrown him a party to commemorate the twentieth anniversary of *Charlie Rose*, his much-praised interview program on PBS and Bloomberg TV. His friends had turned out in force: Google's chairman Eric Schmidt, News Corporation's chief Rupert Murdoch, *The Hangover's* Bradley Cooper. Bloomberg (the man) had heaped praise on Rose's extraordinary record of quality TV—"This program has been one of the few places where you can find smart, stimulating conversation," he'd said, offering a toast. It had been a lovely event. But that night Rose, although pushing seventy and five years past open-heart surgery, was thinking more about his next challenge, weighing an offer for a project that demanded much and promised little. If he said yes, he, along with Gayle King, an editor at large at *O, the Oprah Magazine* and a longtime pal of Winfrey, would be leading CBS's latest assault on *GMA* and *Today*.

*CBS This Morning*, as the network would name it, was envisioned as a brand-new kind of morning program, something unlike anything attempted on American television in the last twenty years. This show would have no pop-culture quizzes, cooking segments, outdoor concerts, or late-breaking news about reality show stars. It would have no street-level studio from which crazed tourists could be seen yearning for the sight of a cast member, proposing to each other, or waving homemade signs. No, the all-new program Rose was considering would be produced by Licht, the *Morning Joe* maker, and it would put a premium on political, public policy, and foreign news stories. It would be an interview show. It would buck tradition by being what journalism professors call "good."

Licht started in early June and had until the end of the year to assemble a new cast (Fager and Rhodes were helping with that), hire new staffers, prepare a new studio, come up with a new name, record a new soundtrack, and do dozens of other things that there really wasn't time for. The makeover was extensive because, as one survivor from the staff said, "there was a thirty-five-year culture of losing" at the network, and Fager and Rhodes wanted Licht to get rid of every last trace of it. Practically the first thing he did was fire Shalev's bespoke couch. In its place he put out a glass-topped table with seats for five. "It should feel important, yet intimate," he wrote in a memo for the set designers. "As if the viewer has a chair at the table."

One especially intriguing part of the launch plan involved starving the old *Early Show* of resources so that it would be especially bad—and thus low-rated—in the second half of 2011. No one would cop to doing this, of course, but it was pretty obvious once CBS literally boarded up the windows on the street-level

Fifth Avenue studio it was about to abandon. Erica Hill and the other women and men still inside the studio felt as if they were anchoring a funeral. The idea was to drive viewers away, and thus ensure that the new show would look more popular by comparison. Creating a sense of momentum was important because, as you may recall, every additional hundred thousand viewers between the ages of twenty-five and fifty-four were worth roughly ten million dollars in annual advertising revenue.

No one could accuse Fager and the other executives involved with the new show of lacking boldness. Indeed, after they signed Rose as their new team leader in November, some of them got just a wee bit cocky. When reminded by annoying reporters that CBS had never been successful in the morning hours, they were likely to reply that that was because the network had never before asked them to take a crack at the task. They saw themselves as not being constrained by conventional TV thinking.

Rose—who has the perpetual air of a man who stayed out too late last night with a bunch of other bon vivants who would never deign to watch a network morning show—was certainly not a textbook choice for an a.m. anchor. "I get up every morning with a new adventure," he once said—and then after he called her a cab there was, before the CBS gig came along, a television-less morning routine: a dog-walk, a workout, and some quality time with the newspapers that fed his never-fully-satiated fascination with the world. Rose, it is true, has humble roots (his parents owned an old-fashioned country store in rural North Carolina) and journalistic cred (he freelanced as a TV writer and producer until Bill Moyers hired him to work on *Bill Moyers' International Report* in 1974, and he appeared on CBS's *Nightwatch* and *60 Minutes* after that); what's more he is very smart (Duke University) and very charming (he vacillates between the temperamental Southern cavalier and the courtly Confederate gent). But any focus group worth its salty snacks would chew him up and spit him out in a Paramus, New Jersey (the Paris of focus groups) minute, for he has virtually nothing in common with the flyover-country ladies who make up the bulk of his potential parishioners. Like the jazz musician who was asked to get up early for that famous photograph "A Great Day in Harlem," Rose seems unaware that there are two ten o'clocks. (That's how he looks, anyway; for the record, Rose says he's always arisen between five thirty and six a.m.)

For Fager, Rose's increased role on commercial TV was the culmination of a long-dreamed dream. CBS executives had talked informally with ABC White House correspondent Jake Tapper and CNBC host Erin Burnett about the new show, but like Irish seamen they kept coming back to their somewhat fogbound first love. No one in the television press wrote about the network's courtship of the PBS star, perhaps because no one who covered the medium could believe it was actually happening, even though Fager, in his enthusiasm, might have readily confirmed the rumor of their long lunches at Michael's and added that Moonves agreed with him that Rose "could be a guy who could change the way you think about the mornings."

The wooing of Gayle King, a more conventional choice for the CBS cohosting job, began in June, two months after Fager's first lunch with Rose. She, too, had solid TV experience—as a longtime anchor in Hartford, Connecticut, and a talk show host on OWN, Winfrey's struggling cable network—but she also possessed a more traditional morning-friendly manner. Having booked her on *Morning Joe* several times, Licht suggested to Rhodes that they all meet. Rhodes chose the spot—the 21 Club, the same Manhattan institution where Matt Lauer was brought when WNBC wanted to sign him—hoping for the discreet tête-à-tête of legend. But the restaurant was making a promotional film that day (June 30) and their rendezvous was bathed in klieg lights and caught by the cameras. Rhodes said that he thought to himself, "This is really not getting off to a good start if we're being taped recruiting talent."

King left the meeting intrigued enough to talk it through with Winfrey. What should she do, King wondered, if they offered her the job? She worried that OWN would garner more bad press if she left. But Winfrey told her, "You must take it! You must, you must!" Said King, "She knew it was a huge opportunity and it was tailor-made for me."

The next time the trio convened, about a month later, it was in a private room at the Capital Grille. There the executives dropped Rose's name for the first time. "I was like, 'Wow, wow, wow'—capital letters, exclamation points, and flashing," she recalled.

By this time nearly all of Rose's friends, including Mayor Bloomberg, were telling him not to do the CBS show, saying he could not possibly juggle both it and his nightly interview program, and that the latter should be considered sacrosanct. Rose responded by saying that everything in his career had prepared him for this. He talked of "reimagining the morning" and bringing his brand of in-depth interviews to the breakfast hour. If he and King were a marriage made in the mind of Les Moonves, neither he nor anyone else at CBS seemed to care. "I knew a big part of us getting any kind of traction," said Licht, "would be about viewers saying, 'That's unexpected. I'm going to actually tune in to see what that looks like.'"

The competition thought they knew very well what it would look like. "Insanity," said the CEO of a rival network. "People are doing a happy dance over here," said a senior executive at ABC. "When you're CBS, you have two choices: try to get a bigger slice of the existing pie, or bake a new pie," said Steve Friedman, the *Today* producer in the eighties who had tried twice to resuscitate CBS's morning show in the 2000s. But he saw the Rose-King show as a third alternative: "No pie." Retrenchment.

Of course, there's nothing like a chorus of doubters to motivate a new team, which saw itself as pivoting back to the basics. Licht told his staff that he wanted to beat the *Today* show by 2015, giving them three years to do it. At a November 15 news conference to introduce Rose, King, and Erica Hill, who'd been spared execution as part of *The Early Show*, the big shots were almost giddy as they described how they'd be breaking the conventions of twenty-first-century morning TV by eliminating all the silly stuff. "Where will the weatherman sit? Oh...wait," said Licht, pretending to forget that the show would have no weatherman. There was no kitchen for cooking segments, either. "Watch the *Today* show if you want that," Licht said. "They're great at that stuff. Or watch the Food Network."

So much for those who don't know how it is done—assuming by *it* you mean not necessarily putting on the most intellectually stimulating show but gathering eyeballs in sufficient quantity to get you into first place in the ratings. *CBS This Morning* is a great show. But you couldn't win the morning game in 2012 by trotting out Charlie Rose and telling people to go watch something else if that's what they want, not when the numbers indicate all too clearly that America is already focused on the many other options beyond your time slot—not just other shows, but Web sites, apps, or simply sleeping in—and when so many of its citizens would truly like to find out how to caramelize onions. If the growing success of *GMA* was teaching us anything from mid-2011 onward about the unwritten rules of morning TV, it was that, whether you imitate *Today* or not, you've got to play to the heart of America as much as the mind. You're helping teachers and lawyers and secretaries wake up in the morning—and that takes a lot of skills that aren't taught in any journalism classroom in this country.

There's no one on the staff of *Today* or *GMA*—where, by the way, some producers make two hundred thousand dollars a year and show-runners make over a million with ratings bonuses—who has not heard an exasperated parent say, "Ohmygod, for this you went to college?" Yet their parents almost always watch every morning—and can't wait to hang out backstage when they visit New York.

Would you like to take a little tour?

It's May 22, 2012, a typical Tuesday in some ways and yet in others a very special evening for *GMA*. The season finale of *Dancing with the Stars* is being broadcast live on ABC, and eighteen million viewers, the network's biggest prime-time audience in months, are expected to tune in to see Donald Driver, Katherine Jenkins, and William Levy compete for the show's mirror-ball trophy. *GMA* will get an automatic boost in its ratings by virtue of all the televisions that will still be tuned to its network when people turn their sets back on in the morning. But the real bonanza, the real benefit of there no longer being thick walls separating self-promotion, entertainment, and journalism, will come as a result of exclusive interviews with the winners and losers at the studio in New York City the next morning, after the competitors are flown overnight from the West Coast but before Americans have had a chance to gather 'round the water cooler and hash out what happened.

*Dancing with the Stars* ends at eleven p.m. East Coast time, and the charter flight with the valuable payload of guests is supposed to touch down at Teterboro Airport in New Jersey at six a.m. During the broadcast Ariane Nalty, a *GMA* producer in charge of getting the dancers onto the plane, calls Jay Shaylor, the overnight producer, with good news. Len Goodman, the competition's persnickety British judge, has, after a little bit of cajoling, agreed to say, "Coming up next, the *Good Morning America* dance party." This to you may pale in comparison to, say, the victory of General P. G. T. Beauregard at First Manassas, but when you work the graveyard shift in morning television, it's the little wins that get you through the night.

Postgame interviews with reality show stars are the stuff of which ratings coups are constructed. They are one of those things, like chocolate, that always work. CBS has done them with *Survivor* and *Big Brother*. *GMA* has been doing them with *Dancing* for years. (NBC, inexplicably, doesn't do them with *The Voice* as well as it should.) But this time, just to keep things fresh and fancy, the producers want to stage an early-morning red-carpet arrival at the *GMA* studio in Times Square. They want to turn it into an "event." That is, if the plane arrives on time.

In the almost-empty sixth-floor production office of *GMA*, twenty blocks north of Times Square, *Dancing* is playing silently on an overhead TV. So far it's a slow news night—though Shaylor, superstitious in the manner of many TV producers, won't say the word *slow* aloud.

At 11:25 p.m. Shaylor is about a third of the way through his workday, and the show is falling into place, as neatly as it ever does. A special preview of the movie *Men in Black 3* is ready to go; a news story about Facebook's bungled IPO is about half-finished. There are still a couple of blanks on the rundown. That's by design: Shaylor has to leave space for the unexpected.

Shaylor, a talkative Columbia Journalism School grad wearing black-rimmed glasses, a T-shirt, and jeans (the dress code is one of the perks of this shift) is about to screen a rough cut of a story about a missing Louisiana girl when a production assistant tells him to pick up the phone. "The dog," he says, "is having a problem."

"*GMA*, this is Jay."

The dog is a two-year-old coonhound named Maddie who has achieved online fame for standing atop things—canoes, trucks, cabinets, people. Yep, just standing there on four legs, on top of things. Maddie is morning show gold—just the kind of surprise in-studio guest who will keep people watching even as they text their friends and tell them they ought to watch, too. Morning show viewers love animals, especially dogs. (Even Stephanopoulos, who feels it is his job to lobby for more serious segments, sometimes e-mails his wife when there's a cute dog coming up. "Tell the girls," he writes.) The dog, like the dancers, was a go for the next morning's show, but now Shaylor can't believe what he's hearing.

There is no way to sugarcoat this, gentle reader. Josh Elliott's "Play of the Day" segment may be in danger.

On the line is Theron Humphrey, a thirty-year-old photographer who is Maddie's proud and opportunistic owner. When *GMA* discovered Maddie on the Web and asked to have her on the show, Humphrey rushed Maddie to Los Angeles International Airport on his own dime, ready and willing to take a red-eye flight to New York for a TV appearance that will last three minutes at most. But at the gate he discovered that Delta requires the owners of pets to have a health certificate from a veterinarian, even if the beast travels with the luggage. After years of booking lizards and turkeys and cats and dogs, some heroes, others more into tricks and such, no one at *GMA* had known about the requirement. Now it looks as if it'll prevent Maddie from arriving in time for the show. Suddenly there's a poignant, dog-shaped hole where Segment 7 used to be.

"How is that possible?" asks Shaylor. "I mean, people fly with their pets all the time..."

With the help of Humphrey, Shaylor calmly but persistently wrangles a Delta representative, Jerry Hughes, onto the phone and begins his negotiations. "How can I get this dog on the plane?" he asks with practiced seriousness. Skilled in the ways of fluff-management, he's listening for inconsistencies and gradually applying more and more pressure.

"Where is this in the paperwork? I've never heard of this..."

Pause while he listens.

"If I go across the street to United or American are they going to treat me this way?..."

Pause.

"I'm platinum on Delta. Happy to give you my number..."

Shaylor wants to find a "creative way," as he puts it, to fly Maddie to New York. If you've ever been stopped for speeding in northern Georgia, or Sardinia, you may have heard yourself saying this same sort of thing. But the Delta rep isn't wavering, in fact is claiming that by federal law he can't waver—and time is running out. It's 11:34 p.m. now, and the flight is scheduled to take off in fifty-six minutes. If Maddie misses this flight, Shaylor tells the Delta man "then the dog will miss its hit time," as if an airline customer-service rep might know what that meant. The man then asks if Shaylor can hold. Things are not looking good, and yet whatever happens with Maddie, tonight will probably not go down as a night of historically bad proportions. It will not rival the time in 2005 that a *GMA* producer was detained for trying to stop the *Today* show from interviewing the hostage victim he thought he had booked first. Or the time in 2011 when *GMA* landed the first big interview with Gary Giordano, the suspect in the disappearance of his female companion on a trip to Aruba, but Giordano wouldn't leave his hotel room. A producer sped to the Ritz-Carlton, coaxed him outside, and delivered him to the studio with just about two minutes to spare.

A minute later Shaylor is still on hold. While he waits he explains to me that this, right here, is why he never says the word S-L-O-W.

※　※　※

Like its main rival, *GMA* is on a twenty-four-hour clock. The first formal meeting of the day starts at ten a.m., when the top producers gather in the office of Tom Cibrowski to get their assignments. Cibrowski, a bald, fatherly guy who could talk anyone off a ledge, became the executive producer of *GMA* in March 2012 when Goldston moved up to the VP job he had wanted all along. Goldston remained involved, but it was understood that the show was now Cibrowski's baby.

The top producers reconvene at four p.m., this time to speak more specifically about their expectations for each segment—how to approach the story, how to sell it to viewers, how to get it done by airtime. They also talk holistically about the mix of segments planned. Is the balance of "light" and "dark" right? Is there time baked in for chitchat between the hosts, showing off their chemistry?

Some of these producers, like Cibrowski, have been up since four a.m., so they head home by five or six p.m. Senior producer Angela Ellis oversees things until Shaylor arrives at about eight thirty. Before Ellis leaves they run through the stories being stitched together overnight, like the correspondent Bill Weir's segment about Facebook. "I think Cibrowski likes it as the lead," Ellis says.

"Totally," Shaylor says.

Shaylor's night is always busy. He edits the scripts submitted by producers and screens early versions of the next morning's pieces. Besides making sure that no story will bore the audience at home, he looks for legal and ethical booby traps: Have we licensed that video? Have we called that lawyer for comment? Have we included both sides?

"We want our viewers to wake up to something they haven't heard," Shaylor explains. So in scripts he crosses out words like *yesterday*, and encourages the correspondents to say what happened "overnight" or what's going to happen "later today."

Shaylor's been on the overnight shift for a little more than a year. He sees it, just as his predecessors did, as a stepping-stone to a job with better hours.

Until then, he has to solve the late-night dog dilemmas.

Thinking synergy, Shaylor wonders if he can get Maddie on the charter flight that's whisking the *Dancing with the Stars* entertainers to New York in a few hours. But as it turns out the charter is full.

In a few moments he is back with Delta Guy. "Can we carry the dog on?" he asks. "What if we put a raincoat and a hat on the dog?"

"For that, you'd have to go through passenger service," the rep mysteriously says.

Then Shaylor thinks, If it's a health certificate that the dog needs, let's find a damn veterinarian.

By 11:54, Shaylor is on the phone with a vet in Los Angeles. "They're willing to accept faxed paperwork," he says, but the doctor says he must physically examine the dog.

"How far are you from LAX?"

"Twenty minutes."

"Yeesh, that's cutting it close."

Shaylor asks the vet to start driving. Miraculously, the man makes it in less than twenty minutes and gives Humphrey the necessary paperwork. But the process takes just a few minutes too long, and the flight leaves without Maddie. Humphrey calls back a couple minutes later with the bad news. Shaylor, undeterred, asks if he'll fly to New York tomorrow instead. "Tomorrow's more than fine with me," says Humphrey.

Shaylor has one more question.

"You would continue to honor doing it exclusively with us, right?" he asks, not wanting to see Maddie standing on Al Roker any time soon.

Humphrey says, "Certainly."

※　※　※

Booking battles are the war within the war on morning TV. *GMA* and *Today* duke it out over presidents and eyewitnesses, over A-list actors and teens who've been expelled for tattoo-related reasons, going to extraordinary lengths to reel in great "gets." If the bookers have any shame, they have suppressed it. They will drop off homemade cookies and handwritten notes on a crime victim's front porch. They'll take campaign strategists out to dinner and get them drunk. They'll strike up months-long friendships with the family members of the jurors in a sensational murder trial. They'll flirt, cajole, cry, beg, and their bosses don't want to know what else, because they believe ratings and their own paychecks are at stake. (The bookers at ABC barely flinched when one of their own bragged of sleeping with an adult witness in a child abuse trial to secure an interview.)

For the biggest bookings, the hosts themselves often make calls and write notes by hand. But the bookers are happy to go a step further for the right guests, and guarantee the interviewer of his or her choice. Is that ethical? Not exactly, but it is closer to the line than a lot of the other stuff they do, such as tailing a guest like a private investigator, sequestering a guest in a hotel room and standing guard at the door—or pretending to be someone else and canceling the other guy's guest's plane tickets. "One of my producers nabbed Ted Williams—the homeless man with the 'golden voice'—when he walked out of a competitor's studio for a smoke. We basically kidnapped him," Santina Leuci, the head booker for *GMA*, bragged in 2011. Leuci, according to a colleague, looked for three attributes in her booker hires: "They had to be hot, able to talk their way into or out of anything, and be a chameleon."

If the circumstances call for it in their opinion, the two leading shows will spend enormous sums of money on bookings. Someone like Humphrey, Maddie the dog's owner, would just receive free airfare and a couple of nights at a hotel. (Humphrey later complained that *GMA* never paid him back for his flights.) But higher-profile guests are treated to lavish dinners with the producers and personal attention from the hosts. To win the first interview with David Goldman when he brought his eleven-year-old son back to the United States from Brazil after a highly publicized custody battle between 2004 and 2009, NBC paid for a charter flight and put him up in a presidential suite at Universal Studios, an amusement park partly owned by its parent company. The network's investment, a clear violation of traditional journalistic ethics, paid off handsomely in the ratings.

The shows say they don't directly pay for nonperforming guests, but they will sometimes license photos or videos from the subjects of news stories—a backdoor way to secure an interview. One of the most embarrassing incidents involved the "Botox Mom," a California woman who claimed in 2011 to have injected her eight-year-old daughter with Botox. A *GMA* producer called her after her story appeared in the British newspaper the *Sun* (British papers are founts of free story ideas for morning shows) and subsequently offered to pay a broker ten thousand dollars for photos of the eight-year-old receiving injections. The story was assigned to Spencer, who had been back at *GMA* for only a few days. "It does sound unreal," Spencer said on the air—but then introduced the segment anyway. It *was* unreal, the woman later claimed in an interview with TMZ. "Honestly, I don't even know what Botox is," she said, alleging that the newspaper had scripted the whole thing and paid her two hundred dollars to participate. ABC executives didn't know what to believe, but they admitted privately that the episode was embarrassing for Spencer and for *GMA*. The ten-thousand-dollar payment, thankfully, never went through. Ben Sherwood came out two months later and said he'd banned the licensing practice, with exceptions to be granted only in extraordinary circumstances.

Sometimes the networks publicly condemned booker behavior, but said very different things behind the scenes. See, for instance, what happened in 2002 when NBC, ABC, and CBS all vied for the first on-camera interview with two teenage girls who were abducted and raped north of Los Angeles. *Today* secured the first interview thanks to Couric and Gloria De Leon, a star booker in NBC's Burbank, California, bureau. Twenty-six years old at the time, De Leon was in charge of "babysitting" (her boss' word) one of the girls before the interview. "Katie was on a plane from New York," De Leon recalled, when she took the girl shopping. Normally NBC's standards prohibit giving gifts to interview subjects, for gifts can be construed as indirect payments. (Of course, so can airline tickets and hotel accommodations and licenses for photos, but the standards are the standards.) But De Leon bought a sixty-dollar pair of jeans for the girl, knowing that the girl's favorite pair were in police custody because they were stained with blood. "She wanted to wear jeans in the interview to show she was the same woman that she was before the rape," De Leon said. The family of the victim couldn't afford to buy her a new pair, so De Leon did. "I thought it was a nice gesture," she said. It was their little secret—until one of the bookers from the other networks called the girl's mother in another attempt to snag the interview away from NBC. The mother told the booker that her daughter had gone "shopping with Gloria from the *Today* show."

That tidbit must have made its way back to the rival network, because within hours reporters from *USA Today* and other news outlets were on the line with Jonathan Wald, the top producer at the time, demanding to know whether NBC had paid for a pair of jeans. Wald thought no—but after talking to De Leon, he had to call back and say, "I was wrong, I was misinformed, we bought the pants." Wald had to call back De Leon, too, and say, "We're going to have to suspend you."

"This was a rape victim!" De Leon said years later, still amazed by the sequence of events. "Back in those days we were doing thousand-dollar dinners" with potential guests, she added. But the standards are the standards. She was publicly slapped on the wrist with a week's suspension; the newspaper reporters were told that. They weren't told this: "When I got back, NBC gave me my first six-figure contract for being, in their words, 'a bulldog,'" De Leon said. "I can go to war thanks to the lessons I learned," she added.

* * *

At 1:21 a.m. in New York, Nalty calls in from LA. "Wheels up!" she announces over Shaylor's speakerphone. The *Dancing with the Stars* cast members are now on their way here.

"We've never left this late," Nalty tells Shaylor. "William Levy"—one of the dancers—"was taking his sweet little time in his trailer."

Shaylor says he's worried that they are not going to make it on time. To have the dancers at the *GMA* studio in Times Square by seven, to shoot their red-carpet entrance, the charter needs to land by six fifteen a.m.

"I just told the pilot, you have to make this," Nalty says. "They'll catch it up in the air."

"They're not drinking?" Shaylor asks.

"No."

After he hangs up, Shaylor looks at me and says, "Sometimes they drink."

At 4:40 a.m. Shaylor's boss Cibrowski arrives at work at *GMA*'s Times Square studio. At 5:04 Stephanopoulos walks into Cibrowski's office. He asks the same question he asks Cibrowski every morning at this time: "What's happening?" And today, an extra question: is the charter on time?

At six thirty Cibrowski and Denise Rehrig, the senior broadcast producer, relocate to the show's bunker-like control room.

Around them a dozen producers, writers, and technicians fiddle with graphics, camera angles, and scripted intros. They get good news: the *Dancing* cast members are off the plane and in a convoy of cars on the way to Times Square. The red-carpet arrival will go off without a hitch. One floor below, in the studio, Robin Roberts and the other hosts are practicing their lines and touching up their makeup. And a few blocks away the *Today* hosts and crew are doing exactly the same things. Thanks to a small television monitor in a corner of the *GMA* control room that streams the feed *Today* is sending out to its network affiliates, Cibrowski and his crew can see them in their ritual labors. Right now Matt Lauer and Ann Curry are proofreading scripts and primping. NBC no doubt has a similar peephole into *GMA*. In this business, you always keep one eye on the other guy.

# CHAPTER 12

---

# Invincible

SOMETIMES IT SEEMED as if the only difference between a big-time college football coach and a network news president was that the coach made more money. "We're going to win the championship!" Ben Sherwood assured the team at *GMA* many times in late 2011 and early 2012. "Two things have to happen—we have to keep growing and they have to keep declining," added the ABC News chief. "But we can do it! It can be done!"

Taking this position, it should be noted, put Sherwood in direct opposition to Steve Capus, his former colleague at NBC News who had no small amount of antipathy for him. Capus dismissed ABC—and particularly Sherwood—as being desperate for a win, and swore that NBC wouldn't let them have one. Asked what would happen if *Today* ever dropped into second place in the ratings race behind *GMA*, Capus told Bill Carter of *The New York Times*, "That is a hypothetical that we are not going to have to deal with. It's not going to happen." When Capus talked this way, though, he was in a sense drowned out by the sound of Sherwood, over at ABC, chanting, "It. Can. Be. Done." In an interview for this book, Sherwood said, "If you ask my colleagues what sentence they've heard come out of my mouth more than any sentence, it's 'We're going to win the championship.'" Then

he leaned in close and said, "We're going to win the championship." Sherwood has excellent taste in cologne.

Sherwood's confidence and enthusiasm were all well and good,
but cohost Robin Roberts kept looking at the numbers in January
and early February 2012—as almost everyone associated with
both shows did—and for her this negated the effect of the ABC
News president's rousing locker-room-style speeches. The numbers were barely budging. Despite the fact that the *GMA* team
was starting to jell, and the research showed that the audience was
liking the softer stuff the show served up with a smile, the ratings
gap remained stuck between half and three-quarters of a million
viewers. Still.

"I've always felt" that *GMA* could beat *Today*, Roberts said.
"Honestly." But why, she wondered, hadn't it happened? Would
it ever?

By this time, ten years into her tenure at *GMA*, Roberts found
all the Nielsen talk numbing. "When I came over from ESPN,
where we were just such a dominant force, we didn't talk about
ratings; we didn't have to; we just killed everybody," she said.

In 2005, when Roberts became the third anchor at *GMA*, with
Diane Sawyer and Charlie Gibson, and the show got within about
forty thousand daily viewers of *Today*, a lot of people at ABC had
predicted a tidal wave of numbers that would sweep the alphabet
network to victory. But then the tide had gone back out, the gap
had gone to half a million and then a million again, and a sense
of profound defeat had hung over the set. The dark clouds never
overwhelmed Roberts, though. "I always felt good about what
we were putting on the air," she said. Still, she admitted, "it was
disappointing that we weren't making inroads."

Eventually, she said, she resigned herself to the difficulty of
changing people's viewing habits. "I had longtime friends, *great*
friends, who were not watching my show. Why? Because that's
morning television." (Translation: her friends were watching

*Today.*) "I'm thinking, if somebody that *knows* me won't watch . . . then I started thinking, 'Well, you can't take it personally. People do have their routines.'"

Of all the great battles in history, the one the morning show wars of the last few years most closely resembled was the Rumble in the Jungle, the fight between Muhammad Ali and George Foreman in 1974. Foreman was lean and mean in those days, and Ali went in as the decided underdog. But Ali came up with a game plan—the famous and never-before-seen rope-a-dope technique—and he stuck with it, and finally there was an unforgettable moment in the eighth round when all of a sudden you saw that the big guy was in trouble. Something had happened—a particularly well-measured punch from Ali, perhaps, combined with the cumulative effect of all that earlier rope-a-doping—that made the champion wobble, and gave the challenger fresh energy, and made the spectators gasp.

For *GMA*, the equivalent of that table-turning eighth-round moment was the 2012 Academy Awards, broadcast by ABC to nearly forty million viewers on the evening of Sunday, February 26. Roberts was on the red carpet in front of the Kodak Theater, interviewing nominees George Clooney, Melissa McCarthy, and Viola Davis, and later winner Octavia Spencer. But more significantly for *GMA*, Roberts also, despite feeling especially fatigued, anchored the next morning live from LA. That broadcast, during which she took viewers behind the scenes of the post-awards-show parties, drew a year-high rating. The next day Roberts was back in the New York studio to help announce that spring's *Dancing with the Stars* contestants. The show was on a roll.

*GMA's* ratings remained elevated through Thursday, March 1, the day Tom Cibrowski formally replaced James Goldston. *GMA* was doing well because it had great guests and because it was drafting in the wake of the Oscars. But just as important to its ratings fortunes was the palpable tension on the *Today* show set between Curry and Lauer, which was making the show hard to watch for some longtime fans. *GMA* was starting to convert at least a few of them. *GMA* was probably also benefiting from the shakeup at CBS—Rose and company's new show had premiered in January, and some viewers were now channel surfing, trying to choose who and what to wake up with in the morning.

So it was partly for things that others had done that Goldston and Cibrowski were hailed as mighty conquistadors and cheered with a champagne toast in the newsroom on Thursday. The next morning there was another cha-ching moment as Coldplay performed a Friday-morning concert. "Not bad for a first day," Cibrowski said humbly as the band packed up, knowing that it would get big numbers. As much effort and worry as NBC put into the morning race, runner-up ABC put in even more, and one way this manifested itself was in *GMA*'s willingness to pay Nielsen thousands of dollars to get reliable overnight ratings a few hours before anyone else. *GMA* didn't do it every day or even every week—but every time the show did, it drove *Today* a little crazy.

Four hours after Coldplay played "Paradise," Cibrowski received this e-mail from ABC number cruncher Amy Miller:

SUBJECT: Thurs GMA - Fast Final Numbers
For the week among Total Viewers averages are as follows
ABC - 5,437,000
NBC - 5,513,000
We are behind NBC by only 76k P2+...smallest gap since the week of May 9, 2005 (Robin Roberts' first week as co-anchor of GMA/DC security scare - plane in restricted White House air space).

One week earlier, *GMA* had been down by 519,000 viewers. But this week, after four days, it was seventy-six thousand viewers away from beating *Today*.

Cibrowski kept the numbers secret from all but a few of his senior colleagues. Managing the staff's collective psyche was important, and he didn't want expectations to get out of hand. He knew that Friday's results would probably tilt back in the *Today* show's favor—the competition tended to win on Fridays for some reason. But because the final weekly numbers didn't come out until Monday (for *GMA*, which was paying extra—normally the weeklies didn't come until Thursday!), he'd have to wait all weekend to find out for sure. "Makes you a bit crazy inside!" he wrote in an e-mail on Saturday.

Cibrowski's immediate goal as *GMA*'s new boss was to win just one week on the back of promotable events like the Oscars, the *Dancing* announcement, and the Coldplay concert. Just one damn week. After that his goal would be to win another week, and so on. Although it felt daunting to put even two back-to-back wins together, he knew it was possible, because, after all, *Today* had done it for more than 840 weeks in a row.

The big test for Cibrowski would be the third week of May. He had already circled it on his calendar. That's when the *Dancing with the Stars* finale would air on ABC, giving *GMA* a temporary bounce the next morning. With a little luck, and the right celebrity booking or two, *Dancing* could be a springboard to first place. "We store up all our ammunition," he said, "and then we fire." Cibrowski figured he had to fire then because—to stick for another moment with the testosterone-fueled language favored by the male network executives who strive to produce shows that will appeal to women—in July, NBC would be making its shock-and-awe move with the Summer Olympics. The Olympics have, at least since 1980, been a trump card for whatever morning show is lucky enough to be on the same network as them. The London Games this year would give *Today* a sure three weeks of wins and maybe even stop the slow fade for good. If *GMA* didn't win a week during the spring, it might not, in 2012, win a week at all.

On Monday Cibrowski found out that *GMA* had closed out the previous week with a daily average of 5.36 million viewers, 164,000 fewer than the *Today* show. Friday had, indeed, helped *Today* widen its lead. The gap was now NASCAR-speedway-size, not football-stadium-size, as he had hoped in midweek. But the results were still encouraging. *GMA* had not been this close to its archenemy in four years.

Certainly these gains were not only due to the meshuggaas over at *Today*. The *GMA* team deserved credit for playing the game well, for remembering the venerable morning rule about good chemistry, and for seeing that the deeper we got into the twenty-first century, the more the morning audience disdained the savory in favor of the sweet. If there was ever a team for the times it was (in order of wake-up time) Stephanopoulos (2:35 a.m.), Roberts (3:45 a.m.), Champion (3:45 a.m.), Spencer (4:00 a.m.), and Elliott (4:01 a.m.; the extra minute, he said, gave him a "psychological lift").

The *GMA* hosts had their petty differences, to be sure; they squabbled sometimes about who was hogging airtime and who would be interviewing the A-listers who rotated in and out of the studio like walking, talking billboards for their movies and albums. But that they stayed friends in the end seemed obvious on air, thanks in part to the time they spent eating and drinking together during off hours. "We like being together, we genuinely like hanging out—as difficult as people might find that to believe," Champion, the show's weatherman, said.

Executives at NBC tended in the early months of 2012 to mock such claims and note that the *GMA* hosts more closely resembled, to borrow a phrase from Don Imus, a pack of backstabbing weasels. Josh Elliott is clearly gunning for Stephanopoulos's job, they would tell you, and Lara Spencer has it in for Robin Roberts. But in private those same people would sigh and say they wished their cast had the same chemistry that *GMA*'s had.

The *GMA* cast even had a favorite restaurant, Café Fiorello, that they frequented after work. Sometimes the producers still at work at ABC would see their Twitter messages about hanging out together and wonder if they'd been hitting the vino a little too hard.

Stephanopoulos was the exception—he rarely hung out with the other four, citing his other job, as host of *This Week*, and his family obligations to explain his absences. But he, too, benefited from the ensemble, even though it ate into his airtime. The best advice Stephanopoulos ever got about the *GMA* gig came from, of all people, Jeff Zucker, who at the time was still the chief executive of NBC. The two men struck up a conversation at a party in New York for the Nancy Meyers film *It's Complicated*, which Ali Wentworth had a small part in, and Zucker told him, "You truly have to be yourself." In a word: authentic. Don't try to fake a reaction or an opinion, Zucker told him—react the way you would naturally react off camera, "because the camera's going to see through it anyway." Having more people in the mix—Spencer to his right, Roberts and Elliott and Champion to his left—freed Stephanopoulos to do just that.

By the end of 2011 Zucker was working in the same building as Stephanopoulos and company, running Katie Couric's new talk show, which ABC was producing. He was an advisor and a sounding board for his old friend Sherwood, who was lucky to have him around. Think about it: Zucker was the producer who had started *Today*'s streak in the 1990s, who arguably knew more about morning television than anyone. Now he was helping *GMA*. "You better be ready, Benjy," Zucker would sometimes say to Sherwood. Confident in his prediction that *Today* would some-day slip up, just as it had in 1980 and 1990, Zucker meant that *GMA* had better be ready to take advantage. "You better be ready. You better be great. Because you're gonna have your chance."

After *GMA* came within 164,000 viewers at the end of February, *Today* rebounded in the first week of March, widening the gap to 448,000 viewers. But a week later *GMA* was back within 262,000 viewers. "Ever closer…" Goldston wrote in an e-mail. As for Lauer, who was now talking to both NBC and ABC about his future, Goldston said, "We are just putting more money in his pocket!" But apart from renewing its vows with Lauer, and plotting a divorce from Curry, NBC didn't seem to be doing much of anything about the threat. The executives at ABC were absolutely baffled by the flat-footedness. "I just don't understand it," Goldston said. "You can't just expect to keep winning. The difference in energy between our show and their show is very stark." That was true—I noticed it, and so did the publicists and crew members who had opportunities to set foot in both worlds.

As Goldston saw it, NBC was not being blasé—but rather was frozen by fear. "As we started to do better," he said, "I think they became incredibly fearful because everything was at stake, including the streak."

Roberts usually takes off the first week in April, to go to a home she has in Key West to watch the Final Four. She might not have done that in 2012, because the race with *Today* was getting closer and she didn't want *GMA* to lose any momentum. But she hadn't been feeling well since the Oscars, and had been going for check-ups and tests. The results had so far been inconclusive, but her doctor advised her not to pass up her regularly scheduled break. "I felt really, really tired," she said. On March 29, ABC announced that Katie Couric would be filling in for Roberts the following week. The network tried to bill the maneuver as simple common sense: Roberts was taking a week off, so a proven pro was coming to keep the seat warm. But the television cognoscenti thought they knew better, and the word went out that Cutthroat Katie was making another dramatic career move—and that ABC, hoping to put itself over the top in the morning, was playing along.

Here's the truth: Couric was six months out from the premiere of her daytime talk show, to be produced and distributed by ABC, and was enjoying some time off in March when Sherwood proposed that she come fill in for Roberts. Couric was game, though she wanted her spokesman Matthew Hiltzik and his counterpart at ABC, Jeffrey Schneider, to make sure the stunt wasn't mistaken for a run at Roberts's job. "I really genuinely just saw it as an opportunity to help *GMA* out, and quite frankly to reintroduce me to an audience that hadn't seen me in that format in quite a while, which would be helpful for my new show," she said. And so April 2 through 6 would be Katie Couric Week on *GMA*. "More than anything else, this is about Ben wanting to kick *Today*'s ass," said a confidant of Couric's after the announcement was made—and yet, said the same person, "There's something that she enjoys about this, too."

Not everyone at *GMA* was happy with what was being acknowledged throughout the TV industry as a brilliant gimmick. Elizabeth Vargas, Roberts's normal replacement, felt she was being passed over, and didn't hide her displeasure. "She's walking around saying that her contract has been violated because she's supposed to be Robin's backup anchor," a rival network executive said during Couric Week.

The Couric announcement sideswiped NBC. None of the senior leaders of the news division were in New York when it was made. Capus was on vacation, as was Lauren Kapp, his most trusted advisor. Bell was in Stamford, Connecticut, in planning meetings for the Olympics. Now, suddenly, their underlings had to scramble to come up with counterprogramming—which put them in a foul frame of mind. "Couric's a very rich woman thanks to the *Today* show," one NBC employee said. "She's trying to win a week when we're down," said another. "It's a particularly personal, ugly thing." Others called Couric a traitor outright. One of the first ideas to come out of the *Today* war room was to counter Couric with another "legend" from the *Today* show's past: J. Fred Muggs. Since Muggs hadn't been seen in public for years, and NBC hadn't been successful in inviting him and his trainers to the sixtieth birthday bash in January, the producers thought to dress up some other chimp instead. "We called every zoo within forty miles of Manhattan to find a chimp to borrow," a staff member recalled, stifling laughs at the absurdity of it all. "It reeked of desperation."

Some thought Couric's stint did, too. Roberts wasn't happy that ABC was turning her absence into a buzz-making Great *GMA* Moment. "But this was a mandate from the top," one of her colleagues said. "She couldn't have stopped it." Besides, she was more worried about her body than her work. Although she wouldn't be officially diagnosed until she came back from vacation, Roberts, for the second time in five years, was seriously ill. "It was kind of funny when everyone was making a big deal about 'Oh, Katie Couric is filling in!' I was like, 'Yeah, I just took a bone marrow test, so I'm not really concerned about that right now.'"

On the air, when Couric showed up for the surprise announcement, Roberts smiled and played along. "Katie, welcome!" she said almost too exuberantly. "It's great to see you!"

Roberts tossed a faux *GMA* key to her fill-in, who went out of her way to say, "Have a great vacation!" Before Couric left, Roberts pointed at her with both hands. "You are doing me a solid, thanks."

"I'll keep the seat warm," Couric responded.

"Do that!" Roberts said.

Reflecting on the sequence of events later, Roberts said, "Never had an anchor going on vacation been so public. We had the whole campaign, like, 'Katie's filling in, here are the keys.' That had never been done before. Again, I understand the reasoning behind it, but it was kind of like, 'Geez, really? Oh-kay.'"

If she hadn't been waiting anxiously for the results of those bone marrow tests, Roberts might have been more troubled about the way Couric Week was going down. Did she fear that *GMA* would win without her? "It wasn't a 'fear,'" she said a few months later. "It was kind of like...I and others, we had been fighting fighting fighting fighting. And knowing that the head-line would have been 'Katie Beats,' not '*Good Morning America* Beats.' So it was more of like, 'Wow, *we*, who have been here, will not get the credit.' But I didn't fault her or ABC management—because they wanted to keep us in the game. They wanted to keep the momentum going. So I understood. But yeah, at the time, it was kinda like..." (insert loud groan here).

Couric, to be fair, mostly stayed above the fray and had fun with her temporary return to morning TV, pretending at one point to mistakenly call Stephanopoulos "Matt." By turns flirty and self-deprecating and inquisitive, she was at ease in the mornings, no matter what network she was on, and it showed. Something else showed, too: that the *Today* show could, in fact, step up its game when threatened. It reacted to Couric Week by hyping a "mystery guest" on Couric's first day (it turned out to be Meredith Vieira), bringing in Sarah Palin to guest-host with Lauer on Tuesday, and flying in Ryan Seacrest on Wednesday. (The chimp idea was abandoned because animal experts warned that chimps are not accepted anymore as entertainers. PETA would have been protesting outside Studio 1A.)

But no one at ABC thought that NBC, in reacting to Couric Week, got it right. Goldston, in the control room a day later, spoke of the competition's "fatal mistake." By acting desperate, he thought, *Today* had alerted more people to the morning race and had encouraged its fans to channel-flip, to see what all the fuss was about.

NBC, however, had to fight back. What was it going to do, roll over and let *GMA* win? "We didn't know whether *Today* would win or lose the week, but we wanted to be armed with the best programming possible," said Don Nash.

But by bringing back Vieira in a time of crisis, *Today* had underlined how much the show had suffered without her and inadvertently drawn new scrutiny onto Curry and Lauer's nonexistent relationship. *The New York Times* television critic Alessandra Stanley wrote the following on Monday afternoon:

> Monday's display was more savage than a ratings contest or a booking war; at times it looked as intimate and creepily intrusive as the elimination rounds of a particularly cutthroat reality show. It's been a long time since NBC put Deborah Norville on the couch alongside Jane Pauley and Bryant Gumbel and turned "Today" into a morning show version of "All About Eve."
>
> These days it is Ann Curry, who inherited Ms. Vieira's place but not her popularity, who looks vulnerable.
>
> Ms. Curry had to sit, silent and smiling, on the "Today" set on Monday, alongside Matt Lauer as he urged Ms. Vieira to announce that she would help cover the 2012 summer Olympics and be his co-host, with Bob Costas, for the opening ceremony of the London games. (He did not say what role Ms. Curry would play, if any.)
>
> Earlier, when Mr. Lauer began announcing that Ms. Palin would be a guest host, Ms. Curry smiled grimly, then looked down at her desk, patting papers.

The *USA Today* TV critic Robert Bianco noticed it, too: "If there's a loser in all this, it's *Today's* current co-host, the unctuous, floundering Ann Curry."

In the end the week was a wash. Couric hadn't led a charge to the summit, exactly, but neither had *GMA* lost any ground during a week when its most beloved cohost was absent. "I'm surprised Katie did as well as she did, because NBC threw the fucking kitchen sink at her," said an ABC executive.

✳  ✳  ✳

The record shows that it was actually April 9 to 13, 2012, the week after Couric's appearance, that mattered more to the future of morning television. This was also the week that Capus was quoted in *The New York Times* saying that *GMA* beating *Today* was a hypothetical that was "not going to happen." Lauer, having just re-upped, was on vacation, which guaranteed that it would not be a banner week for *Today*. In fact, on Monday it beat *GMA* by a now-routine 150,000 viewers—but at ABC some executives saw something encouraging in the quarter-hour ratings. *GMA* won from seven forty-five a.m. all the way through to eight thirty a.m. (Neither show was rated after about 8:20 a.m.) That meant, as one producer there said, "If we can add seven thirty, we win."

During his year running the show Goldston had adopted a backward strategy. Rather than rebuilding *GMA* from seven a.m. on, Goldston had concentrated at first on the eight thirty a.m. half hour—the back door instead of the front door. Goldston believed that many viewers would start out watching *Today*, then switch to *GMA* in the second hour because it did the fun stuff better. By gradually moving up the moment people switched, he felt, *GMA* could eventually win the entire two-hour time slot. This latest ratings breakdown seemed to vindicate his thinking.

*GMA* fared worse on Tuesday, a day when *Today* was helped by NBC's airing of its only really high-rated show, *The Voice*, the night before. But on Wednesday the momentum started to shift, assisted by ABC's airing of *Dancing with the Stars*, which the night before had featured the surprise elimination of contestant Sherri Shepherd, cohost of *The View*. Shepherd appeared on *GMA* Wednesday morning to react to her dismissal—and the show subsequently beat *Today* by more than 360,000 viewers! It even won the seven a.m. quarter hour! Yes, the exclamation marks and "holy shits" were flying. By Wednesday, *Today* was averaging just fifty thousand more viewers per day for the week.

That kind of gap could be closed in a few days. The *GMA* bosses thought they had a chance to win the week—and when they learned that NBC wasn't bringing Lauer back from vacation on Friday morning to stave off a possible loss, they thought they had an even better chance. *GMA* that day featured a heavily promoted interview with Jets quarterback Tim Tebow during which he discussed his Christian faith with Roberts. With a little help from up above, the show could be, for the first time in sixteen years, the number one morning show in television. The weekend-long wait for the ratings had never been so excruciating.

"This winning streak dates to 1995," Jeff Zucker had said in an e-mail to me a few days before *GMA*'s arrival at this precipice. "Every week, 'Today.' Every week. There has never been anything like it in television and there never will be again. Even if it only gets broken one week, it's over. 'GMA' only needs to win once."

On the surface, Monday, April 16, seemed like business as usual—except the eternally chatty executives at both networks had little to say. They were just standing by for news from Nielsen, which would render a verdict on the previous week around twelve thirty p.m.

*GMA* had ripped up its rundown overnight. British socialite Pippa Middleton—Kate's sister—had been snapped in a car with three male friends, one of whom appeared to be pointing a gun at the photographer. By Monday night her friends were saying it was just a toy pistol, but *GMA* led its show Monday morning with the "Pippa paparazzi scandal," first with a live report from Paris, then with an interview of a royal expert. The half hour ended with Roberts promising "more on those shocking photos" later in the show. *Today*, meanwhile, stuck with its lead story about Secret Service officers caught up in a sex scandal in Colombia.

Then the staffs of the two shows just waited. And waited. Ben Sherwood, the ABC News president, was at his desk working with a colleague on the division's long-range plan when Amy Miller called him with the figures. *GMA* had won Friday by 330,000 viewers, enough to win the whole week by an average of thirteen thousand. It was a true squeaker, but the streak appeared to be over after 852 weeks. Sherwood immediately e-mailed Goldston, who was in Las Vegas for a television industry conference: "Call me now."

Cibrowski was standing on West Seventy-Ninth Street with his daughter Caroline, waiting to take the crosstown bus to her preschool on the East Side of Manhattan, when Sherwood e-mailed him the ratings. Looking down at his BlackBerry, Cibrowski thought of the ten years during which he had woken up before dawn for *GMA*, and of what he'd told himself while entertaining the notion of a job with better, saner hours: "Well, if I hang on a little longer I might win the lottery."

Now that had happened. He had the urge to tell someone, but there was only his daughter.

"Caroline," he said, "something really great has happened to Daddy."

"What happened?" she asked.

He thought for a moment, then said, "Daddy's work won."

Caroline smiled, then said, "Daddy's work won, yay!"

# CHAPTER 13

# Inevitable

APRIL 14 AND 15 had added up to a tough weekend for Robin Roberts, too, but not just because of the impending Nielsen news.

On April 9, a few days after flying back from her vacation home on Key West, Roberts had conferred with her doctor and received the results of the bone marrow test. That's when she first heard the phrase *myelodysplastic syndromes*. MDS is a rare and complicated group of diseases that occur when a person's body does not produce enough healthy blood cells. It was once called preleukemia because it can lead to leukemia and other blood disorders. The list of famous patients includes writer Susan Sontag, astronomer Carl Sagan, and Frank Newhauser, who in 1925 won the first National Spelling Bee. But Roberts's doctor wasn't yet 100 percent sure that she had MDS, and her uncertainty led to further tests and more waiting. She was terrified.

On Tuesday the seventeenth of April, Roberts met Sam Champion and Josh Elliott for lunch at Landmarc, one of the restaurants in Time Warner Center, the upscale urban mall that straddles Columbus Circle in Manhattan. Champion, who had known Roberts for about a decade (they met while filling in on *GMA*) arrived before Elliott. As soon as she greeted him and sat down, Champion sensed that something wasn't right. "Sam looked at me as only he can, and I started crying," she said. She hesitated to say, "MDS," but eventually told him about her doctor's strong suspicions that she had the disease, though the diagnosis wouldn't be confirmed for a few more days. Champion later recalled that "I felt like I'd heard some bad news about my mother or my sister."

"Don't say anything to anybody," Roberts said to Champion before Elliott arrived. She didn't want to spoil what was supposed to be a celebratory week.

On Monday, after dropping his daughter Caroline off at preschool, Cibrowski couldn't get back to work fast enough. He was elated, but he knew he shouldn't be—these ratings were the equivalent of a rough draft. On a conference call with Sherwood and Goldston, the three executives agreed to be circumspect about the win until the final ratings arrived on Thursday, April 19. It was possible, though not likely, that the week would flip back in the *Today* show's favor then, since the margin between the two shows was so slight. Cibrowski's statement to the media at one fifteen p.m. read, "This is an exciting day but we will save any celebrating for when the final numbers come in."

It was all but impossible, though, to stifle the emotions that were welling up in staffers who used to slap each other on the back and go out for drinks when *GMA* came within 350,000 viewers of *Today*. Now they *really* had a reason to get drunk. One young producer sarcastically renamed *Today* "the *Yesterday* show," while a *GMA* veteran bombastically said that this early-April win was just a "warning shot" across NBC's bow, and that they, the ABC guys, had barely begun to fight. After all, they'd won a month and a half before the week in May that Cibrowski had targeted.

There were in truth a few not-so-minor technicalities for the *GMA* people to ponder. Their victory had been extremely slim, and in the "demo," the group of twenty-five-to-fifty-four-year-old men and women most coveted by advertisers, they had, in fact, lost to *Today* by something like 254,000. Still, these complications didn't change the basic fact of the matter, even in the eyes of the *Today* show's Jim Bell, who issued a statement to the media at 1:25 p.m. that read like an elegy for the streak.

> *Today*'s 852-week winning streak had taken on a life of its own and as odd as it is to see it end, we should acknowledge just how remarkable it has been. So as we tip our caps to the team at *Good Morning America*, we can also take a bow ourselves and recognize the work done by countless staffers for so long. It is not an overstatement to call it one of the most incredible achievements in television history, one that is not likely to ever happen again. While the streak has been wonderful affirmation of our work, it has never defined us, and we will continue to innovate, take chances and lead the way.

According to a colleague, when Capus saw the statement, he "flipped" and screamed at Bell over the phone. The final ratings weren't even in yet! Capus would have been even angrier had he known that over at *GMA*, George Stephanopoulos was standing in the reception area outside Cibrowski's office and reading Bell's statement aloud to colleagues. Stephanopoulos was the first to recognize its significance. "He just conceded!"

But Bell was preoccupied: his top deputy, Don Nash, was on vacation, and he had a long-planned lunch with Bob Costas to talk about the Summer Olympics. In the wake of the loss, Bell and his colleagues tried to keep up appearances. "It's business as usual," here, said one publicist; "Nobody's crying here," said another. The party line was that what had happened was inevitable. "We knew it was going to happen sooner or later. It couldn't go on forever," Al Roker said later. Capus, looking back, said similarly, "There is no question that there was some slippage in the ratings and they were going to pass us at some point." But Capus had said just a few days before that the streak would never end.

As will happen in such circumstances, a conspiracy theory took root: Bell, it was said, had accepted—or perhaps even cunningly engineered—a temporary dive in the ratings to pave the way for Curry's removal, assuming the ratings would bounce right back afterward. Others at NBC heaped the blame on the network's new parent, Comcast, for not taking the war as seriously as its previous parent, General Electric. Why didn't Comcast yank national commercials from *Today* on Friday, repeating the dirty trick used against *GMA* in 2005? Why didn't someone drag Lauer back from vacation? Still others at the network credited ABC for simply wanting the win more. That explanation was the most honest of them all.

In the second wave of spin, NBC people said—as Joe DiMaggio had in 1941, when his record hitting streak came to an end—that coming up short after all that time was actually a good thing. Capus, at a party two weeks later, told me that *GMA*'s one-off victory "frees us of the burden of the streak." ("Now that the streak is over," the great DiMaggio had said, "I just want to get out there and keep helping to win ball games.")

After the loss there was—strangely, in the opinion of some—no rally-the-troops meeting at NBC. "Jim's just not that kind of guy," one of his allies said. There was instead a kind of stoic silence, a lot of closed doors and quiet cubicles. The mood was summarized by a replica of a British World War II propaganda poster hanging on the wall in the production offices between two rows of cubicles. It read, "Keep Calm and Carry On." Capus, who had held a town hall a week earlier, fumed that Bell didn't do more to motivate his staff.

At *GMA*, meanwhile, they were planning their Thursday-night party—but keeping the details a secret, in case the revised numbers, due early that morning, left them with nothing to celebrate. Jeffrey Schneider, the top spokesman for ABC News, wouldn't let anyone buy champagne ahead of time, lest they jinx themselves. "We were optimistic," he said later, "but didn't want to get caught out between the early numbers and the final numbers." Schneider, a twelve-year veteran of ABC, took the war especially personally, since he'd absorbed a lot of the bullets fired by NBC—and fired even more back. That's why it was stunning, yet entirely sensible, for NBC to try to poach him. *Today* needed a lot of things, and aggressiveness was one of them. An NBC executive had called a few days earlier, right after Lauren Kapp, the news division's PR chief, said she was leaving. But Schneider had made it clear that he bled ABC News blue. He'd invested too much in *GMA* to leave now, when the show was on the cusp of becoming number one.

On April 19, a week after that call, Schneider was huddled in his office with Julie Townsend, his No. 2. The final ratings were due between eight and nine a.m. The two PR people sounded like political speechwriters crafting two speeches, one for victory and one for a remotely possible defeat. "I don't think I can take it if this goes south," Schneider told Townsend. "I'm so tense right now that if I got a paper cut I'd bleed to death."

Townsend tried to tell him it'd be all right. "No," Schneider said. "It's going to suck worse than anything. The world already believes that we won." That much was true. To the reporters who covered television, Thursday was just a formality—unless, of course, *Today* came back from the dead and beat *GMA* for week 853.

A mile south at the *GMA* studio, Cibrowski joked that it was just "another day at the office," and in some ways it was. Both *GMA* and *Today* led with the death of broadcasting legend Dick Clark. *GMA* later had an update on "Gungate," as they called the Pippa Middleton photo scandal. Just after the eight a.m. break, the five hosts were in Times Square teasing a discount shopping segment. At 8:28 a.m., as they were walking back into the studio, Roberts whooped loudly and said, "Oh my God!" Elliott, who had been just ahead of her on the sidewalk, was so startled he nearly left his feet.

Cibrowski had just told Roberts, through her earpiece, that the absolutely official results were in and *GMA* had won the week by thirty-one thousand viewers, about twice as many as Nielsen had originally estimated.

Then Cibrowski flipped a switch and spoke into all five hosts' ears at once. "I'll never forget that moment," Lara Spencer said. "I mean, it brings tears to my eyes." The hosts shouted, "Yes!" and hugged each other as the eight thirty half hour was about to begin. "The crew didn't know why at first," Spencer recalled, because Cibrowski had wanted the hosts to know before anyone else. An ABC photographer Cibrowski had stationed on the set shot a photo of the quintet together a moment later, their index fingers raised in the air to say, "We're number one!" Roberts, who alone clenched her right hand in a fist, looked the happiest of all.

Elliott later said that he felt it was "symbolic" that Cibrowski had told Roberts the good news a moment or two before the others. Both Cibrowski and Roberts had been at *GMA* for a full decade. They were "the people who had worked so hard just to, you know, get us in position," Elliott said. The new anchor saw the Nielsen challenge as something akin to climbing Mount Everest, where "there are like three or four base camps," he said. "You don't just leave camp and go up to the top. There's something like the Death Zone. It's the last camp to the summit when, you know, you've already gone up twenty-five thousand feet. But the last few thousand are the hardest. And boy, did we prove that." Roberts, as Elliott saw it, was both their Sherpa and their Edmund Hillary, guiding and inspiring them toward the top. Even those less fond of tortured analogies agreed. The loudest applause was reserved for Roberts when a couple hundred ABC News staffers gathered on the fifth floor at eleven a.m. for a champagne toast hastily arranged by Schneider, who had cried tears of joy—and relief—in his office when the win was confirmed.

Sherwood began the celebration by naming the young *GMA* producers who had been in elementary school when the *Today* show started its winning streak. He mentioned the length in weeks, 852, and practically roared, "It ended officially this morning."

Almost all work in the newsroom stopped for the next thirty minutes. A camera crew beamed the celebration to ABC bureaus in other cities. A staffer along the back wall wondered, "How long have they had that champagne here?"

Sherwood said the day represented a "victory for the whole organization" and credited, among many others, Goldston, who he said had "reimagined and reinvigorated this program." Goldston, in turn, called for another round of applause for Sherwood: "We would have never gotten here without him."

Sherwood, reading from index cards, thanked his predecessor David Westin and former *GMA* host Diane Sawyer, among many others, and also thanked prime-time shows like *Desperate Housewives* and *Dancing with the Stars*. "How about a round of applause for Marc Cherry?" he said at one point, referring to the creator of *Housewives*. When Cibrowski spoke, he added one more thank-you: for Tim Tebow, the show's well-hyped guest the prior Friday. It was then the hosts' turns, beginning with Roberts, the woman Sherwood introduced as "our captain."

"Ben," she said, "when you came in we had a conversation, and you promised this moment. And you are a man of your word."

Then, to those assembled, she said, "If you have been on *GMA*, if you have cut a piece, if you have answered a phone, if you've had anything to do with *GMA* over the last sixteen years, please raise your hand." As nearly everyone within sight raised a hand, she smiled and said, "You see that? You see that? It is all about team. And all of you share this very moment."

Later Elliott remarked, "I feel almost as though I should apologize. I only had to wait fifty weeks for this." As those in the room chuckled, Spencer, the other new kid, agreed and said they looked forward to the weeks when they wouldn't have to wait until Thursday to know the show had won.

"This is one important step," Sherwood said when he got the microphone back. "But here's the deal. Back in 1994, when the *Today* show beat *Good Morning America* after a five-year run by *GMA*, what happened then, through 1994, was this brawl. They fought it out. What happened this week is that we knocked down the undisputed heavyweight champion. So what happens when you knock down the champion for a week? What do they do? Are they going to stay down? No. They're going to come back at us and they're going to want to kill us." There was knowing laughter around the room. "So a brawl is about to ensue, and it's gonna be a fight. And that's what we want. Because before we can get to a place where we win consistently and we don't gather every time we do it, we're going to have to fight very, very hard for a very long time."

Sherwood led a toast to NBC. "They were the champs for 852 straight weeks. We owe them respect and we owe them a big round of applause for what they did." A not-quite-as-big round of applause followed. Stephanopoulos, raising an unopened bottle, said, "Let's start another streak!"

✳ ✳ ✳

Roberts had to hurry to her doctor's office right after the champagne toasts. There she was told definitively that she had MDS. "That's usually life," she told me a couple months later, right between a *GMA* taping and a chemotherapy session. "You can dream, hope, and pray for how you think something's going to be, and how it actually happens or doesn't happen is usually so far from what you thought it was going to be." Roberts, resting in her dressing room after the show one day, looked at the photo taken of the cast together on the nineteenth, with her fist in the air and Elliott's and Champion's arms around her back. Copies of the photo had been placed in silver frames and given to all the hosts. "I so look at that picture differently than everybody else," Roberts said. "Because that is the day that it was like, 'Yeah, it's MDS. Yes, you're going to have a bone marrow transplant. Yes, you're going to be out for a chunk of time. We don't know when.' It was all this... it was such a gray area. It was just maddening."

On the day of the historic win, no one at the show except Champion and a couple of her personal producers knew she was sick. After the doctor's appointment, at about two, Roberts texted him and Spencer. "Where are you guys?" They happened to be getting a manicure and pedicure together about half a mile away. Roberts walked up to the nail salon, Spencer recalled, "and she just burst into laughter and shook her head, because there we were, Sam and I, with our feet in the tub."

Roberts headed home, and Elliott met up with Champion and Spencer for an afternoon of pre-celebration before the staff party at six p.m. Cibrowski's secret party planners had reserved a rooftop penthouse overlooking the Hudson River on Sixty-Seventh Street, an easy walk from the office. It also happened to be a few doors down from Roberts's apartment building.

Roberts knew she had to go. But, understandably, "I wasn't really into it," she said, and as soon as she hit the street she thought of turning back. Then her doorman said, "Hey, your friends are here!"

There in front of her were Champion, Spencer, and Elliott. It looked like a self-referential post–eight a.m. spot on *GMA*. "I thought, 'Oh my gosh, they came to come get me!'" Actually, they were lost, and a little tipsy, but Roberts didn't realize that at the time, and she was moved by their seeming thoughtfulness. "So I think, like, 'Oh c'mon Robin, suck it up and go to the party.' I hugged them and we're walking down the street and people are shouting out at us. Then I realized, 'You guys didn't come to pick me up, did you?' And they say, 'Oh, you live here?'"

The six-to-eight party went until nine, then ten, then eleven. There were no speeches this time, just drinking and dancing. (Though there was a little bit of work done: ABC had obtained an exclusive photo of George Zimmerman taken the night of the Trayvon Martin shooting, so a few producers had to confer about it. The photo wound up being the lead story the following morning.)

"We had worked so incredibly hard for that moment," Roberts said. She didn't want to spoil it by telling anyone about her diagnosis. She came close to telling Sherwood, but "I was like, 'How in the world can I say something right now to him?' I mean, this is his shining moment. He came back for this." Still, Sherwood said later that after spending time with Roberts that evening he "went home with a sense of apprehension that something was up." It would be six weeks before Roberts told anyone else at ABC but Cibrowski about her condition. ("I needed somebody to know," she said, "in case I woke up one morning and I didn't want to come in.")

Roberts was back at work the next morning for a hungover edition of *GMA*. "These people are dragging today," director Jeff Winn said at the end of the first hour. In the control room a row behind Winn, Cibrowski and his lieutenant Denise Rehrig discussed how to handle the show's on-air announcement of the big win. "I don't want to mess it up," Cibrowski told her, knowing that his boss, Sherwood, and his boss's boss were taking it very seriously. They would divide the happy task: one host would thank the viewers, another ABC's stations—after all, they, too, had been in second place for so long—and another would mention the Other Place. During a commercial break at 7:25, the writer stationed next to Rehrig, Simone Swink, typed out, "We tip our hat to our colleagues at NBC for their amazing streak..."

ABC didn't hear much from NBC the week the win became official. *Today* flirted with the idea of congratulating *GMA* on air, but decided that would just draw more attention to the war. Cibrowski did get an e-mail from Bell on Thursday that said, "We want to send you something, where do we send it?" Bravely, he gave them a correct address.

Later that day a bottle of champagne showed up, not from NBC or from Bell, but from Matt Lauer. His congratulatory card called the win "a big deal" and added jokingly, "Not sure if you want to drink this or hit yourselves over the head with it."

If Cibrowski chose the former option, he needed to chug the stuff quickly. While *GMA* was celebrating its historic victory, *Today* was... winning. Lauer and his colleagues vaulted right back to first place April 16 through 20, winning by 243,000 viewers and raising the possibility in the minds of some at NBC that the prior week's fall to second place had just been a lucky break for ABC. NBC's news release about the ratings noted that *Today* had been number one for "853 out of 854 weeks." And for even longer in the twenty-five-to-fifty-four-year-old demographic: 886 weeks. The gap in the demo was 379,000—*GMA* still had a long way to go in the viewer category that mattered most.

# CHAPTER 14

# The Call from the White House

"FOR NEW DEMOCRACIES," George Stephanopoulos said in April, "the second election is more important than the first."

The *GMA* host knew that his show's single victory in April wouldn't mean much to executives and advertisers unless the same result could be achieved again (and again). Which is why April 23 through 27, 2012, was one of the single most important weeks in *GMA*'s thirty-seven-year history.

"Great News!!!" the ABC researcher Amy Miller e-mailed Sherwood and the other network executives on Thursday afternoon, the twenty-sixth, when the second draft of Wednesday's ratings arrived. She wasn't kidding: after three days *GMA* was ahead of *Today* by 220,000 viewers and in the twenty-five-to-fifty-four-year-old demographic it trailed by only fifty-six thousand. *GMA*'s streak-breaking win earlier in the month was looking less and less fluke-ish.

ABC was going all out to win the week at hand. Robin Roberts, feeling bone-tired but trying to hide it from her colleagues, was on a flight to California when Miller's encouraging e-mail arrived. Roberts was set to interview Mark Zuckerberg about Facebook's new organ donation initiative for a segment that would air on *GMA* the following Tuesday. She was scheduled to talk to him in the afternoon, then sleep Thursday night at the home of close friends who lived near Facebook's headquarters in Palo Alto. Friday she had planned to take off. She sorely needed to gather her strength. But with a second weekly win within reach, Roberts and Tom Cibrowski decided that it would be best for the show if she was back at the anchor desk in New York on Friday morning. He scurried to line up a charter flight that would get her back in time.

The brawl-for-it-all that Ben Sherwood had predicted was now on. The two shows had battled the weekend before over Meow the cat, the morbidly obese tabby. *Today* had won, and flown Meow and a veterinarian from Santa Fe to New York (the cat had its own seat) for a Tuesday-morning segment. When Cibrowski found out about that early on Monday morning, he had ordered his staff to crash a segment about Meow for his show. Using video from a New Mexico TV station, they did, and got it on the air by 7:20, beating *Today* by half an hour. True, only *Today* could boast that it had Meow in person, sprawled right next to Matt Lauer (who, sensing the sentiment of the average viewer, tuttutted over her imperiled health). A *GMA* segment producer said semi-seriously that she had tried to steal the cat from *Today*, as producers have been known to do with guests (sending a car to the hotel sometimes works). Another producer replied playfully, "Probably hard to do a grab-and-run with Meow."

Later that day the two shows scrambled to book a University of Colorado student, Kolbi Zerbest, who had been blamed for accidentally spilling yogurt on President Obama during a campaign stop. The photos of Obama good-naturedly cleaning up the mess with a napkin were the closest the morning shows would get that day to covering culture. But *GMA* got outfoxed by a young *Today* producer named Wesley Oliver, who spotted Zerbest's sorority sisters writing about the incident on Twitter and contacted them there. Zerbest, they told him, was by chance being initiated into the sorority the same day; Oliver learned how to reach her and arranged for her to be on the next morning, from NBC's station in Denver. A *Today* booker handled the follow-up, which involved pleading with Zerbest not to stay up late drinking the night before: "We can't put you on the air drunk! You can celebrate tomorrow." On the show, Ann Curry earnestly praised the young woman who was known for fifteen minutes or so as "Yogurt Girl" for coming forward and accepting blame for the spill.

With a bleary-eyed Roberts back from California, Cibrowski decided to try something new and, by morning show standards, bold on April 27: have all five hosts of *GMA* on set when the show started at seven a.m. Normally Lara Spencer didn't appear until seven thirty or eight a.m., but Cibrowski wanted to emphasize the friendliness of his cast—all the more so since *Today* was getting grief from viewers for Lauer and Curry's dysfunctional relationship. One *GMA* producer said that seeing the two of them together was like watching a "hostage video," but he didn't say which he thought was the hostage. In e-mails and tweets, said people at NBC, it was Curry who got the more unrestrained criticism. The sight of the *GMA* hosts together, Cibrowski hoped, could serve as an antidote to that toxic atmosphere. The arrangement soon became a daily thing. Chirped Spencer, "I love that we are saying from the top of the show, we are a team."

But could they once again be the A-Team? By 6:57 a.m. on Friday the twenty-seventh, all five hosts were on set, but Spencer didn't have the "hellos"—the partly scripted, partly ad-libbed introduction to the show. "Guys, Lara needs the hellos right now," writer Simone Swink said. While the paper script was rushed to Spencer, Cibrowski spoke to all the hosts through their earpieces. "Lara has a very quick tease . . . and then we get right to the headlines." "Here we go," said Denise Rehrig. With ten seconds until airtime, Cibrowski spoke in the hosts' ears one more time. "Good luck, everybody," he said solemnly, as if addressing space-bound astronauts. With the stakes unusually high, the tension in the control room was palpable.

For the most part, *GMA* that morning stuck to its formula of teases and kills. The teases are so frequent that they can make a morning show seem like one long promise of what's coming up in a minute; the kills are stories that start out on the rundown but get lost along the way. *GMA* is purposely overbooked to make it seem faster and more brimming with great stuff than *Today*. "If we slow down in the first half hour, people flip the channel," a producer said matter-of-factly. A couple minutes into the Friday show, Cibrowski killed one correspondent's introduction and told legal analyst Dan Abrams, who was on to talk about the John Edwards trial, "We're very tight so we're going to give you about a minute twenty." Fifteen minutes in, with the show still running over, Rehrig, the timekeeper-in-chief, cut another intro and complained aloud when Sam Champion's weather forecast ran a few Canadian cold fronts too long. "You're killing me, Smalls," she said. During a commercial break, which they miraculously hit on time, Cibrowski briefed Stephanopoulos on the *Today* show, as he did every morning. "They had a real weird hodgepodge of stuff," Cibrowski said. "They did [alleged Travyon Martin shooter George] Zimmerman, a long segment on a missing girl in Arizona, and now they're doing Will and Kate. And," he added, with a note of giddiness, while staring up at a muted monitor carrying the *Today* show, "no Matt!"

It was shocking but true. Once again, as Operation Bambi slowly commenced, and *GMA* loomed ever larger as a threat, and Robin Roberts, despite a serious illness, flew back and forth across the country on successive days to be on the *GMA* set, Lauer stood firmly by his contractual right to a four-day workweek. He'd been on the show from Monday through Thursday, but was replaced this time by Carl Quintanilla, a member of CNBC's morning lineup. Around *GMA*, these Lauer-less days only strengthened the assumption that Curry's ouster was a fait accompli. "Is he on strike till she goes?" one producer asked.

After seven thirty, *Today* featured a live interview with a Texas couple whose three-year-old son had had a baseball snatched out of his little hands at a Rangers game earlier in the week. Cibrowski could live with that story selection, he said, because Elliott's taped interview with the same couple had run earlier in the hour. "We felt it was worth what it was, a minute forty-five." On *Today* the story was given about three minutes, a veritable telethon by morning show standards; it ran so long, in fact, that the child seemed to be falling asleep toward the end. "He used all his energy for *GMA*," ABC News spokesman Jeffrey Schneider quipped. "Off camera, you know they're hitting that kid with a cattle prod." Said Cibrowski, sounding as if he were teaching a broadcasting class, "That's why you tape it."

For the full week of April 23, *GMA* surpassed *Today* by 180,000 viewers, a far better performance than the week of April 9, when it had led by only thirty-one thousand. Elliott celebrated by leasing—though not buying—a black BMW X5 at a dealership in Connecticut. (His assistant had bullied him into trading up from the Volvo he'd been driving.) Sherwood celebrated by sending this e-mail:

Congratulations, team!
You won by 180K!
Smallest demo gap (105K) since 1995.
And . . . GMA Saturday won the entire month of April in the demo.
Great work.
Play your game.
Keep it going.

This was the key "second election" that Stephanopoulos had described earlier. What made the win especially significant was that Lauer had been mostly present that week, unlike during the week of the first win, when he had been—as NBC never got tired of pointing out—gone the whole time. *GMA* had proven it could beat the *Today* starting lineup. (Or you could read the results another way, and say they showed that if Lauer was beatable he wasn't worth the truckloads of money that NBC had just agreed to caravan out to his estate in the Hamptons.) To any kind of doubter, however, *Today* show spokeswoman Megan Kopf offered the same response: "We're still winning in the demo!" True, thought Sherwood, but you're also living in denial.

May 2012 was a seesaw month in the a.m. ratings. Some mornings, *Today* showed some of its old spunk. On April 30, for instance, the NBC show teased three exclusive interviews: the mother of a missing Fort Bragg soldier; Whitney Houston's ex-husband Bobby Brown, in his first interview since her death; and Ryan O'Neal, Farrah Fawcett's longtime lover, who was promoting a memoir. *GMA*, that same day, pulled off the kind of stunt that used to be a hallmark of *Today*, opening at seven a.m. with Stephanopoulos standing atop 1 World Trade Center, the skyscraper under construction in downtown Manhattan, to mark the day it became the city's tallest building, surpassing the Empire State Building's 102 stories. To the viewer the slugfest may have looked like a draw, and it almost was, but ultimately *Today* won by an average of seventy-six thousand viewers for the week and retook the lead.

As far as ratings went, unpredictability was now the norm. Anything could have happened the next week—until Dan Pfeiffer, the White House communications director, called ABC's Washington bureau chief Robin Sproul on Tuesday, May 8, and offered Roberts an exclusive sit-down with President Obama the next day.

This wasn't just any old presidential interview. Obama had been sidestepping questions about his views on same-sex marriage for several days, or ever since Vice President Joe Biden declared to NBC's David Gregory that he himself was "absolutely comfortable" with the idea. Obama, who had said before that his views on gay marriage were "evolving," had been planning on saying later in the year that he was in favor of such unions. But he and his aides had concluded that because Biden had been so blabby, he now had to speak out sooner.

The White House tends to rotate big interviews among the networks. In this case they wanted an interviewer who'd concentrate on the issue at hand, not horse-race politics. Rivals speculated that Roberts's cordial relationship with the Obamas and factors like her spirituality and her race also came into play. (Religiously affiliated Americans and African Americans were more likely to oppose same-sex marriage, according to polls, and having Roberts as the vessel for the news might help politically, the theory went.) ABC naturally wanted to say yes to the offer right away and start making arrangements for Roberts's travel to Washington. But when Pfeiffer called Sproul, Roberts was at her doctor's office in Manhattan with a drill in her back. Another portion of her bone marrow was being extracted for testing. Cibrowski knew why Roberts wasn't in her office that afternoon, but he couldn't tell his colleagues, who spent three hours frantically trying to find her.

ABC executives feared that if the White House couldn't get a confirmation soon, it would take the interview to another network. Indeed, Pfeiffer was going to offer it to NBC's Savannah Guthrie if Roberts couldn't commit to it. Roberts said, "I just remember coming out of the doctor's office, and seeing all these e-mails and voice mails from all these people, from Ben Sherwood and others, almost like, 'Where the hell have you been?'"

When she connected with Sherwood, he told her, "You're going to be interviewing the president tomorrow."

Roberts was surprised, but on the other hand she was in an emotional zone where really nothing was surprising. "Ben, you have to trust me right now," she said. The interview "sounds great. I'm happy. But I need a few minutes; can I call you back?"

She could tell that Sherwood was shocked by her response, and yet she needed time to get her bearings. She was in pain from the procedure, tired from the MDS, and now she had to prepare for this interview. "It should be the happiest time of my life, career-wise, and I'm just not fully engaged," she said later, recalling how she'd felt that day.

"But I think it made me *better*," she added. "Because you think it's the be-all end-all to be number one, and to have a career-changing—life-changing, for many people—interview with the president of the United States, and for me to be like, 'Appreciate it. It's great. But you know what? In the scheme of things, hmmm, it just really . . .' That trite thing that people say, 'Oh, it puts it in perspective'? There is truth behind that."

She paused for a moment. Since the diagnosis, "I don't take myself as seriously anymore," she said. "I know what we do is important and it's a service that we provide. But it's really centered me and made me—as you know my favorite word is *freakin'*—so freakin' mellow. It really, really has."

After leaving the doctor's office, Roberts called Sherwood back and calmly started to strategize about the interview. The network expected that Obama would "make news" about same-sex marriage, but no one knew for sure. "Honestly, we didn't know for sure until the words came out of his mouth," said one producer.

Roberts was supposed to appear on *The View* and *The 700 Club* on Wednesday the ninth to help promote her mother Lucimarian's new memoir. Both bookings were hastily rescheduled, and Roberts and Cibrowski left *GMA* a few minutes early on Wednesday for a ten a.m. Delta flight from LaGuardia to Reagan National Airport for the interview at the White House.

When they arrived at LaGuardia at nine thirty, they found out the flight had been canceled. They scurried to get on a US Airways flight instead, and landed in DC at eleven thirty, two hours before the interview's scheduled start time. While they were on their way to the Hay-Adams Hotel across from the White House, where Roberts was going to change outfits, a taxi bumped into their town car. While the drivers got out to take pictures of the damage, Roberts abandoned the hotel plan. Cibrowski got out of the car and she changed clothes in the backseat. Then they proceeded straight to the White House. "I think same-sex couples should be able to get married," Obama told Roberts, who hurried onto ABC with the news at three p.m. She made it home to New York in time to make dinner for her mom.

The next morning, *GMA* sought to make the most of her huge presidential scoop. Three minutes before airtime, Cibrowski reminded the hosts of what he wanted: "A lot of chitchat off the top about the interview." That was no problem: the *GMA* hosts did chitchat the way Horowitz did Scarlatti. All the morning shows led with Obama's endorsement of same-sex marriage. James Goldston, watching the NBC monitor above his head while straddling a stool behind Cibrowski, predicted that *Today* would "cut their way around us so they don't have to use our interview." In fact the show did use the ABC interview clips, complete with the graphic that read "EXCLUSIVE," but Goldston pointed out, "There's no Robin! It's as if Obama is talking to himself!" *GMA* aired about five minutes of the half-hour interview, followed by a thirty-second video of Mitt Romney's response. Cibrowski thought it was a good morning's work.

So, apparently, did America. On May 15, *GMA* announced that it had scored its third weekly win over *Today*. And in the demo, its margin of defeat was getting smaller…just 139,000.

But if *Today* was demonstrating that it didn't know how to gracefully inhabit the number two role, *GMA* was perhaps revealing itself as an inexperienced winner. Caught flat-footed by its own success, it passed up on a chance to promote itself on ABC's *Jimmy Kimmel Live*. Nor did *GMA* act fast when its long-time concert booker quit in the spring, leaving *GMA* without a summer concert series to rival *Today*'s. Although the booker had a reputation among the staff for being prickly, at least she had secured A-listers like Lady Gaga and Beyoncé the previous year; now *GMA* had B- and C-level acts like Robin Thicke and the Beach Boys and a lot of blank spaces on its schedule. While Usher was kicking off the summer concert series on *Today*, *GMA* unveiled a summer lineup with six Fridays listed as "TBA," for "to be announced." "They really must love this band 'TBA,'" Jim Bell said in an e-mail. (Subsequently "all the great folks here worked their asses off to fill that schedule," Cibrowski said.)

With Curry dispatched to France for the Cannes International Film Festival and Usher on the plaza, *Today* won the week of May 14 by sixty-four thousand viewers. But NBC couldn't keep its mojo going. *GMA* moved back into first place the week of May 21, thanks in part to the season finale of *Dancing with the Stars* (and maybe Maddie the coonhound, who made it to New York by Friday). For the whole month of May, *GMA* and *Today* were effectively tied, with *Today* ahead by just fifteen thousand viewers. What a difference a year had made. "The lead in last May's sweep was 780,000—we reduced it by 98.3%!" Schneider wrote in an e-mail, still amazed that *GMA*, after struggling for so long, was now ascending to first place so fast.

# CHAPTER 15

# "I Am Going to Beat This"

ANN CURRY WAS NOT THE ONLY WOMAN who would take leave of the morning scene in the summer of 2012. Robin Roberts, under strikingly different circumstances, would also be making an exit. Roberts's doctors wanted her to start the chemotherapy that would precede a bone marrow transplant fairly soon, and so the *GMA* cohost would need to tell viewers about her illness, and say what she was going to say about her long-term prognosis and her no doubt prolonged absence in the midst of the wildly seesawing ratings race. But first she had to break the news of her illness to Ben Sherwood.

Roberts and Sherwood sat down in his gray-and-blue-hued office on the fifth floor of ABC on Friday, June 1, for what would turn out to be, as Sherwood told it, "an extremely emotional" conversation. He said later that his message to her was "I need to change your marching orders. 'Cause everybody's marching orders here are to win the championship, to be great, great journalists, great storytellers, and win the championship. But for you the marching orders are different now. It's to take care of yourself first and foremost."

Remember: a little more than a year before, when *Today* seemed permanently affixed in first place, people at ABC had openly wondered whether Sherwood was going to replace Roberts with another female cohost. Maybe Lara Spencer would take her place, they speculated, or maybe ABC would hire Amy Robach away from NBC for the job. Over at NBC, meanwhile, people had whispered that Roberts was unhappy at ABC. (NBC had been intrigued enough by the prospect of poaching her to test her against its own female cohosts in focus groups. Roberts was off the charts: "Robin could do no wrong," one person who saw the research said.) Sherwood's research showed the same thing. Roberts's Q Score was higher than anyone else's on morning TV. She was, simply put, his star. And now she was facing the very real possibility of death. When Goldston heard the news from Sherwood later that morning, he sort of crumpled in his desk chair. "After all that she had achieved, after leading the team in that way, for her to get hit like that, it was unbelievable to me," he said.

What would happen next? Both men were skilled enough in the ways of network television to know that the reality and the perception mattered equally. It was critical that ABC stand by Roberts through her serious illness, and also that it be seen standing by her. It was not that her colleagues all along the hierarchy didn't truly care about her well-being, but the situation had to be carefully managed. She couldn't just disappear from the show one day, then hole up in a hospital somewhere until TMZ got a tip from some disgruntled orderly and broke the news. She would have to tell viewers about her months-long medical leave in a proper way that sent out all the right messages. After that, Sherwood and Goldston knew, ABC couldn't leave Roberts's chair empty; they would need to come up with substitute hosts who were good enough to replace her but who did not appear to be auditioning for her job. If it was done right, Roberts's diagnosis, self-care, and medical treatment could be transformed into a classic television teaching moment and a recruiting tool for bone marrow donors. Done poorly, the episode could turn off viewers and ruin the precious and oh-so-fragile chemistry of *GMA*.

ABC, unfortunately, had some experience in this area. In 2005, Peter Jennings, the anchor of *World News Tonight* for thirty-two years, was diagnosed with late-stage lung cancer. On April 5, shortly after finding out that he had the disease, the sixty-seven-year-old Jennings, who had spent half his life at ABC, shared the news with viewers in a videotaped message. He strained to get the words out. "I will continue to do the broadcast; on good days my voice will not always be like this," Jennings said. But he never anchored *World News* again. He died on August 7 of that year. "So many ABC News viewers experienced the Peter Jennings situation" as a personal tragedy, said a *GMA* producer when Roberts's diagnosis was announced. "We're not doing that this time."

There was no need to. For one thing, five years earlier Roberts had publicly battled cancer and survived it; she'd demonstrated what was possible. This time she faced a very different disease with a very different course of treatment. She had hope in the form of a near-perfect bone marrow match: her older sister Sally-Ann, fifty-nine, a morning news anchor in New Orleans. And she had a deep desire to continue cohosting in the months preceding the transplant. Her daily presence would provide a measure of comfort to her as well as to regular *GMA* viewers.

Roberts knew she would soon have to share her news with her colleagues (except for Champion, who had known since April) and viewers, because pretreatment for the transplant was to begin in mid-June, and the catheter that doctors would be inserting into her arm, to deliver chemotherapy through something called a PICC line, would be visible on television, even when she wore outfits with sleeves. She spoke first with her cohosts, telling Stephanopoulos individually and then Elliott and Spencer jointly.

"It was one of those 'Hey guys, I want to talk to you about something after the show'" moments, Elliott recalled. "But when she went to tell us, she...she couldn't start," he said. "Like, everything caught. So your mind's doing that instant math. Re-calculating, recalculating, recalculating. 'What could this be?' In the span of two or three seconds, you're like, 'Fuck, she's sick.' And at first you think, you don't want to hear her say, 'I have breast cancer again.' But then she starts telling us..."

What Roberts said, sitting in her dressing room, was "I have something really scary."

She took a deep breath.

"It's this disease..."

Pause.

As soon as she said "MDS" and described it briefly, Roberts told her work friends that Googling the disease could be mislead-ing. Since most people diagnosed with it were much older than she was, the public statistics on mortality rates were skewed to-ward depressing. Her doctor, in fact, had told her, "I don't want you to look it up," Roberts told Elliott and Spencer, adding, "Any questions you have, you must ask me."

Spencer called the moment "classic Robin"—more worried about her castmates than about herself. "She was like, 'I don't want you to get upset.' She was so worried about burdening us. I just remember her total confidence, which, consequently, made us totally confident that she's going to beat it."

Cibrowski and Roberts scheduled the on-air announcement for Monday, June 11, one day before she was to begin pre-treatment. The top producers and Schneider, the news division spokesman, spent the preceding weekend in meetings and on conference calls hashing out what to say and what not to say. (They were careful, for instance, never to put a timetable on Roberts's treatment and return.) While they discussed issues of tone and timing, the network's medical correspondent, Dr. Richard Besser, wrote an explanation of the disease for ABC's Web site. That same weekend, Stephanopoulos e-mailed Roberts a long, thoughtful note that staffers later said brought the two of them—the odd couple of *GMA*—closer together. "This—in a tragic way—has helped to strengthen the team," said one producer.

To preserve security—most of the staff still didn't know—Roberts's announcement appeared as a blank spot on the *GMA* rundown at 8:50 a.m. Cibrowski put it there, at the tail end of the broadcast, because he thought it would be difficult for both the on-air talent and the viewers to return to regular morning show business afterward. One of the *GMA* stage managers, Eddie Luisi, had the forethought to Velcro a box of tissues onto the couch where the five hosts would sit for the conversation.

"I am going to beat this," said Roberts, sitting between Stephanopoulos and Elliott, as she gripped both their hands. Then, perhaps trying to preempt criticism of ABC for keeping her on the job, she assured viewers, "I *want* to be here. I don't have to be here. I want to be here while I can." Everyone around her confirmed that was indeed the case.

Roberts, while making the announcement, didn't say how long she would stay on the show before leaving for her bone marrow transplant. She wanted to make it clear, though, that she would be back. She was a fighter, she said, and she'd fight off MDS the same way she'd fought off breast cancer in 2007. Tens of thousands of supportive comments soon piled up on Facebook and Twitter, the vast majority from the women who comprised about 70 percent of the regular *GMA* audience. Some shared their own personal experiences with MDS, and others changed their profile pictures to pictures of Roberts. One person wrote, "God will be inundated with prayers." In the coming days and weeks Roberts would scroll through the comments and, buoyed by the support, occasionally reply to them. The contrast between this use of social media and the tarring and feathering of Matt Lauer on social media could not have been more striking.

After the show, at ten a.m., Roberts addressed the understand-ably anxious staff of *GMA*, dozens of whom gathered around a row of desks to hear her speak. Besser was on hand to describe the rare disease—it affects only one in thirty thousand Americans each year—in detail, and to answer questions. Standing in front of the staff, Sherwood spoke first and sought to head off any speculation that Roberts was permanently off the show—and any campaigning by ambitious fill-ins. "That is her chair," he said. "When she comes back after her transplant, it will be her chair." Then Roberts, in a red hoodie and jeans, held up a photo from the rooftop party on April 19. "I found out this night," she said, pointing to the photo and smiling at it. She thanked the handful of staffers who had kept her illness a secret, and said, "You saw how they continued to work." She wanted the same reaction from the full staff now. She hadn't told them sooner, she said, because "you crave normalcy when your life is kind of not normal."

Roberts then hugged Sherwood's boss, Anne Sweeney, who was leaning on a desk nearby. Sweeney, she said, had "assured me that every possible resource is available to me." For ABC, Roberts's illness was a family crisis, but also a network . . . what? Was the right word here *problem* or *opportunity*? On the one hand, the absence of a principal player from a morning show lineup has rarely if ever been a positive thing; host vacations almost always lead to lower ratings. Roberts's open-ended med-ical leave, some people at ABC were saying, could wreak havoc on the momentum that *GMA* had clearly been building since at least March. "Robin is so essential to what we do, we just don't know what effect this will have long-term on our audi-ence," an ABC News executive said at the time, insisting on anonymity because even speculating about the effect on the rat-ings was taboo. But on the other hand, personal dramas and adventures experienced by the hosts have always been viewer honey. Joan Lunden's very public pregnancies in the 1980s and

Katie Couric's crusade against colon cancer in the wake of her husband's death in 1998 both resulted in ratings spikes for their respective morning shows. And, though she's not a morning show host per se, the attention Oprah Winfrey reaped as she sometimes tearfully fought the battle of the bulge is the stuff of TV legend. Said Chris Licht, the *CBS This Morning* producer, a few days after Roberts's announcement, "On a human level you think, how much more can this woman go through? On a network scumbag level you think, this must drive the *Today* show nuts. Because *GMA* will get a lot of attention."

How calculating the *GMA* producers were or weren't about Roberts's illness is hard to say. Roberts remained more than slightly interested in the overnight ratings, and people at ABC said they took their cues from her about how to cover her illness. She was clearly happy to draw attention to the cause of bone marrow donation. The network let the press know that the day after she spoke on the air about having MDS, the national marrow donor registry Be the Match had recorded more than 3,600 new signups, up from a daily average of two or three hundred. Later in the month ABC News held a bone marrow donor drive at its headquarters. No one could say that a lot of good hadn't come from the network's involvement, yet some people at NBC were whispering about the ways ABC was milking the situation for ratings. The smack-talking truly never stops between the Big Two.

Be that as it may, a big problem for ABC in June, on a network scumbag level, was that the *Today* show also had a woman in distress. Ann Curry, who the research showed was perceived by viewers as being not terribly good at the craft of morning television cohosting, was also perceived as being treated as if morning television ineptness were some kind of felony. She was being leaked about to the gossip press (which said her days were numbered and her colleagues hated her), handled sometimes coldly and sometimes roughly on the air, and (though the at-home viewer was not privy to this) mocked and/or ignored by the show's staff.

This sounds awful, and, as we have seen in an earlier chapter, it most definitely was—but just as Conan O'Brien's audience swelled when his job was at risk in 2010, the *Today* show's ratings benefited from the unresolved questions about Curry's fate. The perennial ratings leader won the weeks of May 28 and June 4, and even squeaked by the week of June 11, when Roberts made her announcement about MDS, taking the prize by a mere thirty-five thousand viewers per day. *GMA* was back on top when the week of the eighteenth started, but on Thursday the twenty-first *Today* beat *GMA* by more than half a million viewers, the biggest daily gap in months. The flip-flop happened because Curry's negotiations to leave *Today* had become front-page news. Curious viewers were flocking to NBC, wanting to see if she'd keep showing up for work.

*Today* wound up winning the week by 133,000 viewers, its fourth straight weekly victory. At the time this was puzzling to some observers who had come to see the *GMA* victories of April and May as something more than a spontaneous surge, and who thought the status of both major shows was rapidly morphing. In retrospect, though, what was happening seems clear: even as a new era in morning television came to pass, the townsfolk were congregating in the public square to witness the torture that precedes the execution.

Its unpleasant reasons aside, the quartet of consecutive *Today* wins, even if they were by a mere one- or two-tenths of a ratings point, put the show much closer to its goal, modest by the standards of the late 852-week streak, of making it to the Olympics (starting July 27) without faltering and falling back to second place. The London Games would give the show a guaranteed ratings lift lasting all the way until August 12. By then, the executives at NBC felt, *GMA* would have cooled off so thoroughly that it might not be a threat again for—who knows?—maybe another fifteen or sixteen years. Or at least for that many *weeks*. *GMA*, during the same pre-Olympics period, had a goal of its own: to finally hit the bull's-eye of the demo, a sweet spot it hadn't struck since the week of September 11, 1995. That was not going to happen, NBC News president Steve Capus told *USA Today* on the eve of Curry's weepy sign-off, because "every week in the last month we've started a new streak!" Alas, apart from not quite making sense, that statement was unfortunate in at least one other way: its cockiness aroused the ABC team and caused them to redouble their efforts. "If there's one quote that riled up everybody here," said *GMA* boss Cibrowski, "it was that quote."

The TV train wreck viewers had simultaneously been hoping for and dreading came, as we have seen, on June 28, when Curry was fake-promoted. How any executive worth his nearly seven-figure salary could have let the wounded cohost go on the air live, without tissues, and make a speech in which she asked forgiveness from all "who saw me as a groundbreaker" for failing to "carry the ball across the finish line," and then squirm away from Lauer's attempted kiss, would for months afterward remain a subject of bitter debate. Curry was still in a town car on her way to the airport (she was flying to California for a wedding) when the spinning and rationalizing began. "She deserved the right to say goodbye to everybody," said one of her few remaining defenders, who would speak only on condition of anonymity. More voluminous were her detractors, some of whom compared Curry's exit speech to a suicide bombing, designed to inflict maximum professional damage on all the people around her on the couch that day, especially Lauer. "The execution wasn't of Ann," said one television veteran, challenging the conventional wisdom that Curry's goodbye had been a public execution. "Ann was the executioner, and the victim was the *Today* show."

✵ ✵ ✵

Talk about must-see TV: *Today* beat *GMA* by three hundred thousand viewers that Execution Thursday—but a day later NBC's mini-streak was no more. Jim Bell had warned some colleagues that the ratings would be "a roll of the dice" in the period following Operation Bambi, and, sure enough, they quickly came up craps. As one viewer put it in a Twitter message to Lauer, "If NBC thought the 'Today' show ratings were bad with Ann Curry, wait until they see them without her." The day after Curry's departure, June 29, *GMA* went from a trailing position to a victory, with 614,000 more viewers than *Today*. It was as if Ann Curry's fan club, more than half a million viewers strong, had changed the channel in unison. The head-snapping number on Friday completely offset *Today*'s Monday-through-Thursday superiority and turned the weekly race into a tie—"a really unbelievable move," said Cibrowski, justifiably. No one could remember the last time the two shows had tied. Said one *GMA* producer: "NBC may have done more to help *GMA* by the way they threw her out the door than had they kept her." Another said he saw the ratings as "a total fuck-you to the *Today* show for firing Ann."

Producers at NBC saw it as something else, too: a rude welcome for Curry's pretty, bright, and well-intentioned replacement, Savannah Guthrie.

# ACT 3

# (ALMOST) INSTANT KARMA

# CHAPTER 16

# The New Girl

SAVANNAH GUTHRIE WAS a Nice Person in a Terrible Position. On June 20, as the leaks about Curry's impending departure were about to morph into the kind of double-edged publicity that can be dangerous to both sides of an argument, Capus called Guthrie, then the nine a.m. cohost of the *Today* show, to his corner office on the third floor at 30 Rock. He had to let her in on a secret.

"There's a story coming out," he said, "about Ann Curry."

In retrospect, it's remarkable how little Guthrie actually knew about Operation Bambi up until this point. Then again, executives like to keep talent in the dark—that's one way they maintain some power over the people who make vaults more money than they do. And sometimes talent keep themselves in the dark—as Guthrie had. She had heard the scuttlebutt about Curry, of course, but she had tried to block it out. Now that was no longer possible.

When Guthrie left Capus's office that Wednesday afternoon, she wasn't quite sure what was going to happen next. It sure sounded as if she was the chosen one for Curry's job—but no one had called her agent to start the necessary negotiations. (Guthrie was represented by Michael Glantz, who also represented

Meredith Vieira.) The end of the week came and went without any word from NBC. The network finally called the following Monday, the twenty-fifth, after Capus had spoken to Guthrie once again—in much the same vague and zigzaggy fashion. At one point Guthrie—still not quite wanting to believe that the *Today* show family was on the verge of a major overhaul—got tired of the suspense and interrupted her boss.

"Are you offering me the *Today* show?" she asked.

"Yeah," said Capus, now smiling broadly. "I am."

This was the fun part of the job—giving people good news and helping them have fulfilling careers. Sure, the joy was tempered a bit in this case by the fact that Burke and Bell had forced this transition to happen far sooner than Capus would have liked it to. But on balance he'd much rather be sitting with the next star of the *Today* show than bargaining with Curry's lawyer, Bob Barnett, who'd been in and out of his office for days on end at that point. Capus told me later, "It's cliché to say it, but in this world, when you can do good things for good people, those are the best days. You know what? That was a good day."

Guthrie tried to smile along with Capus—but she wanted to cry. She was in some ways an odd fit for the cohost job at a major morning program because she is not a schemer, not overly ambitious in what Chris Licht has so helpfully dubbed the network scumbag way. She doesn't trash her rivals, nor does she employ a publicist to plant flattering stories about her. She'd heard talk about Jim Bell and other executives having a kind of professional crush on her, but when confronted with or teased about this she had the habit of clamming up, looking at the floor, and saying…nothing. Her abiding flaw was that she was, by her own admission, an over-worrier. When something happened on or to the show, her brain didn't go to "How can this help me?" but rather to "Will this hurt me?" She was vulnerable, not awful, even when especially sleep-deprived. Which was one of the reasons so many people had a crush on her, strictly professionally of course.

As wonderful as Capus's offer was, she dreaded taking the job under the circumstances. She knew very well what would come next if she said yes: outrage from Curry's fans and people (like herself) who were supporters of women's rights, attacks on her for being the bi-otch who'd benefited from Curry's bumbles, criticism of her performance by both critics and colleagues when the ratings weren't instantly repaired. She felt—rightly—that she deserved better than to be cast as the villain in some play she had never sought a role in.

Capus, through his slightly too-large and -long-lasting smile, asked her if she wanted the cohost job.

"I don't know," she said.

Guthrie's main concern, as she told Capus, was "lowering the temperature," by which she meant getting beyond the current crisis mode and regaining a sense of normalcy on the set. Guthrie had no idea, for example, how Lauer felt about her being promoted, or how Morales—theoretically the woman next in line for the job—would take the news. And she had to at least consider the possibility that she'd be ushered off the couch in a year, just as Curry had been. As we've established, morning TV could be notoriously hard on its women. Indeed, in just a few weeks Erica Hill, a cohost of the still-third-place *CBS This Morning*, would simply not be on the set one morning, and her absence would go utterly unexplained; a new cohost, Norah O'Donnell, would join a month later. (But CBS sidestepped controversy by removing Hill swiftly—"they decided on Wednesday and told us on Thursday; it happened so fucking fast it didn't have time to leak," said one senior producer—and then introducing O'Donnell slowly. NBC's mismanagement of Curry made CBS seem more humane by comparison.) Taking a tack that surely would have made her agent Glantz nauseous, Guthrie suggested that the network reintroduce her to the audience as just a temporary cohost. "I'll fill in for you for a year" and then they could decide where to go from there, she said to Capus.

This idea did not sit well with the news chief. He wanted NBC to look as if it knew what it was doing, and was proceeding with confidence according to a plan, as opposed to groping its way through the kind of difficult period familiar to anyone who has ever accidentally shot himself while cleaning a firearm. Although he had been a staunch Curry supporter, especially in his secret war with Bell, he could tolerate only this much indecision for so long. His boss, Steve Burke, wanted this done before the Olympics, so that's what he had to do: get this done.

At forty Guthrie looked as if she was right and ready for the role. She hadn't always been a high achiever; in high school, shockingly, C's had been the norm for her. But in college she had begun to step up. "I was not always a big gunner academically or anything," she said, "but over time I think I raised the standards for myself of what I thought I should do or be able to do." After graduation her first TV job was at an NBC station in Butte, Montana—which shut down just two weeks after she started. Undeterred, she found a job at an ABC station in Columbia, Missouri. And after two years there she moved back to Tucson for a job at KVOA, the NBC station in town. But she had a nagging desire to go to law school. "She knew she didn't want to be in local TV forever," said her friend Ted Robbins, who taught her broadcast journalism in college and now reports for NPR. Robbins encouraged her to enroll. "I don't say this to everybody, but I said, 'Dream big. You've got the chops. There's no reason you shouldn't do it.'"

In 2000 she did, studying at Georgetown University but keeping a foot in the television world by freelancing as a reporter for WRC, the NBC affiliate in Washington. She recalled, "I would be at law school all day and then they'd call me and say, 'Can you work the three-to-eleven shift?' I'd be covering some murder in

Gaithersburg or something, waiting for the eleven o'clock news, and I'd have my law book on my lap, studying."

Guthrie earned the top score on the Arizona Bar Exam after graduating in 2002. "It was in law school that whatever was hiding in the background in my personality, in terms of wanting to be at the top of my game, rushed to the forefront," she said. "Suddenly I was studying really hard. It wasn't because I wanted to get an A, it was because I didn't want to get an F." She added, almost apologetically, "I don't do all this to try to be Miss Perfect or something, it's because I'm afraid that I'll fail."

Guthrie at that point was still torn between television and law. She had a prestigious clerkship lined up with a federal judge in Washington, but, gathering her courage, she turned it down and started sending out audition tapes. Some agents told her she'd be lucky "to get in the forties," meaning a TV market like Austin, Norfolk, or Oklahoma City. But with help from a believer at the William Morris Agency she landed a trial correspondent job at Court TV.

The job was "perfect, written in the stars," Guthrie said, for it blended her interests in television and law. Guthrie traveled across the country covering events like the Michael Jackson child molestation trial in 2005 in Santa Maria, California, where she cute-met the BBC producer Mark Orchard: the Court TV and BBC live shot positions were side by side, and, well, the rest was B-roll. Orchard at the time had just split up with his wife Anne Kornblut, a *New York Times* reporter, which would later lead to unfair claims that Guthrie was a home-wrecker. In fact the two women are friendly: when Kornblut remarried in 2010 and had a child in 2011, Guthrie was invited to the baby shower.

Guthrie and Orchard were married in 2005, but they divorced after three years. By then Guthrie had moved on up to NBC, thanks in part to Court TV's publicity strategy. As a way to generate attention for itself, the channel sought to book correspondents like Guthrie as guests for legal news segments on other networks. So Guthrie started appearing on MSNBC and on the *Today* show. "That's how I think I came to the attention of NBC," she said.

When her Court TV contract came up for renewal in 2007, NBC snapped her up and made her a correspondent in Washington, as well as an occasional fill-in daytime anchor on MSNBC. Her first experience in that latter post came on March 10, 2008, the day of New York governor Eliot Spitzer's spectacular downfall. "Someone handed me a piece of paper and it said, 'Eliot Spitzer involved in a prostitution ring.' And they said, 'Go' and I said, 'There is nothing here. Involved in? What does that mean?'" Her years at law school and on Court TV had borne fruit. She chose her words carefully on the air, making a smashing first impression.

Later in the year, after briefly covering Alaska governor Sarah Palin's vice presidential campaign, Guthrie was made an NBC correspondent at the White House, backing up Chuck Todd. She was obviously being groomed. Todd and Guthrie hit it off, and a year later they started cohosting a post–*Morning Joe* morning newscast, *The Daily Rundown*, on MSNBC. Not long after she got the White House beat, however, she'd started looking for a way out of it. The reason, she said, was hard to put into words, but it's clear that she internalized the stress of the position. "You can never feel that you know everything, that you've talked to everyone, that you have enough sources. I just put a ton of pressure on myself," she said.

The toughest career move she ever made, though, was probably the one she made by not fleeing Studio 1A after Curry had her on-camera meltdown on June 28.

Guthrie's ascent at *Today* had started slowly, with a morning or two reading the news on *Weekend Today*; then a morning or two filling in as a weekend host; then a morning or two reading the news on the weekday show. Baby steps. At first she didn't see *To-*

*day* as a career trajectory for herself. She *was* looking for a way off the White House beat. But for a while in 2010, Guthrie feared telling Steve Capus about her desire to get the hell off Obama's lawn. Although those around her knew that Guthrie was a rising star at NBC, someone the network wanted to keep happy, she, in full Debbie Downer mode, was afraid he'd say, "Well, that's your job—it's the White House or nothing." If she wanted out, she said, "I honestly thought, 'I'm going to have to leave TV.'"

As usual, her worst fears about herself weren't realized. "To my surprise and happiness, when I finally confessed, 'OK, I kind of think I want to be moved off the White House at some point,' he didn't say, 'Get outta here,' he said, 'OK, we'll have to come up with something for you.' I was relieved." That "something" became the nine a.m. hour of *Today*, cohosted by Curry, Morales, and Roker. With Curry being bumped up to cohost in June 2011, the hour needed a new cast member.

When Capus came to Guthrie's office in Washington to talk through the possibility with her, she was leaning back in her chair, reading a law journal.

"Really?" he asked.

"This is catnip to me. I love this," she told him, though when interviewed for this book she added, "Don't get the wrong impression—*People* magazine was probably hiding inside of it. I've fully reconciled my flighty side and my nerdy side."

When offered the nine a.m. hour and then a second title, that of chief legal analyst, Guthrie didn't hesitate. She loved the mix of stories on the show—"It fits all the different facets of my personality"—and all the opportunities to apply her law degree to boot. "The reason I love the *Today* show is because we do real news, we cover politics, do legal things, but it's really fun to clown around on a cooking segment, too, or to go to a concert and dance," she said. Guthrie's ability to dance and profound inability to cook became running jokes on the nine a.m. hour. She quickly bonded with Roker (despite his playful tendency to call her Samantha instead of Savannah) and Morales.

Guthrie said that when she was given the nine a.m. job, "There was no part of me that thought, 'Oh what's the next thing?' I was so happy to be there." Not only wasn't she striving for the top job on *Today*, her friends said, she feared the perception that she was. Yet when Capus told her that Curry had failed her yearlong stint in the seven and eight a.m. hours, and asked her to move up, she knew she had to accept his offer. No network journalist says no to the president—certainly not when one of the most prestigious jobs in the television world is there for the taking, no matter the circumstances.

Four minutes after Curry signed off, Guthrie took her place on the couch, right near where the tissue box should have been. It was time to start the nine a.m. hour of the *Today* show.

Normally the super-soft third hour starts outside on the plaza, with the cohosts surrounded by a sea of adoring fans. It was a handoff of sorts, a time when Lauer and Curry would say good-bye and Morales, Roker, and Guthrie would take over. On June 28, though, Curry had already left and Lauer chose not to participate. So Guthrie, Morales, and Roker sat on the couch and pretended nothing out of the ordinary had just transpired.

Part of one's job as a morning show host is to divine what the viewers are thinking ("This fat cat may be cute, but what about his health!"). Guthrie sensed right away that Curry's sign-off had gone not quite as well as Evel Knievel's Snake River Canyon jump, but she had no time to figure out even what her own feelings were, or to compose a proper face. She wrapped up the nine a.m. hour by leading a cooking segment, then immediately joined Lauer at the anchor desk—which, if Curry's supporters had had anything to say about it, would have been sealed off with crime scene tape at that very moment—for a network-wide special report at ten a.m., when the Supreme Court's ruling on the Obama administration's health care overhaul was announced. Guthrie's versatility reminded a lot of people at NBC why they'd elected to go with a legal analyst and former White House correspondent rather than a red-carpet chatterbox from the E! network. As Capus pointed out, "If we wanted to pursue someone perhaps flashier from the show business world, we could have. But we weren't aiming for an immediate ratings surge. We were thinking long-term."

The next day, Friday, Guthrie cohosted *Today* with nary a hint of how awkward she felt. A few hours after the broadcast, NBC confirmed with a press release what everyone already knew: that she was the chosen one. She'd start the new job on July 9, a schedule that allowed for emotional recovery and the banking of some sleep. Under the terms of her new contract, Guthrie would be paid about three million dollars a year to cohost *Today*, one-eighth as much as Lauer, the show's veteran, who, it turned out, had renewed his contract and gotten his raise during the very last week of the *Today* show's streak back in April. Guthrie's lack of long tenure was one of her most attractive qualities in the eyes of NBC execs. At age forty, she could have a long career. If everything worked out.

✳ ✳ ✳

In the immediate wake of the Ann thing, as it became known around Studio 1A, the mood around NBC was . . . well, a mixture of numerous emotional elements, but perhaps most notably relief. Yes, the nasty messages continued coming in to Lauer, who was wrongly seen by many as being 100 percent responsible for his cohost's departure. And yes, Curry herself was in hiding: her closed office door bore a red Post-it note that read, "DO NOT

ENTER." Yet as horribly as her send-off had gone—and as sure as a lot of people at NBC were that a lot of other people at NBC were to blame for the on-air debacle—there had been almost universal support for the change itself...which was, let us thank the Lord, now behind them. Lauer "looked relieved," said a staffer, "because he was." And why shouldn't he be? He would no longer need to load his eyes with daggers before each broadcast. Guthrie, a woman who cared deeply about turning the *Today* show around, was now on the case. "It's like the weight of the world had been lifted from his shoulders," said another staffer.

In a memo to his twelve senior staff members dated July 10, Jim Bell tried to rally his troops and find the bright side of his show's fall to second place in the ratings:

FROM: Bell, Jim
SENT: Tuesday, July 10, 2012 7:30 AM
SUBJECT: Private
IMPORTANCE: High

Because I think they can be an unnecessary distraction, I've asked research to stop sending metered market data [early ratings from the major cities] for now. This information is wildly unreliable, almost comically so at times, and every minute that it fuels chatter, phone calls & e-mails is time that could be spent focusing on the next great show idea or coming up with fun ways to highlight our new team and get others, like Hoda [Kotb, the ten a.m. cohost], Tamron [Hall, a fill-in host], Willie [Geist, a fill-in host], Ryan [Seacrest, a special correspondent], into the mix. It's time that could be spent mentoring junior members of the staff. Hell, I'd even prefer it if we spent this time on personal business, call a loved one, get some balance, whatever.

We've allowed ourselves to be somewhat manipulated by

the noise of the last 3 months and it is completely under-
standable; the streak was a big deal...Matt's contract was a
big deal...and the Ann situation has been a big deal. Those
things all had negatives attached...losing the streak...the
concern that Matt would leave...and Ann's last day as anchor. But there are positives here too; we are freed from
the burden that the streak had become...Matt's committed and is here for a while...and Ann was out of position
and we now have a much better show. And you are a very
strong, talented and experienced group. There have been
times when I think we, and I start with me, have acted
like careful custodians of a legacy instead of bold shapers
of that legacy's future. We should all now feel motivated,
invigorated and engaged about getting the chance to create this show's future at a critical time. Who is coming up
with Savannah's first big interview? Who has an idea that
will get Matt excited? Whether it's graphics or bumpers,
contributors or trips, politics or pop culture, let's take some
chances...we are the underdogs now.

We have a tough road ahead to be sure and, though it
won't happen overnight, I know we are entirely capable of
meeting the challenge. We are featuring the best co-anchor
team in the business and their excellence should eventually drown out any residual bad vibrations caused by recent
times. But we are tackling this challenge at a time when
GMA is using Robin's illness and the accompanying public interest in her health as a new weapon in its arsenal.
In addition, our competitors have already shown that they
are prepared to use the press and social media in combat-
ive ways previously unimagined. Let's make sure there are
better things for everyone—the staff, the viewers & the
press—to focus on, and we are going to leave this chapter
far behind us just as quickly as possible. We can and should

take reassurance from the fact that if we are judged on our merits, we cannot help but win.

\* \* \*

It was six thirty a.m. on Monday, July 9—Savannah Guthrie's first official day as cohost. The *Today* show had tied *GMA* during the week of Curry's departure and, with Willie Geist and Natalie Morales filling in, had lost the following week by an average of 243,000 daily viewers. Still, as Lauer strolled into Studio 1A he looked happy and relaxed. Inside he chatted with the crew and read the morning's teases for local stations. Twenty minutes later he was joined by Guthrie, who had picked out a dark-blue Diane von Fürstenberg dress for the occasion. Lauer and Guthrie had done this together dozens of times, when Curry was on vacation or off interviewing refugees, but this time was special.

A makeup artist walked in at 6:56 and applied a little blush and powder to Guthrie's face. Lauer took off his reading glasses and practiced his introduction for the show. "Bright and early, it's a big day around here as Savannah Guthrie takes her place at the anchor desk," he said.

No one mentioned Curry or the travails of recent weeks. The new duo smiled while an NBC photographer snapped a picture of them at the anchor desk. With a minute to go before air-time, Lauer suppressed a cough and Guthrie sat up straighter and brushed back her hair. Then, holding a script, she placed her hands on the desk and looked straight into Camera 1. "Have fun," Don Nash said in her ear. The clock struck seven a.m.

For those who remembered the elevation of Curry to the co-host spot thirteen months earlier, the opening moments of the broadcast brought on a feeling of déjà vu. Lauer celebrated her arrival and had the control room replay the audio clip of her name. "We're happiest," he said, "because you bring a great attitude and what we like to call a weird sense of humor." Guthrie played along, and immediately showed an ease with Lauer that many viewers thought Curry had lacked. "Seven oh-two," she said, gesturing to the camera, "and he's already calling me weird."

The whole broadcast on Monday was designed to show off Guthrie without seeming to say, "Look, we've upgraded!" to the show's many confused and angry viewers. Jim Bell, who'd been away over the weekend on Olympics business, flew back from London for the day to supervise. Guthrie was given the first interview of the morning, with the Obama campaign advisor Robert Gibbs, who talked about possible tax hikes on millionaires like Lauer and Guthrie. Later the cast moved over to what is no doubt the only couch in America that could itself get a mid-six-figure book deal, for a long segment welcoming Guthrie to the family, including a highlight reel reintroducing her to viewers. There was Guthrie the legal correspondent, Guthrie the interviewer, Guthrie the jokester, Guthrie the amateur guitarist. She cracked up when the video included a clip of her singing Bob Dylan's "You're Gonna Make Me Lonesome When You Go."

The *Today* show knew how to do this kind of thing—and maybe that's why some people found the tribute hard to watch: it was slick and professional, but a little by-the-numbers, as Curry's had been the year before. After the video, Guthrie smartly acknowledged the odd circumstances of her promotion. "I just want to say, in all seriousness: this was a little unexpected, as we all know. But I just want to say, I'm so proud and honored to be in a place occupied by so many women that I admire: Ann, Meredith, Katie, Jane, Deborah, Barbara." As her official welcome came to a close, the sun suddenly broke through the clouds in midtown Manhattan and shone straight into the windows of the studio. Those NBC people think of everything. Later in the show Guthrie was surprised by one of her musical idols, the singer-songwriter Shawn Colvin, who invited her to play the guitar and sing a song with her. (Unbeknownst to Guthrie, her boyfriend Michael Feldman had helped a *Today* producer sneak into her apartment and pick up her guitar after she'd left for work.) The whole show went off without a hitch. And the Olympics were only three weeks away!

Operation Bambi?

As that infamous banner above George W. Bush's head read, "Mission accomplished."

✳ ✳ ✳

Or, actually, as more than a few people said back to George W. Bush, "Maybe not."

On Monday, Guthrie's first day, *Today* lost to *GMA* by 356,000 viewers, and it lost again, by 151,000, on her second. It lost in the demo, too. Her third day was even worse, a 582,000 viewer margin. "Killed them yesterday," read an e-mail from Schneider, the ABC spokesman. Guthrie turned off the Google Alert for her name and tried mightily to ignore the daily ratings reports.

Kopf, the *Today* spokeswoman, reminded reporters that Stephanopoulos had had a tough go of it when he started on *GMA* in December 2009, and no one should expect anything different of Guthrie. But no one in the business thought that the viewers were rejecting Guthrie per se—they were rejecting *Today* for hurting Curry. Kopf was blind to how severely the show was damaged. "This," said a top ABC executive, "was always the real bind these guys were gonna find themselves in. Ann was taking them down. But actually taking *her* down alienated a whole other group of people. They were damned either way." Could Guthrie repair it? Clearly she was a more comfortable companion for Lauer than Curry had ever been. But there were a couple of knocks against her—patently unfair ones, maybe, but knocks nonetheless. Guthrie was unmarried and had no children. Every time she cracked a joke about knowing nothing—*nothing!*—about cooking, she reminded moms at home how little she and they had in common.

With *GMA* pulling ahead among viewers ages twenty-five to fifty-four, Cibrowski began, for the first time, to contemplate whether—and how—he should celebrate a weekly win in the demo. When I asked whether he'd hold another rooftop party for the staff, he admitted, "I was thinking about that last night in bed." It was Thursday of Guthrie's first week. "We gotta wait till that happens, though. It's very close, it's very close," he cautioned. Then he looked up at the monitor in the *GMA* control room showing *Today*, and saw a tease for a story about Jesse Jackson Jr., the charismatic Illinois congressman who had been hospitalized for depression. "We did that story yesterday," he said with a chuckle. Cibrowski said he wasn't surprised that *Today* was losing to *GMA* every day, despite the press hoopla around Guthrie's arrival. "Nothing, zero, has changed on that program," he said. "They've offered nothing new." *GMA*, meanwhile, continued to push hard. Although she was in the midst of twice-weekly chemotherapy treatments, Roberts, who'd been in Atlanta the night before for a ceremony honoring a local anchor there, flew back overnight on a charter flight to be on *GMA* by seven.

At seven thirty Cibrowski and Denise Rehrig looked up at the monitors and saw that all three network morning shows were simultaneously teasing the same amateur video of a South Carolina couple who were shocked when they reeled in a shark on a fishing trip.

"Look!" Cibrowski exclaimed. "All three shows. A trifecta."

"Oh my God, amazing," Denise Rehrig said.

*GMA* was the only show that would bring you the couple live, though. They were going to come on via Skype for a short chat at 7:47. The Internet video connection was ideally informal for such a segment. "To roll a truck to them for two minutes, it's just not worth it. It's too much money," Cibrowski said. Through his earpiece, Cibrowski instructed Josh Elliott to brag on air about the exclusive nature of his upcoming chat with the still-astonished anglers.

Scoff if you must, but the American public likes its sharks and its exclusivity. *GMA* wound up winning on Thursday by more than four hundred thousand viewers. For the week of July 9, Guthrie's first as the cohost of *Today*, the ABC show enjoyed its largest lead yet—a daily average of about 350,000 viewers. Yet *GMA* still couldn't quite break the *Today* show's 898-week streak among twenty-five- to fifty-four-year-olds. *Today* stayed ahead—if only by a mere 1,496 viewers—in the demo. The loss, small as it was, rankled. "Total viewers was cool, but this is the money streak," said one senior *GMA* staffer, who admitted to being tired of reading about how *Today* had made nearly five hundred million dollars in advertising revenue in 2011, 150 million more than *GMA*. The demo, as Jim Bell had once said, "is the only number that matters" to the executives, their bosses, and their bosses' bosses, because of the huge cash premium associated with first place. If *GMA* started winning in the demo, it would not just be the most popular morning show—it could become by far the most profitable.

Ann Curry had a hard time sleeping in, just as she'd predicted she would when she left *Today*. She couldn't shake the habit she had formed fifteen years before, when she became the show's news anchor. So she would rise early in her home in Connecticut and start thinking.

Weeks after her departure, Curry still struggled to make sense of her slow rise and sudden fall. Looking back on her year in the cohost chair, she recalled certain moments that, in retrospect, seemed like clues. Or maybe they were best described as non-moments, because it was mostly a lack of support from producers and staff that she most painfully recalled. More than she'd realized at the time, it had been an ugly situation, with Bell, fearful of losing his own job and his pristine reputation, freezing her out to save himself.

That, at least, was one of the theories she entertained as she talked the matter over with family members and friends. Her husband of twenty years, Brian, a software executive, was particularly incensed by the network's treatment of his wife. He wondered, had she been set up to fail, like Deborah Norville and Lisa McRee before her?

When TV critics and anonymous sources blamed a lack of "chemistry" for Curry's bad year with Lauer, she heard a euphemism for something else. Several friends recalled her saying, "Chemistry, in television history, generally means the man does not want to work with the woman." They said she added, "It's an excuse generally used by men in positions of power to say, 'The woman doesn't work.'" Historical examples abound: Connie Chung and Dan Rather; Barbara Walters and Harry Reasoner. Chemistry, Curry argued, is when both people want to play catch—when somebody isn't interested in playing catch, that's when there isn't chemistry. She, at least in her own mind, came to work every day with her glove on and her throwing arm all warmed up.

Curry's friend Nicholas Kristof said he believed Curry had been unfairly made the scapegoat for the show's declining ratings. "They had to pin the blame on somebody," he said, and they couldn't pin it on Lauer, given the size of his paycheck. "She was the new kid on the block and they turned on her." While Kristof described himself as being "just enraged at NBC" after Curry's demotion, he said she herself "had no venom in her." NBC, he said, "couldn't have found a better person to treat so brutally. She at one point said that while it was very painful, it was better to happen to her than someone else because she's very resilient," he said. "And it's true. She is very resilient. But it was sort of an incredible thing to say."

Executives at NBC had trouble feeling sorry for her, given that she had been given a contract worth five million dollars a year to essentially change jobs, but had instead reacted by crying and petulantly disappearing from the NBC scene. Even Capus sounded angry. "She burned her only friend," one observer said, by breaking down on live television. Capus, though, mostly faulted Bell and Burke. If they hadn't honed in on what he said to one friend was their "ridiculous, artificial Olympics deadline," maybe viewers would have been spared the tears. Bell, meanwhile, was back in London. When *Today* lost to *GMA* during Guthrie's first week, he issued a statement—"We are incredibly confident in the new *Today* anchor team. Although it's premature to look at one week of unofficial numbers and draw any conclusions, we just made a big change that we didn't take lightly, and we are in this for the long run"—and got right back to his Olympics work. Capus, back in New York, resented having to clean up Bell's mess.

By all indications, Curry harbored little ill will toward either her replacement, Guthrie, or Morales—who maintained an upbeat attitude even though she had arguably been first in line for the cohost chair. "Natalie could have made this so much more difficult," said one of Guthrie's friends. Instead Morales was openly supportive of Guthrie, whom she had known for more than five years, telling her after the promotion, "I'm so happy for you. This is great for us, it's great for the show." It's hard to believe, I know, but their friendship actually flourished in the summer of 2012, a truly bizarre thing in the cutthroat TV business. Speaking of bizarre, NBC medical expert Dr. Nancy Snyderman arranged a ladies' lunch for Curry, Guthrie, Morales, and several others during Guthrie's second week as cohost. Curry showed up, and the participants all described it afterward as cordial. Tense, yes, but cordial. No one would say what had been discussed. (Other than Guthrie's migraine headaches, which came up early on in the meal; she had to wear sunglasses much of the time because she was sensitive to light.)

But viewers wouldn't let the matter of Curry's dismissal drop. Her fans kept up their campaign against *Today*, riddling the show's Facebook page with requests that she come back—or that Lauer leave as compensation. Clearly they were reading the tabloid stories with titles like "Matt Lauer Was '100 Percent' Behind Ann Curry's Ouster." Said one observer, "The story line is, Matt is a bad boy who's pushed out a good Christian girl." Some of the Web commenters turned around and asked Lauer, via Twitter, whether the rumors were true. They deserved credit, at least, for their persistence. Lauer maintained his silence while Kopf basically ignored the stories. But that was a mistake because on the Web, where all links are equal, many people didn't distinguish between TMZ, which was sometimes wrong but often right, and NBC News, which was almost always right but occasionally wrong. Meanwhile, the incriminating video clip of Curry crying on the couch was always just a click away thanks to YouTube. And Lauer's silence wasn't helping.

Gumbel, Lauer's best friend, came out swinging on July 18, saying what so many people at NBC had wanted Capus, Bell, or some other executive to say. "I'm surprised and disappointed at this idea that Ann was a martyr, that she was thrown under the bus," Gumbel said in what seemed like a random interview with the *Los Angeles Times*. "I don't know why she's being portrayed as a modern-day Joan of Arc. In every job, in every walk of life, people are hired to do a job, and if they don't do it well they are relieved of that job." He added, "It's a big-boy business, and when things don't work out, people are asked to leave. It's happened to me; it's happened to almost everyone in this business."

Privately Gumbel seethed at how badly NBC had botched the transition, just as it had when he was in Lauer's position in 1989. Had the people in charge learned *nothing*? He and everyone else in the TV industry had ideas about how the network could have done it differently. They could have taped the goodbye, for Christ's sake, and dodged a live television meltdown. Or they could have issued a terse press release on a Friday night and refused her any airtime at all. In hindsight a number of people at NBC agreed with Capus that the network should have scrapped its pre-Olympics plan and waited until the end of the year before changing hosts. "We rushed her; we shouldn't have rushed," an NBC executive said in December.

By mid-July 2012, NBC's promise that Curry would be back on the *Today* show as an "anchor at large," covering highfalutin stories around the world, was starting to look like a lie. Curry hadn't seemed to believe it when Lauer said it during her on-air farewell; and partly because *Today* hadn't asked her to contribute anything, and partly because she hadn't piped up with any suggestions, she seemed as gone from the show as Joe Garagiola. NBC hadn't even set up her new office space yet. As viewers brooded about the standoff, Lauer's popularity steadily sank. *Today*, moreover, was losing to *GMA* every single day in the total viewer ratings and barely maintaining its 898-week-long streak in the demo.

The question of whether Curry would ever return to the show was answered on Friday, July 20. At a midnight showing of the latest Batman movie, *The Dark Knight*, in the Denver suburb of Aurora, Colorado, a crazed twenty-five-year-old gunman opened fire on the audience, killing twelve people and injuring fifty-eight others. With Bell doing his Olympics thing, Don Nash was in charge. The deadliest mass murder in the United States in over a year was obviously a big story, one to rival Tucson and Fort Hood and Virginia Tech and Columbine. On a six a.m. conference call with Nash and others, Capus decided not to send Lauer, since he was due in London on Saturday to begin preparing for Olympics coverage. Instead, he dispatched Guthrie, *NBC Nightly News* anchor Brian Williams, and another NBC news employee whom he hadn't seen in a while, but who was in the forefront of his mind. "Anchor at large" Ann Curry, he decided, would anchor a special edition of *Dateline* from Colorado on Friday night, then cohost a special edition of *Today* with Guthrie on Saturday morning. This was, in some key ways, Curry's kind of story. What better way to begin repairing the damage done by Curry's departure than to have her symbolically join hands with Guthrie at the site of a national tragedy? It sounded like a foolproof plan—except for the fact that neither Guthrie nor Curry knew the other was going.

First *Today* had to get through Friday's show. By six thirty that morning Lauer and Guthrie were at the anchor desk. They were scheduled to debrief Jace Larson, a reporter for NBC's station in Denver, by phone at the top of the seven a.m. hour. And then what? They didn't know. The shooting news might consume the whole show. Then again, New Jersey governor Chris Christie was on the way to the studio to talk about Mitt Romney's presidential campaign. For a politician, Christie was a tough get. Should the interview go on? Lauer and Nash talked through their options while the pop rock band Hot Chelle Rae warmed up outside on the plaza. That was another predicament: should the concert go on?

As the seven a.m. airtime approached, nothing had been firmly decided. Then at 6:59:30 a production manager ran up to Nash. The correspondent in Colorado wasn't answering his phone.

"We don't have Jace," the manager said.

"Thirty seconds," the assistant director shouted.

Nash pressed the button that put his voice into Lauer's and Guthrie's ears. "You guys may have to talk about this for a little bit," he said, "I have no one to go to." He let go of the button. The clock struck seven. About ten seconds later the production manager was shouting that Jace was on line one. That might have been the *Today* show's first lucky break in months.

Nash wound up devoting virtually the whole Friday morning broadcast to the Aurora shootings. He scrapped the Christie interview and recorded the concert so it could be shown another day. During a commercial break, he told Guthrie she'd be flying out to Colorado that afternoon. She understood that parachuting into tragedies is a part of the *Today* cohost's job, right up there with interviewing presidents and presenting holiday party planning segments, and she was ready to go—as soon as her boyfriend packed her a weekend bag and brought it to Rockefeller Center.

Two charter flights were booked, one for Curry, one for Guthrie—purely for timing reasons, their colleagues insisted, not because either of the women had refused to share a plane with the other. Indeed the strange truth was that, in all the confusion surrounding the fast-breaking story, no one had told either Curry or Guthrie about the reunion plan. NBC put out a triumphant press release about their pairing when both were in the air. But when Curry landed in Colorado and found out, she said she wasn't going along with it. If Guthrie was here, too, then what was the point of an "anchor at large"?

NBC News executives spent Friday night trying to coax Curry into cohosting (Guthrie was fine with the idea), and they held out hope, into early Saturday morning, that she'd come around. But with a couple of hours before seven a.m. on Saturday, she was still holding out. Her allies said she was offended that NBC was trying to use a national tragedy for PR purposes. Her critics said she was just trying to score points in an ongoing battle with her bosses. Meanwhile *Today* show staffers, unaware of the mix-up and thus of Curry's newly re-bruised feelings, were shocked when her name was removed from the rundown; one senior producer laughed, thinking the edit was a mistake. But it wasn't: Curry was going to come on *Today* for only one four-minute-long segment. A young staffer was told to delete all online references to Curry's cohosting—to pretend, in essence, that NBC had never announced it. Another was told to see whether Guthrie and Curry could be booked on separate flights back to New York.

Guthrie and Curry were separated by several miles during the *Today* show on Saturday. The former was near the crime scene, the latter was at a hospital. Instead of repairing the damage caused by Curry's demotion, their one segment together somehow made it worse. Curry appeared stone-faced as she introduced her story about a young couple who had survived the shooting. It wasn't Guthrie with whom she had a problem; the women would wind up flying back to New York together later in the day. But the split screen at the end of the segment—with the show's past on the right and its present on the left—was a bitter reminder of all that had gone wrong for *Today*.

# CHAPTER 17

---

# Total Victory

NBC NEEDED THE OLYMPICS the way Smokin' Joe Frazier needed the final bell in the Thrilla in Manila, the way George Washington needed nightfall in the Battle of Brooklyn. *GMA* was beating up on *Today* every single morning among total viewers, and was now surpassing its once-glorious rival dangerously often in the precious demo (although it had still not won a full demo week). The Olympics were two weeks of guaranteed wins for *Today*, sitting right there on the schedule, looking delicious. Reaching the Games, even in a degraded state, was all that mattered.

Lauer flew over to London first, on Saturday the twenty-first of July, because he had to prepare to cohost the opening ceremonies coverage the following Friday. Guthrie, Morales, and Roker joined him there on Wednesday the twenty-fifth, having flown overnight from New York. On location at the Tower of London on Wednesday for its first pre-Olympics broadcast, *Today* pretended to have the castmates pull up to Lauer's location in one of London's iconic black cabs. "We're always looking for some good shtick to open up the show," Morales said afterward, calling it a "classic little opening scene."

The hosts then scurried up to a small stage overlooking the Thames. They were sweating heavily in the thick British heat. As a makeup artist patted Guthrie's face during the first commercial break, she joked, "I know, I'm sorry, it's like a full-time job right now."

"When people come to visit the show, even in the studio, they're always surprised by how much activity there is," Lauer said, off camera, to me. "How much running around there is. How much moving from one place to another. It's a little bit like a two-hour workout. We like it that way. We like the chaos and the spontaneity of morning television. But we're supposed to make it look easy. Even though it's not as easy as it looks." Conjuring up the viewers at home, he said, "These people are in their curlers, they're brushing their teeth, they don't want to see us frantic over what's happening. They want to see us in control and calm, starting their day off on the right note."

Lauer was a different man with Guthrie than he was with Curry, at ease and ready to tease, on the air but even more so off. Twenty minutes into Wednesday's show in London, when there was a glitch during a live shot with Ryan Seacrest—his first appearance ever as a contributor to *Today*—Lauer said "Sorry, we thought we lost you," and Guthrie joked, "We're going to blame jet lag." Right after the commercial break started, Guthrie and Lauer fake-debated off the air about who had rescued the segment. "As far as I'm concerned, I saved it," Lauer said. Guthrie sarcastically answered, "Yes, yes, you were the life preserver of that."

Back on the air, Guthrie started the 7:24 a.m. shill for upcoming stories, then looked in Lauer's direction, expecting him to finish with the words "After your local news." He, for some reason, didn't, so after a slight pause she said them. This sparked another round of off-camera teasing between them, with Guthrie pretending to be the veteran host: "Am I going to have to teach you ev-er-y-thing?" Lauer grinned.

The three hours of *Today*—even the nine a.m. hour emanated

from London—were a sweaty blur for the cast and crew, who sprinted from interview to live report to Olympics party planning segment, but a comfortable blend of news, entertainment, and Olympics promotion for the viewers at home. "It's great to get out of the studio every now and then," Nash said. Picking up on that thought, Roker elaborated: In New York, "You don't get this extended period of time to be together. This is almost like we're at camp. We get to hang out with each other." Lauer, sitting nearby, chimed in, "The good news is, it's almost like camp. The bad news is, it's almost like camp." Roker laughed and added, "Matt short-sheeted my bed last night!" The hosts seemed to be saying, "See, *GMA*? We have chemistry, too."

On Thursday, July 26, the atmosphere was a lot less like camp because Steve Burke, the NBCUniversal chief, stopped by the Tower of London set during the broadcast to shake hands with the cohosts and watch the production. Burke was a well-dressed reminder of the role that politics and hierarchies play in the lives of even those people who have what are generally regarded as dream jobs. Right beside him was Pat Fili, the business-savvy former head of ABC and WebMD whom he had just appointed to oversee NBC's news operations.

Eighteen months had passed since Burke had taken over NBC, and it seemed fair to say he wasn't having much fun yet. NBC News, he told his colleagues, had turned out to be a time sink. It had consumed countless hours thanks to the *Today* show contract negotiations, the conflict between Bell and Capus, and other miscellaneous botherations. So Burke had decided to combine NBC News, MSNBC, and CNBC under a new umbrella group, the same way he had strung together the company's various sports units. He named it the NBCUniversal News Group. To run it he'd picked Fili, one of his most trusted administrators. Internally the pick was hugely important, because it signaled that neither Capus nor Bell was being promoted. Capus would now have to report to her, not Burke. It was time for him to consider packing up his office.

While Fili watched *Today* work its production magic at the Tower of London, the final ratings for the prior week, July 16 through 20, reached BlackBerrys there and in New York. There had been some special concern about the numbers recently, since NBC had run its streak of winning demo weeks to 898, and reaching the big round number of 900 would be a psychologically significant moment—empowering for *Today*, deflating for *GMA*. But when the powers that be looked down at their handheld devices, they saw that in week 899 *Today* and *GMA* had... tied. According to Nielsen's estimate, each show had averaged 1,737,000 viewers in the demo.

Both shows immediately claimed a victory, calling to mind the famous headline "Harvard beats Yale 29–29." At a press conference (previously scheduled with TV critics, part of a twice-annual event in Los Angeles) ABC News president Ben Sherwood purposely peppered his remarks with Olympics references, adding up all of *GMA*'s "silver-medal finishes" before saying his cast now stood "at the gold-medal podium." The last time *GMA* had been number one in the demo, he said, "I think the Lillehammer games had just finished the year before." He didn't "think" that; he knew. Almost lost in all the gloating was *GMA*'s huge win among total viewers: the gap between the two shows was 353,000, the widest yet.

For NBC there was worse news to come. In the days leading up to the opening ceremony, July 23 through 27, *Today* did everything it could to stomp out *GMA*. That's why it produced elaborate shows from the Tower of London and Olympic Park with famous contributors like Vieira and Seacrest. It at first seemed to work—the rough drafts of the ratings put *Today* ahead in the demo for most of the week. Even the staff of *GMA* thought their show would win again among total viewers but lose in the demo. So ABC employees were stunned on Thursday, August 2, when Sherwood sent them an e-mail with this subject line:

LAST WEEK—VICTORY IN THE DEMO! AND TOTAL VIEWERS! THE 25-54 STREAK IS OVER!!

Sherwood himself was shocked. The rough drafts had under-counted *GMA*'s audience, especially in the twenty-five-to-fifty-four-year-old demographic. This final draft showed that *GMA* had eked out a twelve-thousand-viewer win over *Today* in the demo—ending the streak-within-the-streak that dated back nine hundred weeks to 1995.

Cibrowski was at Bomboloni, an Italian coffee and dessert shop on Columbus Avenue a few blocks north of the ABC News office, with Chris Vlasto and two other colleagues. They were waiting for their orders and talking about how tough Thursdays are in the land of morning TV (they're the worst—everyone is tired but everyone knows the weekend is still a full day away) when Cibrowski saw the e-mail from Sherwood. In large type highlighted in yellow, it read:

TOTAL VICTORY!!
Demo 25-54: 12K+
Total viewers: 542K+ !
FIRST TIME IN 2 DECADES TO WIN THE WEEK BEFORE OLYMPICS SINCE 1992 (BARCELONA)!

Cibrowski smiled and held up his iPhone so the others could read it. "No more ties now," he said. Vlasto wondered about NBC: "How are they going to spin this one?"

The answer was, as hard as they could. In its press release a few hours later, the network claimed—absurdly—that its streak continued into week nine hundred because the two shows had received the same ratings point, a 1.5. The problem with that argument is that, as people in the business know, ratings points are imprecise—like measuring a person's height in feet rather than inches. *GMA* won outright, surpassing *Today* by twelve thousand viewers in the demo, even though the ratings points rounded up to the same number. No knowledgeable industry observers were buying NBC's version of events.

This was Cibrowski's e-mail to the staff:

GMA WINS!!!!!!!!!!!!!!!!!!!!!!!
#1 MORNING SHOW TOPS TODAY IN THE 25-54 DEMO OUTRIGHT!!!!!!!!!!!!!!!
YOU DID IT!!!!!!!!!!!!!!!!!!!!!!!!!!!!!!!!!
I LOVE YOU ALL!!!!!!!!!!!!!!!!!!!!!!!!!!!!!!!!!!!!!!!!!!!!!!!!!!!!!!!!!!!!!!!!
!!!!!!!!!!!!!!!!!!!!!

The morning game had been upended in the year since Curry had succeeded Vieira. In July 2011, Curry's second month as cohost, *Today* had won by about seven hundred thousand viewers. But in July 2012, Guthrie's first month, the show lost by nearly half a million—a swing of 1.2 million viewers. To put it another way, before Curry's exit *Today* was number one in the ratings; after it *Today* was number two. It would be cruel to begrudge Cibrowski his hard-earned exclamation points, yet the bungling of Operation Bambi was arguably just as responsible for *GMA*'s new success as anything he, Sherwood, or Goldston had done.

As the demo victory sunk in, Sherwood was the first to acknowledge that twelve thousand viewers ages twenty-five to fifty-four, in a country of 312 million, wasn't a meaningful amount. Then again, as he also pointed out, *GMA*'s first victory in the total viewer category had been by a mere thirty-one thousand viewers. Now *GMA* was winning in that category by more than half a million. You have to start somewhere. At lunchtime Sherwood e-mailed all of ABC News to declare *GMA* to be "the Undisputed Champion of the Morning."

When the Olympics started, the *Today* show's ratings soared, as expected, as the games steered tens of millions of viewers to NBC in the evenings and the athletes showed off their medals to Lauer and company in the mornings. Kopf issued a press release after just one weekday of Olympics coverage, celebrating the fact that *Today* had "crushed" *GMA* by 1.5 million viewers. But *Today* was *supposed* to crush *GMA* during the Olympics. That wasn't news. Besides, as ABC happily pointed out, the *Today* show's lead over *GMA* had been wider during the 2008 Summer Games in Beijing. The real test would come *after* the closing ceremony. Would viewers stay with *Today* or come back to *GMA*?

Even with its ratings success, the Olympics were not a particularly blissful time for NBC. Bell was a superb producer of the prime-time broadcasts, but he and his colleagues were mercilessly criticized on Twitter and radio call-in shows for NBC's decision to tape-delay some big Olympic sports like swimming and track and field until prime time in the US. The fact that tape-delay seemed to work wonders for NBC—by encouraging prime-time viewership, the network broke Olympics ratings records and even eked out a profit after forecasting a loss—did not appease anyone except NBC employees and shareholders. And then there was that concurrent and somewhat distracting little side event that might be called the Ann Curry Games. Many had wondered whether Curry would show up in London, as Lauer on her goodbye broadcast had assured viewers that she would. Before her demotion she had been working on stories that were supposed to air during the Games, but those had been scrapped. There had also been talk about having her travel to the Syrian border the first week of the Games to cover the conflict there from her warmhearted perspective. But that didn't pan out, and Curry wasn't seen once on NBC during the first week of the Games.

She was eventually heard from, though. On August 1 she popped up on Twitter, writing at 6:51 a.m., "Good morning Twitterverse. Your unbelievable kindness resonates. You have made me love YOU even more." She posted a couple of Gandhi quotes, including one of her favorites—"When I despair I remember that throughout history, truth and love have always won"—and replied to a follower who asked her to tweet when she knew she'd be back on TV. "PROMISE," she wrote. She was, it seemed, hosting her own little morning show online.

Curry finally made an appearance on the *Today* show on August 9, fronting a story about a sports photographer. This was supposed to be another moment for healing—Lauer planned in advance to say some nice words about Curry. But there was nothing nice about this. Curry walked onto the show's indoor-outdoor set at Olympic Park with her head down, hiding tears. Lauer, perhaps picking up on her body language, didn't stand up to shake her hand or hug her. Once the show came back from commercial, Lauer went out of his way to seem welcoming, saying it was good to see her and mentioning her own photography skills. Naturally NBC executives later went out of *their* way to point out how nice he had been. But Curry, perhaps assuming Lauer was just playing to the cameras, didn't reciprocate. No one seemed to sense just how much pain she was still in. Television critics called the reunion "icy," "tense," and "awkward," and most everyone agreed that it probably set the healing process back considerably. It would be another month before she would make another *Today* appearance.

*Today* came back to New York on August 13 with a new sense of optimism about the ratings race. It had spent two refreshing weeks back at number one, and in front of an audience that ranged between five and six million it had shown its best face and promoted its new lineup of hosts. During its first week back in Studio 1A the show featured an all-star cast of Olympian contributors and five straight days of concerts by acts like the Fray and Nicki Minaj. *Today* felt good about its chances, as did the top producers of *GMA*, who thought *Today* would benefit from a few weeks of Olympics afterglow and stay at least that long at number one.

But the audience had other ideas, and once the closing ceremonies were over it promptly resumed carrying its grudge. Said an ABC executive of the Olympics fans, "They came, they watched, they left." On Monday the thirteenth *Today* had 4.5 million viewers, about three hundred thousand more than *GMA*. But the next day, Tuesday the fourteenth, *Today* slipped to 4.2 million and *GMA* regained the lead. On Wednesday, buoyed by actor Robert Pattinson's first interview since the revelations about his girlfriend Kristen Stewart's affair, *GMA* won by half a million viewers. It was all the more notable because Roberts, the biggest star of *GMA*, was on vacation. Maybe the ensemble was becoming the "star."

*Today* that day dipped below the four-million-viewer mark for the first time in more years than anyone cared to count. When numbers like that happen, somebody usually has to be taken out back and shot. With Curry gone, the morbid attention was now focused on Al Roker, who was patently guilty of having been on the show longer than anyone but Lauer. A personal friend of Curry's, he had been horrified by the way she was treated. On Thursday, August 16, four days after the London Games ended, he and Lauer interviewed members of the rowing team from the Olympics. When the athletes mentioned their tradition of celebrating a win by throwing teammates in the water, Roker said to Lauer, "Which is different than *our* tradition...which is you throw one of us under the bus, but that's another story." A moment of awkward laughter followed, and then, mercifully, a commercial break. "Mr. Roker!" Guthrie exclaimed, as if she were a schoolteacher chastising a student. Roker later claimed it was an innocent joke, one he had made on the show dozens of times before. But his colleagues knew better. Right after the segment he said to a staffer in the control room, through his microphone, "I thought you'd like that." TMZ quickly picked up on Roker's jab, and then dozens of other media outlets did, too. ABC's early-morning newscast even mentioned it, which pissed off Roker so much he tweeted about it. "Some competitors are classier than others," he wrote. All the media outlets seemed to be framing it as a kind of Freudian ad lib aimed at Lauer for forcing Curry's departure.

On Thursday night, while Roker's remark made the rounds, an NBC executive ordered a round of drinks at a bar a safe distance from 30 Rock and brought up the prior day's resounding loss to *GMA*. A gap of half a million viewers, three days after the Olympics? It was worse than anyone had imagined. "This is rejection. This is rejection," the executive said, raising his voice. "It's over. We're in second place."

# CHAPTER 18

# The Empty Chair

COULD THE BILLION-DOLLAR *Today* show franchise be fixed? Bell and the other executives and producers there could not rewind and edit "the Ann situation," as Bell had called it in his memo of July 10, out of their once-glorious history, but could they make improvements that, as time passed and the audience's anger gradually faded, would result in the re-summiting of Mount Nielsen?

While Bell was busy producing the Olympics in London, Capus and his top lieutenant in New York, former *Nightly News* producer Alex Wallace, started looking into the matter. As we know by now, Capus and Bell had never seen eye to eye about what The Problem at the *Today* show really was. For Bell it was Curry's incompetence as a cohost; as a *Today* correspondent put it, "He thought it was Ann and Ann alone. He didn't see structural problems, he saw one problem." Capus, on the other hand, did not think Curry had been the main issue. Neither did Wallace, the highest-ranking female executive in the news division. Their point of view was gaining traction within 30 Rock: after all, Curry was gone, a patently more adept replacement had been found in the form of Savannah Guthrie, and the ratings were still shrinking faster than Al Roker after his stomach-stapling.

At Capus's behest Wallace poked around *Today* during the

Olympics, treating the show as if it were some rogue unit operating within NBC News (which in some ways it was). The assignment was uncomfortable both for her and for Bell's loyal staffers. "I know I'm not supposed to be here," she is said to have remarked at one point. But Capus wanted her there, and so did Fili, the new woman in charge.

Wallace held a meeting in early August, while the Americans were still racking up gold medals in London, to strategize over what *Today* should do after the Olympics. To Don Nash, who called in to the confab from London, the answer was obvious: more attention-grabbing stories. According to people with knowledge of the meeting, Nash told Wallace and the half dozen producers gathered with her, "*GMA* can do buzzier stories than we can, because Matt won't let us." He recalled giving Lauer a heads-up about an interview Natalie Morales was pursuing with the family of a young American man who was mauled by a chimp in South Africa. The family later decided not to talk with *Today*, but Nash said that Lauer, who was thought to have been exerting more editorial influence since signing his new contract in April, responded, "After the Olympics, I don't know if that's going to be our show." (Nash denies making either of these statements. The show did air the chimp attack.)

Although the alleged exchange may seem insignificant—just another chimp conversation in a genre of television that seems to play the chimp card (funny chimp, savage chimp, hero chimp, endangered chimp, even possible mystery-guest chimp) every time it doesn't have a Missing Blonde Girl to turn to—it was evidence of nothing less than the battle for the soul of the *Today* show. Of course *Today*'s biggest problem could have simply been that *GMA* lusted more fiercely after victory. That *GMA* was hungrier. Consider that night in late November 2011, when *GMA* was still firmly in second place, and a freelance ABC producer spent a lousy night sleeping on the hallway floor outside Gary Giordano's room at the Ritz-Carlton. He was guarding against the possibility that the *Today* show might come in the night and try to steal Giordano. "Of course there's Robin, who's famous, George, who's famous, and these new hosts, and they are the show, no doubt," said Ben Sherwood. "But it is not an exaggeration to say that the kid who slept on the floor to protect that interview is a hero. That kid is the difference between winning and not winning."

Perhaps the other difference was on display not far from Lauer's home in the Hamptons on a Saturday afternoon in July, when Josh Elliott and Sam Champion attended an ovarian cancer charity event that counted Spencer as one of the hosts. Spencer brought her husband; Champion brought his boyfriend. (Champion got married in December, becoming the first openly gay cohost of a network morning show.) At the charity event Denise Rehrig bumped into one of her counterparts at *Today*, Debbie Kosofsky.

"I don't get it," Kosofsky remarked to Rehrig when she saw the three *GMA* hosts hanging out together on a day off. "Did everyone just meet here?"

"No," Rehrig said, "everyone came together."

Kosofsky gave her a quizzical look. She asked, "Are you shooting something for the show?"

It took a little while for Kosofsky to suspend her disbelief. But this was just a typical Saturday afternoon, not some setup for a future segment on *GMA*.

Then Kosofsky gave Rehrig this look of awe. She said, "*That's* why you guys are winning."

But Lauer attributed the *Today* show's ratings weakness largely to content choices, not chemistry: he still felt the show relied too heavily on sensational, scandalous stories of the sort that could be found all over *GMA*. A worldly man of fifty-four, he had basically zero interest in silly stories about performers who were often less than half his age. He wanted his show to concentrate on more substantial subject matter—like the notably chimp-less 2012 presidential election—and thereby raise the level of the competition. Arguably what he wanted was a return to the newsier *Today* of the 1990s, when he was the new cohost, Jeff Zucker was the producer, and the winning streak was born. The day of the meeting, Nash is said to have remarked, "I think he'd rather go to number two than have one more person tell him at a cocktail party that they do too many tabloid stories."

Producers like Nash—who had to answer for the ratings just as the cohosts did, but didn't have twenty-five-million-dollar contracts to fall back on—just wanted to win, baby, even if that meant bringing a stop-the-presses prominence to news of Jennifer Aniston's engagement, as Lauer found himself expected to do at the beginning of his first show after the Olympics. Natalie Morales's story about the actress's impending marriage to Justin Theroux led the seven thirty a.m. half hour. "Matt and Savannah, I'm sure you'll all be invited," Morales said, leading Guthrie to quip, "Matt has been so worried about this." Tellingly, when *GMA* cohost Lara Spencer covered the same engagement news ten minutes later, there was not a drop of sarcasm. "We are so happy for her," Spencer said before teasing a story about Miley Cyrus's makeover.

And that was the problem right there: *Today* was still covering celebrity weddings and lurid crimes and the like, but without the verve or sincerity of *GMA*. *Today*, in fact, wasn't all-in on any specific strategy, despite Lauer's wise admonition at one point that "we need to get on the same page" because "the guys across the street are already on the same page."

Amid these internal debates, *GMA* just racked up wins. The week of August 20, *GMA* beat the former champ by more than half a million viewers; the following week it won by more than eight hundred thousand, and, more importantly, it returned to first place in the demo. Indeed, its lead in that sweet spot was now 150,000 viewers—an exponential improvement over the month before, when *GMA* had won by just twelve thousand for a week. Now ABC could begin hiking its advertising rates. ABC News president Sherwood sent the numbers to the hosts and ended his e-mails with "Keep it going. Play your game." Despite all the progress, he still wanted them to play as if they were a half million viewers behind.

Over at 30 Rock, it was as if Bell and his lieutenants thought the ratings crisis would subside if they just pretended it didn't exist in the first place. The *Today* show production offices were remarkably tranquil—far too tranquil, in the view of many ordinary staff members. Where was the "brawl" Sherwood had predicted back in April? *Today* fought back for a little while, then seemed to stop. At cocktail parties, Sherwood asked his old friends from NBC, "What's happening?" He almost sounded disappointed, as if ABC was winning too easily.

Back at NBC, "there is no leadership" was the phrase I heard more than any other. Bell was keeping a low profile (and squeezing in a little vacation after the Olympics) as rumors revved up that he would soon be replaced at *Today*. He didn't take a side in the debate over the show's future direction until the first week of September, when he spoke out for Lauer's vision in no uncertain terms. "We have to make the anchor happy," one of Bell's staff members recalled him saying. The change was almost instantly apparent on air: in the fall of 2012, *Today* spent more time on politics and foreign policy and less time on entertainment, particularly in the first hour of the show. But the ratings needle barely budged—and to the extent that it did, it was at the *Today* show's expense.

Robin Roberts's last week on *GMA*—the week of August 27—was the first week of her show's winning streak in the twenty-five-to-fifty-four-year-old demographic. Roberts had been planning on saying, "See you soon"—not goodbye—on Friday the thirty-first. But on Wednesday night her sister Sally-Ann called and said their eighty-eight-year-old mother Lucimarian's health was failing (she'd had a stroke in July). Roberts couldn't fly home to Mississippi that night because the airports were shut down while Hurricane Isaac came ashore in Louisiana. So she booked a flight for Thursday morning, right after *GMA* was to wrap, which meant she would be starting her leave for her bone marrow transplant a day sooner than she had planned.

Cibrowski and the other producers scrambled to rearrange Thursday's show and make time for Roberts's sign-off. Two of the hosts were out of town—Champion was in Louisiana covering the hurricane, and Stephanopoulos was in Tampa for the Republican National Convention—but they would participate via remote hookups. Fortunately country star Martina McBride, a friend of Roberts's, was already scheduled to perform a song for her on Thursday's show, so the producers built around that, scheduling time for the hosts to give Roberts gifts and for Roberts to interview her doctor.

"Everyone should head downstairs now," senior broadcast producer Denise Rehrig said in the control room a little after eight thirty. The staff hurried to the studio and gathered behind the couch where Roberts was seated with Elliott and Spencer. As they looked on with barely contained emotion, Cibrowski made a rare on-camera appearance to present her with a bound book of handwritten letters from her coworkers. "We will be with you every step of the way," Cibrowski said, squeezing her hand. "We are Team Robin."

Then Cibrowski stepped off set while McBride sang "I'm Gonna Love You Through It," a song she had written a year earlier for breast cancer survivors like Roberts. He looked at Sherwood, who was standing next to him, and pursed his lips, trying to hold back tears. Sherwood, also welling up, patted Cibrowski's shoulder.

There hadn't been time to script what each host was going to say, so the end of the show was ad-libbed. Each of the hosts gave Roberts a gift for her hospital stay—matching pajamas for her and Sally-Ann, a studio prop to remind her of the show, etc.—and then she had a few seconds to sign off. A stage manager crouched underneath her camera shot and counted down from ten to one with his fingers.

"George, Sam, Lara, Josh, my *GMA* family"—six seconds—"My family there at home: I love you"—three seconds—

Roberts held her fist in the air, striking the same pose as on April 19 when *GMA* was named number one and she was diagnosed with MDS. She looked directly into the camera. "And I'll see you soon."

Roberts, Elliott, and Spencer hugged as the staff applauded—two seconds, one second, and then the broadcast faded to a commercial break. "We're off," a stagehand said.

Then Roberts stood up and said what she really wanted to say. "Now that the cameras are off"—she paused and looked around at the staff—"I want you to continue to kick ass!"

The staff laughed; the tension was eased. Roberts bowed her head and spoke the prayer that her mother had taught her as a child: "The light of God surrounds me; the love of God enfolds me. The power of God protects me; the presence of God watches over me; wherever I am, God is."

Then she looked up and said, "God bless; Godspeed; and I'll get back to you just as *soon* as I can."

Stepping off the stage, she immediately looked for Sherwood, who was standing near the doorway to the lobby. The two hugged for a long time. He whispered in her ear and she nodded her head. Then they let go, and he wiped a tear from his eye.

Roberts's mother Lucimarian died that night with both her

daughters by her side. "Wasn't easy to get here, but glad I made it," Roberts wrote in an e-mail. Cibrowski notified the staff at midnight so they could begin planning a televised tribute for the next morning. Roberts's transplant was delayed for a few days so she could attend her mother's funeral in Gulfport, Mississippi. Stephanopoulos flew in from the Democratic National Convention in Charlotte so he could attend, too. Then Roberts returned to New York and braced herself for the surgery. She was admitted to the hospital on September 10 and put through eight days of chemotherapy before the transplant on the twentieth. The bone marrow procedure itself lasted just a few minutes. If you understand how *GMA* operated, you know this just had to be a TV moment. Diane Sawyer and Sam Champion were in the room, along with one ABC camera. "I will now wait and anxiously watch and see what happens," Roberts said, looking straight into the camera.

*GMA* aired the video the next morning. After that the anchors mentioned her every half hour, every day, reminding viewers that this was still Roberts's show—even though no one could say when she would return. It would be much easier to keep winning what Sherwood called "the championship" with her there: boosted by her "see you soon" broadcast, *GMA* beat *Today* that week in August by an average of 882,000 daily viewers, its biggest margin since 1994. But *GMA* had demonstrated earlier in August, when Roberts was on vacation, that if it had to, it could win without her, too. The future depended not just on whether they could keep their fizz from going flat—but on whether *Today* could recover the formula that had once sold like Coca-Cola.

Some at NBC began to speculate that Lauer was The Problem. His theories about the content of *Today*, and the bossiness he'd projected since renewing his contract, put him at odds with many of his colleagues, who worried, especially after NBC laid off twenty workers from *The Tonight Show with Jay Leno*, that they might lose their jobs if ratings remained low—and that Lauer wouldn't take a salary cut to save jobs, the way Leno had. But these grumblers became insignificant when compared to the dozens and sometimes hundreds who demonized the cohost daily on Twitter and Facebook, or who sent scathing e-mails directly to the show. This Web site comment spoke for the rest of them: "Sadly when I see Matt Lauer on Today I say to myself. 'Where in the World is my Remote.'" The mainstream press mostly went easy on Lauer, but on September 16 the *New York Post*'s Page Six column called him the "anchor animal" and quoted an anonymous source who said, "He has gone so crazy about ratings that staff on 'Today' are not even allowed to mention 'GMA' to him." (Said Lauer in response: "Please print this story—it's the most interesting and dangerous I've ever sounded!") When the *Daily News* reported that his Q Score had dropped 25 percent in the last year, it also quoted Lauer as saying, "Is it only 25 percent? Because it feels much worse." It was one of the unintended side effects of Operation Bambi that Lauer, but not Bell and Capus and Burke, was seen as the villain in the plot against Curry. This was partly because Lauer was not exactly the hero of the tale—although he never demanded that she be pushed out, he could have done so much more to help her—and partly because relatively few people knew who the warring executives were. Outside of a very few upper-level staffers at the *Today* show, no one grasped the important subtleties of the story.

Among the powerful few who did have inside information, however, Bell was in trouble—not at all unlike the trouble Ann Curry had been in months before the ax finally fell. Playing the role of Jim Bell, this time, was Pat Fili, the woman brought in by Steve Burke in July to oversee all of NBC's news brands—NBC News, MSNBC, and CNBC. Fili had let there be no doubt that job number one was fixing *Today*. She sized up the show and right away saw an institution that had fallen for its own propaganda. "It just hasn't evolved," she told associates matter-of-factly—echoing what so many outsiders had been saying for years. Fili believed in changing the show's pacing, its story selection, even its set, but she knew she needed to start backstage—with Bell.

By taking that view, remember, Fili was siding with Capus—the man who had wanted to replace Bell for a while now. Capus was one of her direct reports. Fili, perhaps influenced by him, wondered if Bell, after seven years on the job, had become too much of an expert on how things are done, and cared too little about how they might be done differently. According to Fili's allies, about a month after the Summer Olympics were over she met with Bell and said, in effect, "You have a choice to make." Fili told Bell that he could produce *Today* or he could produce future Olympics broadcasts—but he couldn't do both. Not anymore.

Her allies say Bell balked at first, as Curry had when Bell proposed she leave the *Today* show's cohost chair.

"I can do both," he said.

"No, you cannot do both," Fili responded.

Fili was unyielding. *Today* needed someone who was prepared to sit through no small number of therapy sessions to make "America's first family" whole again. That's what fucked-up families have to do sometimes. "You need to do some soul-searching," Fili told him, "to decide if you have the energy to evolve this show." If Bell didn't want to or didn't think such a thing was necessary, that was fine by Fili. NBC Sports wanted him.

Bell could feel his autonomy being stolen away. Already his staff members were whispering that it had been Fili, not Bell, who'd sided with Lauer's vision for the show and forced everyone else to fall in line. "Jim just tried to make it sound like his decision," said one. Now it looked as if he was losing one of his two jobs. "He's having a hard time coming to grips with the fact that he's being demoted," an associate of Bell's said shortly after his initial meeting with Fili. The whole affair reminded a lot of people of 1990, when Bell's mentor Ebersol returned to NBC Sports after blaming himself for the Deborah Norville disaster at *Today*.

But Bell's allies tell a different version of this tale. Bell, some say, knew when he took the Summer Olympics job that the arrangement was temporary: eventually he'd have to choose one or the other. Others say he knew when he took the job that he would be coming back to sports full-time. But Bell never said that publicly, and he declined to comment here. In any case, Fili may have made it a nondecision (to borrow the phrase used for Curry's promotion) by convincing Burke that *Today* needed a change at the top. "Pat wanted her own person" running *Today*, one of Bell's friends said.

Bell had at least the illusion of choice in September, when Fili and Capus started interviewing candidates for his chair in the control room underneath Studio 1A. On September 26, in a move that surprised many who cover the television business, he summoned a string of reporters by telephone to ask him anything—about Curry's exit, about Lauer's level of involvement, about his own future running the *Today* show. What made this slightly shocking was that Bell had been turning down all interview requests for three months. He had said next to nothing about the circumstances of Curry's departure, which had allowed a thousand rumors to bloom, many of them reflecting badly on Lauer. "Jim had been shirking responsibility at every turn," one of Capus's allies complained.

The day Bell picked for his series of one-on-one interviews coincided with Yom Kippur, the Jewish day of atonement. Bell is a Christian, but atoning is what he was doing nevertheless. "It was all my fault," he said in essence, over and over again to *The New York Times*, the Associated Press, the *Hollywood Reporter*, *TV Guide*, and others. Don't blame Lauer or anyone else for the Curry disaster, he said, blame me. "It was definitely not Matt's call," Bell said to *The Times*, of Curry's dismissal. "He is the host and does not have management responsibility. It was not his call. That was my call."

Was Bell very belatedly trying to take the heat off Lauer, perhaps at Lauer's behest? Was he campaigning to keep his job? Those were the theories at the show. But it was hard to say for sure. In the interviews, Bell didn't express any regret for removing Curry—"it was the best thing for the show"—but he admitted it "didn't go quite as we had hoped." When the *Hollywood Reporter* asked if he had "cleared the air" with Curry, he claimed he had, when in reality she still felt betrayed by him. The *Reporter* followed up by saying, "But no one seems to want to let the transition go." Said Bell, "Well, I'm encouraging you to be the first one! Let's start moving forward." In practically every interview he did that day, Bell only sort of denied the rumors of his imminent departure, saying suspiciously often of his present position that it was "the best job in the world."

Fili talked to almost twenty candidates for that "best job." Herself an example of female leadership in a male-dominated industry, she was keen on hiring a woman or two to remake *Today*. Chief among the candidates was Izzy Povich, a former producer for *The Maury Povich Show* (where she'd met her future husband, Maury's nephew Andrew) who'd worked at MSNBC since 1996. Povich's biggest claim to fame was running *Countdown*, the prime-time show hosted by the famously combustible Keith Olbermann. If she could manage him, the thinking went, she could manage anyone! Povich met with Lauer in mid-September for a job interview of sorts—though no one at NBC dared call it that, since the party line was that Lauer was an artiste and had no management involvement. Then she, like all the other candidates, waited to see what Fili would do.

In addition to ratings, Robin Roberts had a whole new set of numbers to wonder about: her blood counts. After the transplant "I was in a pain I had never experienced before, physically and mentally," she told *People* magazine. "I was in a coma-like state. I truly felt I was slipping away." But her sister Sally-Ann's stem cells were doing their job of rebooting her bodily systems, piece by painful piece. On October 3, two weeks after the transplant, Elliott and Champion (wearing surgical gloves and masks to protect Roberts from germs) visited her hospital suite for the first time. The next day there was great news back at work: *GMA* had beaten *Today* for the entire month of September. In those same weeks *Today* had hit twenty-year lows. Roberts, for one, said she was not surprised. "I know we consistently have the best show," she told me in an e-mail, "and viewers know we care for one another." Yes, even in the hospital, she was still watching the show every morning and scrutinizing the daily ratings e-mails.

Roberts was released on October 11. For at least three months she would have to stay at home in isolation, to decrease the risk of her getting an infection when her immunity was so low. Elizabeth Vargas and a new hire from NBC, Amy Robach, took turns filling in for her. On October 25, when Oprah Winfrey was guest-cohosting in her absence, Roberts called in to the show for the first time. "I am so incredibly blessed to be doing as well as I am," she told Winfrey and the cast. Seeming to address the whispered suggestions that *GMA* was exploiting her illness, she also said, "I think of my dear mother, and she taught me well. It is about being a service to others. It would be a whole lot easier to not be so public when you are going through things like this. The people I have met, who are going through this, their family members who are so appreciative of what we as a family are doing. It's a privilege to be a messenger."

☀ ☀ ☀

In September, NBC's marketing unit commissioned Sterling Brands, a consulting firm that helps companies figure out what they are and what they aren't, to conduct a study that would do just that for *Today*. Sterling interviewed twelve people, including Lauer and Guthrie (but not Roker or Morales); Capus, Bell, and Nash; Jackie Levin, the senior producer in charge of author bookings; and John Kelly, the head of ad sales for NBC News. The product of the interviews, a thirty-six-page report called "Positioning *Today*," was delivered to select members of the show's staff on October 4.

Knowing they wouldn't be quoted by name, the twelve had spoken freely about what they felt was right and wrong about the show. They seemed happy to talk, like a worrywart who has to wait two weeks for a therapy appointment: "There was consistent support for the project," Sterling noted in the report, "as a way to come together around a clear and shared sense of purpose." For some it seemed a much-needed chance to gripe: "If I look at the show, I am not sure I'd know what year it is," said one. "I want to feel like we are watching 2012." But everyone seemed to be expressing thoughts that they had considered and refined over time—and no one denied that they were facing problems larger and more fundamental than the miscasting of Ann Curry. "We must acknowledge the shift in the kinds of stories people want," one subject said, "but how do we do this while remaining TODAY?"

On page one of the report, the researchers listed ten "insights" on which there seemed to be a consensus:

1. we are proud of our tradition
2. at our best, the whole is greater than the sum of our parts
3. we're currently losing the war
4. we're open to change, but it's about focusing more so than changing

5. our family needs to be fun again
6. we must define our purpose, and it can't be their purpose
7. we must deliver a wide variety of stories and payoffs, but with a through line
8. we're most "TODAY" when we advance the story
9. we've lost sight of our audience
10. our passion shows best when our co-anchors connect to the story

Sterling's researchers commented on the fact that the twelve *Today* interviewees barely talked about the viewers at home whose wants and needs they presumably tried to anticipate. The twelve talked in vague terms about "the demo," but not about serving its members in specific ways. "This is a problem for a show whose success is measured daily by its ability to capture the hearts and minds of Americans," the report stated.

But if the participants seemed aloof, they were not oblivious to the way relationships among staffers—and between talent and viewers—had deteriorated. "Our sense of family is broken," one said. "Matt is being blamed, and some in our audience see Savannah as the younger replacement wife," another said. The researchers concluded that "Ann Curry's departure was a public airing of family business that's negatively affected trust in our talent and desire for our viewers to welcome us into their lives. It's also hurt morale internally." Still, there was danger in getting too Curry-centric in analyzing the problems. Said one interviewee, "Ann was only 50 percent of the problem; people were leaving for the content, too."

The main beneficiary of all this misery and miscalculation, everyone involved seemed to acknowledge, was *GMA*. "There are many aspects of *GMA*'s family that we may not hold in the highest esteem," a member of the *Today* staff told Sterling, "but everyone agrees on one thing: they look like they are having more fun, and we need to bring the fun back!" A big part of having fun came down to relaxing and not caring so much what *GMA* did. "We are all over the map," one of the twelve said. "We have to stop reacting and [stop] just doing what they're doing!" "*GMA* beat us with a surgery story at 7:42, we copied and it didn't work."

A good deal of anger came through in the interviews. "'GMA' is a boy band," one person said; "we're a group of professional musicians." But some people noted that the competition had shown a better sense of the zeitgeist. "They went light, just as we were spending too much time on the dark stuff," said one of the interviewees. Another said of *GMA*, "They may be ice cream, but we can't become vegetables."

Sterling found two schools of thought about how the show should change. The first it called the "look at others" school: "Look outside, especially at GMA, to guide how we should change." The second, which they called the "back to the future school," was the one Lauer personified, the one that said the team should "re-discover our sense of self and innovate forward from there." Sterling stated the obvious: that *Today* currently suffered from a lack of a clear self-identity. Conjuring up the voice of the staff, it said, "We know we want to be north of 'GMA' and south of '60 Minutes,' but then we have trouble defining exactly who we are." The consultants seemed to throw their weight behind the more high-toned vision of the show's future espoused by Lauer. "Part of the American viewing diet will always be an appetite for tabloid style journalism," reads the report. "But this appetite can be fully whetted elsewhere. Tabloid journalism is corrosive to our positioning. Corrosive to our soul. They are not who we are." According to a producer who read the report, "Sterling dismissed *GMA* as 'fluff,' merely a guilty pleasure."

"They are an entertainment show that covers the news," the consultants wrote. "We are a news show that tells compelling stories, and we need to be better at this than we have ever been before."

Not everyone who saw the report agreed with Sterling's conclusions. To some it sounded as if the consultants wanted *Today* to morph into *CBS This Morning*: as one staffer put it, "To get back to number one, imitate number three." Sterling had little to say about talent, even though talent was arguably the reason *Today* was failing the Sound-Off Test, something propounded by Fili and countless other television executives to see how two shows stack up against one another. Turn off the sound and watch the shows side by side, they'd say: see which team is having more fun. See which team you'd rather spend time with. The answer in 2012 was *GMA*.

Fili knew that. And that's one of the reasons why, as the fall wore on, it began to look more and more as if Bell would not be part of *Today*'s future. It was not an easy time for the man who had once run a show that had a string of victories going back to the Clinton administration. As Curry had in the months leading up to her sign-off, he resisted the inevitable, avoiding conversations about a new job, talking in public about how much he loved *Today*, and showing up for work every day despite suspecting that his boss—in this case Fili—wanted him gone. The Olympics job was a hugely important job, but it was awfully hard to give up *Today*.

That Bell should wind up a loser in the morning game was, to some observers, ironic, since a strong case could be made that he had jump-started the *Today* show's recovery. Not only did he take out Curry—a hard but necessary thing, many believed—but he brought in both Savannah Guthrie and her friend and occasional fill-in Willie Geist, who was about to join the cast full-time as the cohost of the nine a.m. hour. Both of those hires, almost everyone agreed, had made *Today* better.

Geist, thirty-seven, was perhaps the single biggest beneficiary of Don Imus's stupid 2007 slur. "In the span of five seconds, Don Imus talking about the Rutgers women's basketball team changed my life forever," Geist said. The son of CBS correspondent Bill Geist, Will had already worked all the grunt jobs of TV—he'd logged plays, edited tapes, produced interviews, written jokes, brainstormed shows for CNN and Fox Sports Net. He'd been hired by MSNBC in 2005 to help produce a late-night show for the conservative commentator Tucker Carlson. At the end of every episode of this show, which was titled *The Situation with Tucker Carlson*, Geist came on camera to sum up the day's pop-culture news in a segment with Carlson called "The Cutting Room Floor." "I definitely had the bug," he said. But Geist wasn't on a mission to become TV "talent." It just sort of happened. Olbermann asked him to tape a couple stories for *Countdown*. Joe Scarborough, who was still on in prime time, asked him to do the same. "They were closer to the *Onion* than *Nightly News*," Geist said. But the segments impressed the right people. When Imus was fired, Geist was on Scarborough's list of suggested costars for a new show called *Morning Joe*.

Geist was initially Scarborough's sidekick, a source of comic relief amid serious political debates. But gradually he refashioned himself into the kind of calm voice of reason that perfectly suited the upbeat and aggressively unthreatening environment of the *Today* show. Geist started filling in for Lauer in 2011 and seemed like the designated sub in 2012, just as Geist's contract was coming up for renewal. NBC persuaded Geist to stay by offering him a package deal: he'd helm the nine a.m. hour, continue to fill in for Lauer, and contribute to NBC Sports and its Olympics coverage. He'd even continue to cohost the six a.m. hour of *Morning Joe*, televised across the street.

Capus, Fili, Burke, and even Tom Brokaw were all involved in keeping Geist at NBC, but Bell got to announce the young cohost's promotion. Geist, a beneficiary of Curry's fall (since

Guthrie's rise opened up the nine a.m. time slot for him), tried to paper over all the terribleness. "Right now I see a moment of great opportunity," Geist told me the day his promotion was announced. "And the great news is that everybody over there at the *Today* show feels the same way, too."

Bell by this point was all but gone. By late October, according to people at NBC News, he had stopped resisting Fili's order and started negotiating with NBC Sports for a new contract. He told colleagues that he was opting for "stability," his word, in sports after a stressful year (or seven of them) in news. Fili and Capus, meanwhile, had settled on a new, two-tiered management structure for *Today*. They'd appoint Alex Wallace, the female VP who had conducted an assessment of the show while Bell was producing the Olympics—and whose responsibilities included overseeing Curry's reporting unit—to be the executive in charge. They would also appoint someone—it was unclear who, but Povich was in contention—to be the show's executive producer. This system had worked back in 2005, the last time *GMA* was a threat, when Bell was the producer and Phil Griffin was the executive in charge.

Change was in the air of the *Today* show control room in early November. Bell's deputies put out feelers for work elsewhere, thinking they might fall victim to a corporate bloodbath. His longtime No. 2 Don Nash inquired with ABC about work on Saturday the tenth. And then the shake-up finally started to, you know, shake. When Wallace's role leaked on Monday the twelfth, NBC confirmed the by-now-obvious: that Bell was leaving. He'd have the same responsibilities he'd had over the summer, executive-producing NBC's Olympics coverage, only now he'd have them full-time. The official line, which had also been the official line with Curry, was that he was being matched with a job at which he excelled and relieved of burdens that were almost beneath a person of his extraordinary talents. Bell said the change was bittersweet. "When you start to look at the truly special franchises in television, the ones that have stood the test of time and the ones that continue to not just be relevant but really thrive, it's a very short list," he told *Sports Business Daily*. "The Olympics are on that list. And the *Today* show is on that list."

NBC told reporters that it would be able to name a new *Today* executive producer by the end of the week. First, though, it had to pick one. Fili was intrigued by a pairing of Povich and Tammy Filler, the producer of the ten a.m. hour. It would have been an all-female team, and an innovative one, too. *Today* needed innovation. But Fili encountered resistance—from Lauer, some said. An NBC executive said, "Matt had no veto power," but admitted, "we weren't going to put somebody in that Lauer completely disagreed with." Povich and Filler were never offered the jobs; Fili accepted that such a move might be too disruptive. Instead, Fili and Capus decided to promote from within. Don Nash was in his car, heading home to Connecticut at around four o'clock the next day, when Capus called and offered him the job. "I was overcome with emotion," Nash said. "I was thrilled, I was humbled, I was excited. It was almost a surreal experience."

Nash very much wasn't what some people thought the show needed—a break from the past. He *was* the past. A mild-mannered twenty-three-year *Today* veteran, he had been passed over for the executive producer job in 2005 when Zucker went out and recruited Bell from NBC Sports. He'd reached out to ABC recently when he suspected he was going to be passed over again. But in his conversations with Fili and Capus, Nash had said all the right things about the future: specifically, that *Today* "needed to evolve." "I'm easily bored. I have the attention span of a gnat," he told me on the day of his promotion. "I think one of the reasons why I got the job is, I'm always looking for the next thing."

For Capus, Nash's appointment was a big victory—a long-awaited vanquishing of Bell. He couldn't wait to get the news out. The prose in his press release sounded boilerplate: "I am thrilled for Don and for *Today*," the statement read. "I know firsthand the show will benefit from Don's unmatched morning television experience, control room skill and leadership." But when Capus introduced Nash as *Today*'s new boss at a two p.m. staff meeting amid the show's rows of cubicles on Wednesday the fourteenth, the applause was loud and sustained and the expressions genuinely joyful. "The feeling," said one staffer, "was 'One of our own is up there. He gets the show. He's not gonna come in here and tell us we suck. He's gonna look out for us.'" Lauer and Nash had their share of disagreements, but at least they knew and respected each other.

But simply appointing a well-liked producer was no more a solution for *Today*'s problems than removing Curry had been. The solution lay deeper, somewhere in the shifting reasons viewers reach for the remote control—or don't—when they wake up. Fili alluded to it when she talked to a reporter from the *Wall Street Journal* on the fourteenth. "People wake up with their smartphones, that's their alarm," she said, "so when you are presenting the 'Today' show, we have to keep that in mind." The world had changed, and *Today* had to, too.

One thing had changed already: the arrogant edge was off the voices of producers and bookers handling pitches from book, film, and would-be guests' publicists. The aura of invincibility was gone. Instead of thumping its chest about the ratings, NBC issued weekly press releases noting that it was "closing the gap" with *GMA*. Closing the gap! Imagine how hard *those* words are to write if you've spent the past sixteen years issuing pompous press releases about your gargantuan winning streak. It was true that, with a mix of somewhat more substantial stories (but still with plenty of breaks for fun and games), *Today* was edging a little closer to number one in the twenty-five-to-fifty-four-year-old demographic, now and then—and it managed to beat *GMA* in the demo by six thousand the week that Hurricane Sandy ravaged the New York region (although that week didn't count in the year's ratings because of the widespread power outages related to Sandy). But the larger truth was that *Today* was now the number two morning show, even if it pulled off a win once in a while. On Bell's very last day in charge, Friday, November 30, Nielsen released numbers that showed just how much the TV world had changed, and in which direction it was going. The ratings were for the November sweeps month, sweeps being a vestige of a time when ratings were collected just a few times a year, not every second of every day. During the November sweeps in 2010, *Today* had won by nearly 942,000 viewers. During the sweeps in 2011, it had won by 663,000 viewers. And this November? *Today* lost by 466,000 viewers—a swing of more than a million in one year.

Kopf, the spokeswoman, countered that bad news with the only positive piece of information she could scrounge up: *Today* had won in the demo for the three days leading up to Thanksgiving. After that, though, *Today* looked as deflated as a Macy's parade balloon on Black Friday. Lauer looked exactly the same way. Viewers—make that *former* viewers—continued to assail him for his role in Operation Bambi. And he continued to avoid questions about what his role had really been. Online commenters even ganged up on him when he mispronounced the name of the George and Ira Gershwin song "'S Wonderful" while hosting the Thanksgiving parade. Seriously. He said "S-Wonderful." A week later, a Page Six story provided the year's best reminder of how badly *Today* had been mismanaged, and how seriously Lauer had been hurt by it all. The story was a rebuttal to another gossip column's claim that Lauer would be fired if the show's ratings didn't rebound soon. "There is absolutely no truth to this," Alex Wallace told Page Six.

Of course there wasn't. *Today* was still *The Matt Lauer Show*. But that the question had to be asked—"Will Matt survive?"—and answered by NBC—"Yes"—was nothing short of astonishing. Even Ben Sherwood couldn't have scripted it.

*GMA* returned to first place in the demo the week after Thanksgiving and stayed there for the rest of 2012. This was in spite of ABC's prime-time schedule, not because of it: the network's audience at night was minuscule, while NBC was enjoying a resurgence, yet people were still switching the channel to *GMA* in the morning. America had chosen.

Nash officially took over on Monday, December 3. But Bell came back that day for a televised toast. The cast, equipped with champagne glasses, congregated in the control room at eight thirty a.m., where Bell was sitting at his old desk in the middle of the room. Nash was still standing in his former spot in the front row, running the minute-by-minute production of the show. The body language was telling. Bell didn't bother to stand up while Lauer congratulated him for "seven fantastic years" and Guthrie told him to "enjoy sleeping in." Like a lot of *Today* segments from the last few years, it seemed like something you'd seen already. But Bell clinked his glass with all the cast members and said thanks. Then Lauer, as he had done with Curry, asked Bell to assure him that they would surely work together again, at the next Olympics.

"We'll see you in Sochi, right?" Lauer said.

"Russia and Rio," Bell affirmed.

After the toast, Roker invited viewers to see what was happening in their neck of the woods and Lauer hurried upstairs for an interview in the studio. The other hosts told Bell again how much they appreciated his management over the years. Morales, who speaks Spanish and Portuguese, said, "If you ever need a translator, you know who to call." Roker shook Bell's hand and said, "I'll follow you to the ends of the Earth, baby." All the while viewers were still seeing a local weather report—at least that's what the *Today* hosts thought. Lauer wasn't in place for the interview yet so Guthrie, acknowledging the awkwardness of Bell's goodbye, deadpanned, "Jim would love to be interviewed a little further." Bell laughed and said, "Yes!"

From his seat in the control room, Bell stared ahead at the same wall of monitors that he had faced most mornings for seven years. From this vantage point he could see everything a *Today* show executive producer needed to see: Lauer getting mic'ed up in Studio 1A upstairs, fans waving signs on the plaza outside, correspondents standing by for live shots in other time zones. He could see *GMA* and *CBS This Morning* and *Morning Joe* and *Fox & Friends* and *Squawk Box*.

At this particular moment, though, he could also see something horrifying: *he was on live TV!* NBC's stations had rejoined the *Today* show, but it seemed that no one in the control room had cued the cast. Actually, Nash *had* pointed and told them to "fill" the time, but for some reason no one had taken the new boss's words as a signal to start. Bell saw that a close-up of the left side of his face was being beamed across the country. He swiveled to the left, looked into the camera, and froze.

"Are we on?" Roker asked. "All right, we're on!"

"Just more time to talk with Jim," Guthrie said, breezily applying a dab of professional polish to the gaffe. She asked what it was that Bell had liked best about working on the show, and as America watched he thawed instantly, and said nice things about the cast and crew, just as Curry had on *her* way out of morning television.

# AFTERWORD

In 1980, the same year that *Good Morning America* beat the *Today* show for the first time, stoking the biggest rivalry in television, Woody Allen released a movie called *Stardust Memories*. The movie opens with a black-and-white shot of two trains on parallel tracks. Allen is shown surrounded by miserable passengers on his train. Then he's shown looking out the window, where he can see the glamorous passengers on the other train, full of life, full of joy. That train over there? It's having a party. It pulls away right as a gorgeous passenger blows Allen a kiss.

In 2012, you might say Allen's train was the *Today* show, and the party train was *GMA*. Millions of people were still *Today* people—they enjoyed waking up with Lauer and company every morning. But *Today* gave up nearly a quarter of its audience ages twenty-five to fifty-four, a terrible loss for any television show, and especially for one that had been firmly on top for sixteen consecutive years. Network sources spoke of a devastating fifty- to seventy-million-dollar dip in advertising revenue—the cost, perhaps, of falling from first to second place.

*GMA*, meanwhile, won new converts. The show began 2013 about half a million total viewers ahead of *Today*, its best performance in at least two decades. In February, when the show celebrated six straight months of weekly wins, ABC began to call it a "streak." But in the twenty-five to fifty-four demographic, it was basically tied with *Today*. *GMA* was still technically in the lead, but the demo ratings gave *Today* reason to have hope.

Ben Sherwood continued to tell his hosts and producers to "play each day as if we're half a million behind." Reflecting on *GMA*'s accomplishments, Sherwood made it all sound deceptively simple: "We worked hard, had a clear strategy, and got lucky. We put together a winning combination, on air and behind the scenes. We played every day as underdogs and took nothing for granted. We seized the opportunity when they gave us an opening.

"And we know one thing for sure," he added. "The fight goes on, the battle never ends."

But the players change. On February 1, 2013, Steve Capus said that he was stepping down after seven years as the president of NBC News. The announcement had an air of inevitability, given the fact that Fili was keeping an increasingly close watch over the troubled news division. Fili moved downstairs from the fifty-first floor—where she had an office near Burke—to the third floor, right beside Capus's office, the same week he decided to pack it up.

Some people surmised that Capus was the final victim of Operation Bambi. He didn't see it that way, though. The day after he made the announcement, he went with his son to a music lesson. He played the bass, his son played the keyboard. And he felt tremendous relief.

At home in Connecticut, Jim Bell started waking up at a decent hour again. He made pancakes for his kids and prepared for 2014's Winter Olympics in Sochi, Russia.

The executives who remained at NBC, from Steve Burke on down, were united in the view that they had done the right thing by replacing Ann Curry with Savannah Guthrie. They admitted, however, that they might have gone about it wrong. They feared Matt Lauer's reputation would never recover.

Curry continued to view the whole thing as a profound betrayal by Bell and Lauer. Though bestowed with the title of NBC News national and international correspondent, she rarely appeared on the network. She did, however, have a story on *Today* on Don Nash's first week as the new executive producer—from New Zealand, where she'd interviewed the stars of *The Hobbit*. The fact that she was literally halfway around the world from Studio 1A was not lost on anyone.

Nor was the fact that Lauer was a fallen star. He had managed to renew his contract on the very last week of the *Today* show's sixteen-year streak back in April. Now his colleagues complained that the money had been misspent. They wondered, wouldn't Willie Geist or another cohost attract the same number of viewers for a fraction of the price? If Lauer had any regrets, he kept them to himself. But he did give in to Twitter's charms and start tweeting more often—thereby reaching the growing number of people who woke up with their phones, not their televisions.

Guthrie and the rest of the cast defended Lauer, whose Q Score had fallen even further than *Today*'s ratings on a percentage basis. By January 2013, his score was a nine, down from nineteen in 2011. Previously, Lauer had been the most-liked man on morning TV, according to the data; now that title belonged to George Stephanopoulos. Al Roker, in a CNN interview in January, said Lauer had "had nothing to do with anything that happened on our show," meaning Curry's ouster. Roker diagnosed the media with a sick case of schadenfreude: for the better part of two decades, he said, "They had to write we were number one. And now we're not, OK. Good on *GMA*. Good for them."

※ ※ ※

*CBS This Morning* remained stuck in third place in 2012, right where CBS had stayed for decades. But the news division bosses were proud of the program and they stood by it, believing that it was an appealing alternative for viewers who would surely someday tire of *Today* and *GMA*. Around the time of the show's one-year anniversary in early 2013, the ratings began to look up.

"When we came in, we were challenged to grow these broadcasts. And look what's happening: steady, solid growth. Especially this year on *CBS This Morning*," the news division president David Rhodes said in February. "But what's even more encouraging is we're getting that growth on quality. People know what we stand for. We're more likely to reveal a crisis in Syria than a crisis in a spray-tan booth."

☀ ☀ ☀

Jeff Zucker took over CNN Worldwide in January 2013 and was charged with reviving the company's flailing cable news channel. One of his first priorities, he said, was fixing the low-rated morning show called *Starting Point*. A week later he poached ABC's Chris Cuomo, who been the news anchor on *GMA* years earlier. Then he started casting a female cohost, determined, as he was, to hit the morning show jackpot again.

☀ ☀ ☀

Robin Roberts's bone marrow transplant transformed her from a *GMA* host into a *GMA* viewer, just one of the millions who tune in every morning. "Now I get it," she remarked on one of Josh Elliott and Sam Champion's visits. *It* was the profound intimacy that viewers feel they have with television hosts they've never actually met. "I feel like I've been there with you guys every day!"

In December, after three months in isolation, Roberts began to venture out of her home. She donned a red dress for Champion's wedding on the twenty-first. All the other GMA cohosts were there, too, save for George Stephanopoulos, who was on an out-of-town trip. Later that same day Roberts came to the *GMA* holiday party, marking the first time that most of the staff had seen her since the transplant. The music stopped, and Roberts was handed a microphone. "I *will* be back," she vowed. And sure enough, on January 9, 2013, Roberts received a tentative thumbs-up from her doctors to start the transformation back into a *GMA* cohost. Months would have to pass before she could just show up for work like anyone else. But the fact that she could show up at all was something of a miracle.

ABC arranged for Roberts to announce the good news on January 14, four months and sixteen days after she had signed off. A camera crew arrived at her apartment before dawn to set up a live shot in her living room at home. Roberts would say that her most recent bone marrow test showed no abnormalities—none. She hoped to be back behind the anchor desk sometime in February, assuming that the "reentry process," as she called it, went smoothly.

"Ready?" Tom Cibrowski, in the control room, asked Roberts through her earpiece a few minutes before seven a.m. Her face was projected onto a big screen in the show's Times Square studio—the next best thing to being there.

Cibrowski stood up as the song "Ain't No Mountain High Enough" started playing at 7:01. "Hello, Robin," Stephanopoulos said on the broadcast. "So nice to really see you." The cohosts—and a few people in the control room—burst into applause.

What happened next was Roberts's idea. Before the show she'd told Cibrowski that she wanted to greet viewers right at the top of the show, even though he was saving her formal announcement for the seven thirty half hour. Cibrowski then told Stephanopoulos, who knew exactly what she wanted to say. Stephanopoulos looked across the studio to the big screen and said, "I know you've been waiting 138 days to say this, so go for it."

Grinning from ear to ear, Roberts looked downright effervescent. She threw her arms in the air, held her head skyward, closed her eyes, and proclaimed, with more energy than ever before, "GOOD. MORNING. AMERICA!"

## AFTERWORD TO THE
## TRADE PAPERBACK

So Bell had lost and Capus had won, right? Wrong. On the first day of February in 2013, it was his turn to say goodbye to NBC News.

The announcement had an air of inevitability, given that Fili was keeping an increasingly close watch over the troubled news division. Consider this: Fili moved downstairs from the fifty-first floor—where she'd had an office near Burke—to the third floor, right beside Capus's office, the same week he decided to pack it up. But he was said to be leaving of his own volition. "It has been a privilege to have spent two decades here, but it is now time to head in a new direction," Capus wrote in a memo to staff members.

His new direction wasn't immediately clear—but thanks to the terms of his divorce from NBC, he had no need to hurry into a new job. At home in New Jersey, he joked about being comforted by the fact that Bell had been squeezed out before him.

Meantime, at home in Connecticut, Bell started waking up at a decent hour again. Suddenly he was able to make pancakes for his kids in the morning. Unlike Capus, Bell still had a job—preparing to run NBC's coverage of the 2014 Winter Olympics in Sochi, Russia. There he'd briefly reunite with Lauer and Meredith Vieira, two hosts of the opening ceremonies telecast.

The executives who remained at NBC, from Steve Burke on down, were united in the view that they had done the right thing by replacing Curry with Guthrie. But they started to say more honestly—at least in private—that they'd done it the wrong way. Some of them feared Lauer's reputation would never recover. Others complained that the money set aside for Lauer's fat new contract had been misspent. They wondered, wouldn't Willie Geist or another cohost attract the same number of viewers for a fraction of the price?

The decline of Lauer's Q Score told the story as effectively as anything else. By January 2013 his score was a nine, down from nineteen in 2011. Previously, Lauer had been the most-liked man on morning TV, according to the data; now that title belonged to George Stephanopoulos.

If Lauer had any regrets about renewing his contract, he kept them to himself. As he remarked to one interviewer, "I'm not going to whine or get depressed. Who's going to feel sorry for me? Nobody." But it seemed, to the cynics who follow this stuff a little too closely, that he'd embarked on a New Year's image rehabilitation effort. One day Lauer even replied to a Twitter message about a former *Today* show intern, Mark Zinni, who had described Lauer as "not so nice" behind the scenes. "Huh? Always tried to be nice Mark," he wrote. "Sorry you didn't think so. Hope you're doing well." One of those aforementioned cynics wondered if Lauer would go on a door-to-door apology tour next.

Guthrie and the rest of the cast steadfastly defended Lauer, and by extension the show they loved. Al Roker, in a CNN interview in January, said Lauer had "had nothing to do with anything that happened on our show," meaning Curry's ouster. That, of course, was not true, and the quote stung Curry when she heard it. She continued to view the whole ordeal as a profound betrayal by Lauer and Bell. Yes, she had been very well compensated. Yes, the title of NBC News national and international correspondent had been bestowed upon her. But she rarely showed up on the network. She was MIA, for instance, during NBC's coverage of election night and Inauguration Day. She did, however, have a story on *Today* during Don Nash's first week as the new executive producer—from New Zealand, where she'd interviewed the stars of *The Hobbit*. The fact that she was literally halfway around the world from Studio 1A was not lost on anyone.

March 4 was Capus's last day. He was feted at a party in Studio 8H, best known as the home of *Saturday Night Live*. Some attendees wondered if his successor was somewhere in the room—after all, any of his deputies could have picked up the reins right away. But Fili was looking not just outside the room, but outside the country. She waited months to appoint a new president, leaving the news division in a state of suspended animation in the meantime.

NBC News went ahead with its annual luncheon for advertisers, which happened to fall on the same day that I published a story in the *New York Times* about Lauer and his tenuous future with *Today*. The story—titled "At NBC, a Struggle to Revive the Morning Magic"—described internal deliberations and office gossip:

> The ratings are scrutinized now by NBC and ABC for signs that "Today" is stronger on the days when Mr. Lauer is on vacation.
>
> He is criticized routinely in the media; one columnist this week said simply, "He's got to go." And even members of his own staff are sharply divided: some say he, and "Today," can recover from the last year, while others say his reputation is irreparable.

The employees spoke on condition of anonymity because they feared retribution from Mr. Lauer and their bosses. They all agreed that his contract, thought to keep him at "Today" through at least 2014, would be his last.

While I was fact-checking the story, Alex Wallace (the executive in charge of *Today*) called to provide a comment. While "we are aware of all the ridiculous rumors and gossip," she said, "we would like Matt Lauer to be in the chair as long as he would like to be. We hope that's for many years to come." The comment suggested that Burke and Fili had made a decision: contrary to what some lower-level staffers and many of NBC's competitors thought, *Today could* recover from its self-inflicted wounds with Lauer at the helm.

If Lauer was seething about the article, he didn't show it at the advertiser schmoozefest. Aware that there were reporters in the room with their recorders on, he prefaced his on-stage remarks by addressing what he said "might be a teeny white elephant in the room." The crowd laughed. "We all love covering the news, we hate being the news, and so I would like to say on that subject—from the bottom of my heart—that I promise to spend all of my time and energy over the next several months trying to keep Savannah out of the headlines." At that, the crowd belly-laughed. Lauer had handled it perfectly.

Wisely, and more seriously, he added, "We want to go back to the most-watched morning program and the least-talked-about morning program."

But no one, not even Lauer, could turn back the clock. The advertising buyers in the room knew that *Today* had given up almost a quarter of its audience ages twenty-five to fifty-four, a terrible loss for any television show, and especially for one that had been firmly on top for sixteen consecutive years. That meant ad time on the show had become cheaper. Network sources spoke of a devastating fifty-to-seventy-million-dollar dip in ad revenue—the cost, pretty clearly, of falling from first to second place.

Among total viewers, the bragging rights category, *GMA* had begun 2013 about half a million viewers ahead of *Today*, its best performance in at least two decades. When the show celebrated six straight months of weekly wins, an ABC press release called it a "streak." This was apparently a slipup—the network shied away from using that word again. But the rogue press release was accurate—there was now a new streak in morning TV. *GMA* soaked up the media attention.

Roker, on CNN back in January, had diagnosed the media with a sick case of schadenfreude: for the better part of two decades, he said, "they had to write we were number one. And now we're not, OK. Good on *GMA*. Good for them."

There was still some hope for *Today*: in the critical twenty-five-to-fifty-four demographic, *GMA* wasn't half a million viewers ahead, it was barely one hundred thousand ahead. *Today* won a day here and there, and occasionally even a week. But *GMA* was the show with the momentum. And that was true even *before* Robin Roberts made her triumphant return.

Roberts's September 2012 bone marrow transplant transformed her from a *GMA* host into a *GMA* viewer, just one of the millions who tune in every morning. "Now I get it," she remarked on one of Josh Elliott and Sam Champion's visits. It was the profound intimacy that viewers feel they have with television hosts they've never actually met: "I feel like I've been there with you guys every day!"

In December, after three months in isolation, Roberts began to venture out of her home. She donned a red dress for Champion's wedding on the twenty-first. All the other *GMA* cohosts were there, too, save for George Stephanopoulos, who was on an out-of-town trip. Later that same day Roberts came to the *GMA* holiday party, marking the first time that most of the staff had seen her since the transplant. The music stopped, and Roberts was handed a microphone. "I will be back," she vowed. And sure enough, on January 9, 2013, Roberts received a tentative thumbs-up from her doctors to start her transformation back into a *GMA* cohost.

ABC arranged for Roberts to announce the good news on January 14, four months and sixteen days after she had signed off. A camera crew arrived at her apartment before dawn to set up a live shot in her living room at home. Roberts would be able to tell viewers that her most recent bone marrow test showed no abnormalities—none. She hoped to be back behind the anchor desk in February, assuming that the "reentry process," as she called it, went smoothly.

"Ready?" Tom Cibrowski, in the control room, asked Roberts through her earpiece a few minutes before seven a.m. Her face was projected onto a big screen in the show's Times Square studio—the next best thing to being there.

Cibrowski stood up as the song "Ain't No Mountain High Enough" started playing at 7:01. "Hello, Robin," Stephanopoulos said on the broadcast. "So nice to really see you." The cohosts—and a few people in the control room—burst into applause. What happened next was Roberts's idea. Before the show she'd told Cibrowski that she wanted to greet viewers right at the top of the show, even though he was saving her formal announcement for the seven thirty half hour. Cibrowski had then told Stephanopoulos, who knew exactly what she wanted to say. Stephanopoulos looked across the studio to the big screen and said, "I know you've been waiting 138 days to say this, so go for it."

Grinning from ear to ear, Roberts looked downright effervescent. She threw her arms in the air, held her head skyward, closed her eyes, and proclaimed, with more energy than ever before, "GOOD. MORNING. AMERICA!"

On February 20 she said the words again, this time on the set as *GMA* threw a party for her first day back at work. There were supersize crowds outside the Times Square studio. There were special yellow-and-pink graphics emblazoned with inspirational words from a prayer that Roberts's mother had taught her: *light, love, power, presence.* And there was no shortage of ABC suits, including even Anne Sweeney, the chair of the Disney/ABC Television Group. As staffers gathered in the second-floor studio for a toast to Roberts toward the end of the program, Champion joked, "Is anybody running ABC News right now?"

While one pair of workers rolled out a tall, multicolored "WELCOME HOME ROBIN" cake, another pair arranged an overflowing basket of goodies from the *Today* show. Gifts in the basket were tagged with the names of the anchors—an umbrella from Roker, et cetera. Some at *Today* steadfastly believed what Bell had written in his memo the prior summer: that ABC was "using Robin's illness and the accompanying public interest in her health as a new weapon in its arsenal." One lower-level producer grumbled to me on the day of Roberts's return that ABC was being exploitative; another fretted about the ratings race and said, "*GMA* could use this to pull away." But Nash distanced himself from the anonymous gripes: he had the *Today* show cast give Roberts an on-air shout-out, and he told me in an e-mail, "All of us at 'Today' wish her continued good health and years of hitting the 3 a.m. snooze button!" Roberts was equally gracious when she spoke to a group of reporters after her welcome-back show. When Don Kaplan of the *New York Daily News* asked her, "What's it been like watching the wheels come off the other guys?" she answered, "I'm not going to talk about them" (well, besides wishing them well and calling *Today* a "very strong program").

Truth be told, jealous producers at *Today* weren't the only ones grousing about ABC's handling of Roberts; some people at the alphabet network thought that it was "overkill," to pick out one oft-repeated word. But Roberts seemed genuinely appreciative of the network's support and 100 percent comfortable with the coverage.

After the on-air toast, the staff gathered for a series of speeches, first from executives and then from Roberts herself. ABC News president Ben Sherwood started it off by paraphrasing one of his teachers, who'd spoken about television's ability to transmit emotion. "For the last two hours, and for the last 173 days, you conveyed real emotion; a real sense of family; and today, an unbelievable sense of joy," he said to cheers from the crowd.

Then he singled out Stephanopoulos for a round of applause, citing "your leadership and your growth in this incredible period."

Growth? "Not that much!" Stephanopoulos joked.

The at-least-three-inches-taller Roberts cracked up.

Next Sherwood scanned the studio for Amy Robach and Elizabeth Vargas. As the women hurried up to the front, he said, "We've got two new regulars on this show"—affirming that they'd remain a part of the cast even though Roberts had returned. This was especially important, since Roberts could work only part time at first, and would sometimes have to call in sick with very short notice.

Sherwood turned over the mic to Cibrowski, who told Roberts, "We will follow you anywhere. We will always be with you. We love you."

If this sounds intense on the page, imagine how it felt in person. Roberts told the staff—and the battalion of her doctors and nurses that was on hand—that she felt she'd been given a "third lease on life."

"People ask me, 'Why do you want to go back to work?' I say,

'I want to go back to work because of the people I work with, and the work that we do. We're just getting started.'"

Finally, she uttered what I thought was the best line of the day: "Now we can resume regular programming."

Roberts thanked a multitude of people by name, including Amber Laign, her longtime girlfriend. It was only natural for Roberts to acknowledge her, and it wasn't news to ABC staffers—they'd gotten to know Amber at holiday parties and other assorted functions over the years. But Roberts had never spoken publicly about her sexual orientation before, a fact that seemed to clash with the highly personal stories she shared on television about her health and family. It was as if Amber had been delicately cropped out of the photos carefully chosen to illustrate Roberts's cancer battle and comeback.

After the toasts concluded, I asked Jeffrey Schneider, ABC's public relations chief, if Roberts's thank-you to Laign was her way of coming out—casually, within the context of something larger, the same way Champion had come out in an interview with a *New York Times* reporter while at a same-sex wedding. The question seemed reasonable since seven or eight other reporters had been in the room when Roberts spoke. Schneider squashed the theory, but suggested that Roberts's coming-out moment was coming soon.

At the *Times*, there is an understanding that reporters do not preemptively "out" public figures; accordingly, my story in the newspaper the next day did not mention Amber, nor did the stories written by any of the other reporters.

After Roberts's return, the morning show "war" turned... monotonous. Not to the grunts, mind you—they still battled over every single booking. But for a long while in 2013 there were no shocking cast changes, no game-changing stunts, no sudden changes to the ratings standings. *GMA* extended its streak while *Today* struggled to mount a comeback. Sherwood continued to tell his hosts and producers to "play each day as if we're half a million behind."

For the obsessive followers of this stuff, the most dramatic developments involved the network that was still ensnared in third place, CBS. The news division bosses stood by *CBS This Morning* throughout its first year on the air, believing that it was an appealing alternative for viewers who would surely someday tire of *Today* and *GMA*. This was more than mere wishful thinking, it turned out—around the time of the show's first anniversary, in early 2013, the ratings began to look up.

"When we came in, we were challenged to grow these broadcasts. And look what's happening: steady, solid growth. Especially this year on *CBS This Morning*," news division president David Rhodes told me in February 2013. "But what's even more encouraging is we're getting that growth on quality. People know what we stand for. We're more likely to reveal a crisis in Syria than a crisis in a spray-tan booth."

Was Rhodes posturing? Sure. But he was right that *CBS This Morning* devoted more time to straight-up news than its competitors. And no one could deny that it was working, if "working" means "edging a bit closer to second place in the ratings." Some weeks CBS would be up 15 percent over the same week a year earlier; other weeks it would be up 20 percent. The ratings gains weren't as impressive in the twenty-five-to-fifty-four-year-old demographic, at least not initially, but more and more viewers were giving *CBS This Morning* a chance and liking what they were seeing. Chris Licht, the executive producer, adopted a sort of unofficial slogan for the show that punched up at NBC and ABC: "The news is back in the morning." On Twitter, he and his producers shortened it to three sharp words: "News is back."

With more viewers came more scrutiny, and once in a while CBS had to deflect stories about how the trio of anchors—Charlie Rose, Norah O'Donnell, and Gayle King—weren't the best of friends behind the scenes. But the network had inoculated itself against some of that by positioning Rose, O'Donnell, and King as journalists and not promising some pretend family. Rose's hometown newspaper, North Carolina's *Raleigh News & Observer*, called this a "decidedly adult take" on morning TV in a feature about the rising ratings: "King admits the trio, with busy individual lives, don't hang out when the camera's not on. But O'Donnell adds, they have a mutual respect and admiration for each other." If there's anything to be learned from the *Today* show's misadventures, it's the importance of mutual respect.

In April 2013 this book was published in hardcover, triggering a whole new round of bad press for NBC and some second-guessing about the decision to boot Curry from *Today*. Curry was silent throughout. But Lauer granted a couple of interviews, presumably to get ahead of what he thought this book would say. He told Howard Kurtz of *The Daily Beast*, "I don't think the show and the network handled the transition [from Curry to Guthrie] well. You don't have to be Einstein to know that." You don't have to be Einstein to see what was missing from his comment, either. Everyone knew the show had mishandled the transition—but what about the star of the show? How much blame would Lauer assign himself for the disaster? Either Kurtz didn't ask or Lauer didn't answer. Instead, the *Daily Beast* story leaned on anonymous sources who swore that NBC executives were the Bad Guys and Lauer was the Good Guy, the one who "repeatedly tried to convince his bosses to slow things down and give Curry more time."

The story also included a puffy anecdote about Lauer taking the elevator to NBCUniversal chief executive Steve Burke's office and offering to resign in the fall of 2012.

"If you think the show's better off without me, let me know, and I'll get out of the way," Lauer was said to have told Burke. Burke recalled that he responded this way: "You're the best person who's ever done this. We'll get through this."

The *Daily Beast* story was roundly dismissed as NBC spin. (One blog denounced it with this headline: "Matt Lauer Wasn't Mean to Ann Curry, Says Matt Lauer.") Two weeks later, *New York* magazine published a much more comprehensive story—a cover story, no less, with a photo of Lauer and the words "NOT A GOOD MORNING." In it, reporter Joe Hagan asked Lauer if he'd ever spoken to Curry "about fixing the perception that her ouster was his fault."

Lauer answered, "No, I have not ever had that conversation."

Why? Why not try to patch things up with Curry? Hagan quoted Lauer's excuses, rolled his eyes, and concluded that "the answer is obvious: Matt Lauer was helpless to convince her otherwise."

Curry, by now, was installed in a new office on the twenty-seventh floor of Rockefeller Center, two dozen floors above her former *Today* show colleagues. After I finished the hardcover edition, her colleagues continued to tell me about the daily indignities she faced, perhaps to keep the public on her side; in a *New York Times Magazine* cover story pegged to the hardcover publication, I described one day when Curry trudged into the building's art deco lobby and no one recognized her:

> Curry had spent 22 years, a majority of her professional life, in the hallways of the NBC headquarters. She knew 30 Rock's shortcuts: the side door out of Studio 1A that allowed her to dart across 49th Street and avoid the tourists;

and the exit that ensured she would bump into autograph seekers in the concourse. But on this March morning, according to a colleague, she was standing in the lobby and was unable to find her employee badge. Instead of being waved through by a security guard or rescued by one of the legions of pages or young producers from "Today," Curry queued up at NBC's visitors' center, where the lunch-delivery guys and MSNBC guests announced themselves. Her attempts at being unnoticed, in her trench coat and hat, were backfiring. When it was her turn, Curry immediately apologized to the guard—gratuitous apologies were one of her on-air trademarks. The guard looked at her quizzically. "Name?" he asked. "Ann Curry," she said. Then, after a moment. "A-N-N." Pause. "C-U-R-R-Y."

Now put yourself in the shoes of Anderson Cooper. You're sitting in your office at CNN, with its lovely view of Central Park. You're under contract to CNN for another nine months or so and thinking about the arc of your career. And then you find out that Pat Fili, the chair of the NBCUniversal News Group, wants to meet with you about a position on the *Today* show. How would you react?

NBC's bungling of *Today* must have made Cooper hesitate. But he agreed to meet Fili for coffee—in television, you always take the meeting—and hear her out.

Fili was thinking about a succession plan for Lauer. Someday—be it in three months, three years, or, more likely, sometime in between—he would step down, and NBC would need to have a plan in place. And now, with Capus gone, this fell to Fili to figure out. Willie Geist, David Gregory, and Lester Holt were all in-house possibilities, but she wanted to look outside as well, and

Cooper was a logical option. He'd gotten his start at CNN by coanchoring *American Morning* with Paula Zahn in 2002. He was a night owl now, with an eight p.m. newscast, but maybe he'd try the early shift again?

Fili and Cooper, according to a person with direct knowledge of the meeting, discussed a transition plan that would have had Cooper overlap with Lauer on *Today* for about a year, leading up to the day when Cooper would take over the morning show. But Cooper had his doubts, especially after Deadline.com got wind of Fili's initial phone call to Cooper's agent. Both sides denied interest in such a move, and Cooper ultimately renewed his CNN contract at the end of 2013.

Fili had more luck with her executive recruiting. In May she announced that Deborah Turness, the head of ITV News in Britain, would be the next president of NBC News. By network news standards, this was head-spinning. Turness had seemingly little knowledge about NBC News or about morning television; she was a clean break from the past. And there was this: she would be the first woman ever put in charge of an American network news division.

Here's how I reported her promotion in the pages of the *New York Times*:

> Deborah Turness was the first person interviewed for the prestigious job at the top of NBC News earlier this year. It was a telephone interview, because Ms. Turness was in London, where she oversaw ITV News. The person on the other end, Patricia Fili-Krushel, was so impressed that she flew Ms. Turness to New York for a follow-up.
>
> On Monday, Ms. Turness, 46, was named president of NBC News, ending a search that took months and beginning a new era for a wounded news division that forfeited its top spot in the morning television ratings race last year

to its archrival, ABC News. NBC's "Today," the most profitable part of the news division, has yet to recover...

The decision to look outside NBC and the United States for a president suggests that NBCUniversal executives were yearning for new thinking.

"Yearning for new thinking" was probably an understatement. Fili and her boss, Steve Burke, wanted Turness to turn the place upside down, or rather right side up, starting with *Today*.

Turness didn't start work at NBC until August. (Before she started, she read the hardcover edition of this book, and she told confidants that she'd reached a number of conclusions about what had gone wrong at *Today*. She might have made some of the same mistakes Capus and Bell had made, she told them, but she never would have let Curry on the air that fateful last day.) She tried to make up for lost time by reviewing reams of consumer data, going back to the 1990s, about *Today* and the American morning news landscape. What she saw was a long, slow decline at *Today*, dating back to the Meredith Vieira days. Crucially, she concluded that only a tiny fraction of *Today* loyalists had actually switched over to *GMA*. Others had started to watch *CBS This Morning*, or cable morning shows, or had switched off the TV altogether. "They are recoverable," Turness said in private conversations, and evoked the joy of reuniting with an ex-boyfriend or -girlfriend.

Except that most of those relationships fail. But never mind that.

By September, Turness, in consultation with Don Nash and others at *Today*, had come up with a cheery new mission statement. This, she said, was "our north star," something that would guide every decision about every segment on the show. It wasn't shared with the public, but it said this:

TODAY Mission Statement:

We are a news show. We wake up every morning to give you and your family all you need to start your day. If it matters to you, it matters to us. We are in the people business.

As the sun rises across America our mission is to inform you, to inspire you and to entertain you. These are our priorities....

First, we will break news, and we will set the agenda for today. We will deliver the newsmakers, we will ask the questions that need answers today. We will bring you the latest, and we will tell you why it matters today. We are on your side—helping you navigate a complicated world. We embrace the best of the human spirit, we believe in the power of community. We will share with you the stories that connect us all, and celebrate all that's good about life.

We recognize that at the heart of every story lies a human truth. Even in the darkest places, we will seek the light.

Turness also coined three words that she called "filters" for *Today* show content: Substance, uplift, connection. She repeated the words so often, they began to blend into one: Substanceupliftconnection. Substanceupliftconnection. It was lost on no one that they could be abbreviated as SUC. Thankfully Turness didn't propose a fourth word like *know-how*.

Turness was in the control room every morning at seven a.m. Then she led debriefings with the staff after the show, at ten. She'd arrived in the midst of a face-lift for *Today*, with a multi-million-dollar studio renovation and a spiffy new graphics package already close to completion. So she seized the opportunity to have a housewarming party—to say, in effect, "Come over! We've redecorated!"—by inviting the press to a tour of the remodeled Studio 1A in mid-September.

"Everything's been brightened up," she said, pointing out that the *Today* logo now had light coming out of it, and that the producers would feature pictures of sunrises sent in by viewers. (Later she'd also introduce a new slogan, "Rise to Shine.")

Obviously a sunrise-themed logo wasn't going to solve NBC's a.m. problems. But it was a chance, however slight, to turn the page. The terms Turness used to describe the new studio— "incredibly warm," "inviting," "like home"—were precisely the words she wanted people to use to describe *Today*.

☀ ☀ ☀

Throughout 2013, and especially once Turness took charge, rumors swirled that *Today* show executive producer Don Nash was about to be replaced. That's what often happens at second-place TV shows: the executive producer gets scapegoated, then replaced by someone else who eventually suffers the exact same fate. But Nash held on to his job—not that it was a particularly pleasant job to have.

With Lauer, it worked the same way. Not a week went by without fervent speculation that he wanted to exit his contract early, or, more ominously, that NBC wanted to nudge him out and make it look like his choice, a la Curry. The network's research in mid-2013 showed that losing Lauer would seriously damage the show. Still, his status was a parlor game internally: "How much longer will Matt be here?" When a gaggle of reporters asked Lauer at the open house in September, he wouldn't answer any version of that question. But Fili may have dropped some hints, inadvertently, when the *Hollywood Reporter* asked her one month later if Lauer "would still have a place at NBC News" if he did not want to stay at *Today*.

"Absolutely," Fili said. "He is arguably the most talented interviewer across the morning television scene—there is no one like him. That's a grueling time period—it's a lot of television. It's a lot of prep, and Matt really preps."

The next thing she said may have revealed more than she'd intended to: "We hope he wants to last out at least this contract on the *Today* show."

With that, Fili left open the possibility of Lauer's leaving the show prematurely. Yes, she also emphasized that "I'd keep Matt Lauer as long as he wants to stay on the *Today* show." But it was no wonder Fili was hell-bent on coming up with a smooth succession plan.

For the time being, she and Turness decided to add talent rather than subtract. On open house day, there was a giant surprise: Carson Daly, the former MTV VJ famous for hosting *TRL* in Times Square a decade earlier. Daly had filled in on *Today* numerous times and even sat in Lauer's chair for a day in July, prompting complaints from Twitterers who felt he didn't have the journalistic chops to sit there. Now he was officially joining *Today* as a fifth cohost of sorts, assigned at least nominally to the Orange Room, a new feature intended to connect the social media world to the show and vice versa. Turness tried to bat away all the obvious questions—Was Daly now in line for Lauer's seat? Was Geist no longer the chosen one? Wait, had Geist *ever* been the chosen one?—by saying that Daly brought something new to *Today,* an entertainment quotient that no one else had. But the press instantly played it as a rivalry.

When reporters approached him at the open house, Geist did his best to deny any apprehension about the additional cast member. But it didn't help matters that he, Al Roker, and Natalie Morales were told about Daly's ascension only two days before the announcement. In the months that followed, Geist's fans—and there were many—noticed that his appearances on the seven and eight a.m. hours were cut back, ostensibly so he could concentrate on his nine a.m. hour.

Daly was on at seven a.m. whenever he wasn't hosting the NBC singing competition *The Voice* in Los Angeles. But his social media tie-ins to *Today* were clunky, and skepticism reigned about whether he was really part of the solution to the show's problems. A mere two months after he was added to the cast, the *Hollywood Reporter* noted Daly's low Q Scores and all but wrote him off, saying he was a "long shot" for Lauer's chair. There was *still* no clear heir apparent.

From time to time in 2013, staffers at *Today* would ask me forms of this question: "Aren't we better than them?"

"Them" was *GMA*. The ABC morning show was clearly number one now in the ratings, yet some people at NBC still couldn't comprehend why more viewers were choosing it over *Today*. My answer amounted to this: there was more energy and sometimes real joy on the *Today* show, and the producers and cohosts deserved credit for that, but *Today* still felt wounded somehow.

The staff knew it, too. Particularly after Turness arrived in August, the atmosphere in the trenches, according to several staff members, was toxic. (One person said staffers were "all but exchanging gunfire.") In an early September staff meeting, complaints arose about the frequency of "crashes"—a term for last-minute packages that must be assembled overnight in time for the seven a.m. show. In the past, these kinds of assignments had been much more common at *GMA* than *Today*. Senior producer Matt Carluccio, normally a pretty polite guy, cut off the conversation by snapping, "If you don't like it, you can go knock on Tammy Filler's door." Filler was the producer in charge of the nine and ten a.m. hours—perceived to be the fluffier, lower-profile parts of *Today*. Staffers were outraged by Carluccio's comment, but he was simply relaying what Fili and Turness wanted. And the executives, in turn, were simply trying to prove to NBCUniversal CEO Steve Burke that they could turn around the show. One week in the fall, Turness recalled to an associate, she "let up" on the staff—and immediately sensed "slacking." So she tightened her grip again.

At *GMA,* Roberts returned to a full-time schedule after Labor Day, six months after resuming work part time. The month of September was special for another reason, for it represented the third in what Ben Sherwood called a "trifecta" of ratings wins. The first was a single week beating *Today*; the second was a sweeps month; and the third was a full television season. While ABC kept avoiding the word *streak*, the network promoted the win in this for-the-ages press release on September 27:

"GMA" Wins the 2012–2013 Television Season
First Time in Two Decades "GMA" is #1 in Demo and First Time
in 19 Years in Total Viewers
"GMA" Tops NBC's "Today" by Largest Season Margin in Over
21 Years

The numbers were the single best illustration of the sea change that had taken place in television news. During the 2012–13 season, the one that began three months after Curry's dismissal, *GMA* had averaged 5.3 million viewers per weekday, nearly seven hundred thousand ahead of *Today*. The season before, *GMA* had averaged a little under 4.9 million viewers, compared to the *Today* show's 5.1 million. Third-place *CBS This Morning*, meanwhile, had averaged 2.8 million viewers, up about three hundred thousand from the season before.

In the twenty-five-to-fifty-four-year-old demographic, *GMA* was only eighty-six thousand ahead for the whole season—but that lead had stayed pretty consistent throughout. *GMA* benefited mightily from the premium that came with being on top. Sherwood said his show's immediate goals were "to keep building on our strengths, to stay hungry and humble, and to keep our eyes on the prize." He shortened his two sayings for the *GMA* staff, "Keep it going" and "Play your game," to three letters apiece: KIG and PYG.

Behind the scenes, Sherwood had to KIG by keeping his co-hosts in their chairs. The contracts for Roberts, Sam Champion, Josh Elliott, and Lara Spencer were all approaching their expiration dates, and all four would want the raises and other rewards that come with first-place status. But real life intruded twice in the fall. In October, Elizabeth Vargas, one of Roberts's two designated substitutes, took a leave of absence and sought treatment for alcohol addiction. The treatment became public when the *New York Daily News* found out she was at a rehabilitation facility. At the same time, Roberts's other sub, Amy Robach, was diagnosed with breast cancer. The circumstances, as they were explained to *GMA* viewers, were jaw-dropping. Robach was cajoled into a televised mammogram by a show producer who called her at the end of September and asked her to participate to mark the beginning of Breast Cancer Awareness Month. "Would you even consider it?" the producer asked. Robach initially wanted to say, "No way, never gonna do it."

"I'm forty years old," she explained in an on-camera interview. "I've never had a mammogram. I've avoided it. And I started thinking, 'Wow, if I've put it off, how many other people have put it off as well?'"

So she agreed to go ahead with it. Later, she heaped credit on Roberts, a breast cancer survivor, for telling her that "if one life is saved because of early detection, it's all worth it." The procedure was discreetly televised on October 1. A few weeks later, she said afterward, she was told about the diagnosis. "While everyone who gets cancer is clearly unlucky, I got lucky by catching it early, and there are so many people to thank for making sure I did," she wrote in a blog post on November 11. "Every producer, every person who urged me to do this, changed my trajectory. The doctors told me bluntly: 'That mammogram just saved your life.'"

Robach had a double mastectomy three days after telling viewers of her diagnosis. Doctors found that the cancer had spread to one lymph node, so she began chemotherapy treatments in December. "I'm going to work through it," she said on *GMA* on December 5, her first day back on air. "I saw Robin do it. I know how strong you were. And you give me strength, Robin, because it is important to get up and have something to do each day, even if you don't feel great and even if you feel crappy."

When her hair started to fall out, Robach made an appointment with a stylist and brought along a camera crew to record the haircut. "I decided I was going to take control of one thing away from the cancer," she explained on *GMA* in mid-January. One month later she was in Sochi, Russia, serving as the morning show's correspondent during the Winter Olympics, between her third and fourth rounds of chemo. *GMA* knew the *Today* show would temporarily retake first place during the Olympics—*Today* always relocated to the Olympic host city for the duration of the games and always enjoyed a huge surge in viewership, as did NBC as a whole. With twenty to twenty-five million viewers watching the action in prime time, how could the morning show not get a lift? But *GMA* decided to fight rather than roll over. It tried to cover the Olympics so aggressively that viewers wouldn't think about sampling the *Today* show, with Robach in Sochi, a stable of past Olympians as analysts, and even a slightly misleading "GMA AT THE OLYMPICS" logo affixed to the show's usual set in New York City. Maybe it worked, because *Today* beat *GMA* by only about 350,000 total viewers on the first weekday of the games. And on the second weekday, something extraordinary happened: *Today* lost. It wasn't even close: the gap between the two shows was four hundred thousand. The blog *TV Newser* said "the win for 'GMA' marks the first time since the beginning of electronic records that a network morning show that didn't carry the Olympics won a morning."

*Today* won again the next day, but the loss underscored that even the Olympics—with the Olympic-size audiences they convey—weren't enough to guarantee Lauer and Co. the lead anymore.

If you've read this far, you probably realize that I've left out several headline-grabbing moments. I've done so intentionally—to show how little they really mattered in the grand morning show wars.

The first struck on Monday, December 2 like a bolt of lightning: Sam Champion said he was leaving *GMA*. Executives at ABC had seemed confident that they would reach new deals with Champion and the rest of the cohosts whose contracts were coming due; no one was interested in breaking up the family that had beaten the *Today* show after so many years of trying. So it had come as a true shock when Champion told Sherwood over the weekend that he had decided to take a job at the Weather Channel. Not just any job, of course: he'd be "managing editor" of the channel and the anchor of a "new flagship morning show" that would compete directly with *GMA* and the dozen or so smaller morning shows on at that hour.

There were some practical reasons for the move: being based at the channel's headquarters in Atlanta would put Champion closer to his husband, Rubem, whose art studio was in Miami. And there were profitable reasons: Champion would receive a sizable chunk of stock in the channel's parent company on top of his multi-million-dollar salary. But another reason might have been the most important: airtime. On *GMA*, Champion, like many television anchors, was always hustling for more airtime, but the show had four other hosts and two hours a day. At the Weather Channel he'd be the lead host of a three-hour show—albeit on cable, where he'd be seen by a fraction of the audience that had seen him on *GMA*. It was a classic "bigger fish, smaller pond" situation—both he and Sherwood knew that. The two men agreed to announce the departure after Monday morning's edition of *GMA* and be gracious to one another in the press. And they were gracious, indeed: the press releases and televised goodbyes that followed were the antithesis of Ann Curry's sign-off eighteen months earlier. ABC was praised for giving Champion such a bighearted send-off. (A sample of the dialogue on his last day, from Robin Roberts: "You encompass all that is good and right in this world and you show it every day when you show up here.") And Champion was ebullient about his twenty-five years at the network.

But only a few days passed before anonymous gripes bubbled up. Some at ABC depicted Champion's departure as a talent raid by NBC through the Weather Channel. That's because the channel was jointly owned by two private equity firms and NBCUniversal. "If I'm Deborah Turness, I'm doing whatever I can to disrupt *GMA*. I'm doing whatever I can to snatch people," one executive told me, noting that Turness had also met with Elliott, whose contract was also coming due.

NBC denied that Champion was in line for Al Roker's job on the *Today* show, but that didn't stanch the speculation, especially after Champion began to show up as an occasional weather correspondent on *Today* in January. *Today* used Weather Channel correspondents from time to time, but this was different—this was the weatherman from the first-place network morning show appearing to prop up the second-place show after battling against it for years. Staffers at ABC had reason to be bitter, and so did Roker.

Champion, for his part, was furious when the *Daily News* gossip column said "the real reasons why Champion jumped ship for a spot at the cable network: money and power." The column quoted a network insider who said "the big reason he is leaving is that he can now appear on merchandise for the Weather Channel" and predicted he would make millions of dollars "from merchandise alone." The next day, another gossip column said Champion felt "betrayed" by his former friends at ABC. And on it went—but did any of it really matter? Champion had won himself a high-profile new gig on cable. And *GMA* hadn't missed a proverbial beat in the ratings with him gone. The network moved weekend weather anchor Ginger Zee over to the weekdays on the day after he signed off. Granted, Zee wasn't a full-blown co-host the way Champion had been, but she did have something he didn't: an actual meteorology degree.

While all of this was going on, Roberts renewed her *GMA* contract without any fanfare. And four days after Christmas, with the help of spokesman Jeffrey Schneider, she came out and said what she hadn't quite been ready to say in February: that she was in a long-term relationship with Amber. She tucked Amber's name into an end-of-the-year Facebook post that read, "At this moment I am at peace and filled with joy and gratitude. I am grateful to God, my doctors and nurses for my restored good health. I am grateful for my sister, Sally-Ann, for being my donor and giving me the gift of life. I am grateful for my entire family, my long time girlfriend, Amber, and friends as we prepare to celebrate a glorious new year together. I am grateful for the many prayers and well wishes for my recovery. I return every one of them to you 100 fold. On this last Sunday of 2013 I encourage you to reflect on what you are grateful for too."

The biggest star in morning television, an African-American and a cancer survivor, had identified as gay. Years ago, this might have triggered weeks of media coverage and serious concerns that some intolerant viewers would switch morning shows. But not in 2013. By New Year's eve the press had moved on, save for a bit of online speculation that Roberts might get engaged soon.

*GMA* kept scoring wins. Sherwood kept telling his staff to KIG and PYG. *Today* kept straining for signs of ratings progress. Turness told the *New York Times*, "We will win back our viewers one by one."

And me? I decided to take a job in television myself, reporting for CNN and anchoring the Sunday morning media program *Reliable Sources*. Jeff Zucker, who had led the *Today* show to victory in the 1990s, was now on a mission to revive CNN. He became my uber-boss. During my third week on the job, NBC invited me to the network's annual holiday press party at Rockefeller Center. I hurried over to the party between CNN live shots. I couldn't find Curry in the crowd—I suppose I shouldn't have been surprised by that. But Turness was there, and Lauer, and Guthrie, whom I tapped on the shoulder before scurrying back to work. We congratulated each other on our engagements—hers in September, mine in October—and then she asked about CNN.

"Harder than it looks?"

Yes, I told her—television is indeed much harder than it looks, not to mention much more complicated behind the scenes. But that hadn't come as a surprise—this book had already taught me that lesson.

# A NOTE ABOUT SOURCING

*Top of the Morning* is the product of eighteen months of researching, reporting, and television-watching. I interviewed about 350 people, some of them multiple times. Many of the interviews were conducted on condition of anonymity because the sources—even the ones near the tops of their companies' organizational charts—feared reprisals from their employers for speaking openly.

I interviewed each of the cohosts of *Today* and *GMA*, with two partial exceptions: Matt Lauer and Ann Curry declined to be interviewed for the book in the wake of Curry's ouster.

Some quotes attributed to *Today* and *GMA* hosts and their bosses were recounted later by their colleagues. I tried, whenever possible, to interview sources within minutes or hours of climactic moments like Robin Roberts's MDS announcement and Savannah Guthrie's promotion, in the hope that I'd get closer to the truth that way.

My visits to the control rooms and studios of the morning shows shaped the book in big and small ways. NBC, ABC, and CBS insisted that most of these visits be off the record, with the understanding that they'd decide which quotes could be placed on the record later. They have operated this way for many years. I agreed to the restriction, knowing it was the only way I'd receive any access to the otherwise sealed-off studios, control rooms, and production offices of the shows. I also believed it would benefit my reporting, and in retrospect I know it did. For one thing, labeling the visits "off the record" assuaged the fear of some staff members that I would share information about bookings with their archrivals, and helped me to gain their trust.

These agreements were reached before my other employer, *The New York Times*, forbade the practice of "quote approval." ABC scrubbed a few curse words from producers' mouths but allowed virtually every other quote. NBC was more heavy-handed: every one of Jim Bell's quotes from my control room visits were kept "off the record." So were descriptions of Bell's body language and his demeanor, descriptions of other staffers reacting to Bell, and some quotes from Ann Curry. NBC approved most of the rest of the control room material.

Once in a while, on particularly sensitive days when the PR apparatuses of NBC and ABC denied access to their studios, I simply peered into their street-level windows like a tourist.

Links to the works cited in the book and recommendations for further reading can be found at http://brianstelter.com/morning/.

# ACKNOWLEDGMENTS

In June 2011 I walked into Ben Greenberg's office at Grand Central Publishing with a bad idea for a book about television news. I walked out with *Top of the Morning*.

During the meeting—arranged by my agent Kate Lee, who believed in my ability to write a book a full four years before I believed in it myself—Ben, Kate, and I brainstormed better ideas. Ben asked, "What about the mornings?" The mornings! Ann Curry had just taken over *Today*, and Josh Elliott and Lara Spencer had just joined *GMA*. Surely, I said, *something* interesting would happen in the next eighteen months. "The mornings—why didn't I think of that?" I wondered as I walked out of the meeting. But that's what editors are for.

Among the other things I didn't think: that *GMA* would seize first place, that Curry would be demoted, or that Lauer would be blamed. So thanks are in order to ABC and NBC, for giving me a story worth telling!

Thanks also to Kate, for guiding me through the foreign terrain of book publishing. Thanks, Ben, for seeing a book where I just saw a time slot, for giving me the time and space to tell the story, and for tolerating my inevitable and surely irritating deadline-bending. Every author should hope to be as fortunate as I've been.

When Kate departed ICM agency in 2012, Kristine Dahl adopted the book as her own and matched me with Charles Leerhsen, who worked tirelessly with me to transform my lumpy chapters into a real live book. Not only did Charles know what I was trying to say better than I did, he knew what I *didn't* need to say. (Readers, you were spared sixty thousand words of tangents.) Together, we conceived the zippy three-act structure that opened and closed with *Today*, with *GMA* in between. Charles, thank you.

My greatest thanks of all go to Jamie Shupak, whom I'm lucky to call my girlfriend (and roommate and pen pal, among many other titles). Jamie cured my spasms of self-doubt, red-lined my rough drafts, and asked the questions she knew readers were going to ask, making the book better in a hundred different ways. Jamie, I simply could not have written this without you by my side. Thank you.

Thanks as well to Bruce Headlam, Craig Hunter, and Bill Brink, my editors at *The New York Times*, who never wavered in their support of this second job. They made a hard thing much easier. So did *The Times'* media columnist David Carr, who had my back the whole time, especially when the going got tough. I'm honored to call him a friend. Bill Carter, Jodi Kantor, and Andrew Ross Sorkin helped me figure out how to structure the book and convince skeptical sources to cooperate. Alex Weprin and Scott Kidder kept me sane.

Carolyn Wilder provided invaluable research help. The media monitoring service TVEyes, a virtual DVR for television, was indispensable.

Corporate communications professionals at the networks were enormously helpful when they could be, and apologetic when they couldn't. At NBC they included Adam Miller, Kathy Kelly-Brown, Lauren Kapp, Amy Lynn, Monica Lee, Marie Wicht, and most of all Megan Kopf. At ABC, Zenia Mucha, Kevin Brockman,

Jeffrey Schneider, Julie Townsend, Alison Bridgman, Alyssa Apple, and Heather Riley. At CBS, Sonya McNair and Kelli Halyard. At MSNBC, Jeremy Gaines and Lauren Skowronski. At CNN, Christa Robinson and Barbara Levin. Thank you.

Hundreds of sources, many of whom can't be named here, taught me more about morning television than I ever dreamed I'd know. You know who you are. Thank you all.

And finally: Mom, whatever writing talent I have, I have thanks to you. You nurtured my youthful curiosity about the Web at great cost (I still cringe thinking about those domain hosting and long-distance phone bills) and you encouraged me to write, write, write. After Dad died it was your refusal to give up, your determination to give me and Jason and Kevin a normal life—bluntly, your determination to keep living—that got me to this final paragraph. Thank you.

# INDEX

ABC. *See also* Cibrowski, Tom; *GMA*; Goldston, James; Sweeney, Anne
  Academy Awards 2012 and, 185
  *A.M. America*, 103–4
  Champion's departure and, 320
  Couric talk show on, 61, 189, 191
  Disney ownership of, 61, 116, 138, 303
  *GMA* as profit generator, 10–11, 125, 271
  headquarters, 221
  Lauer wooed by, 61–62, 63, 64, 67, 190
  Lunden firing and, 6
  News division, 45, 61, 80, 103, 106, 115, 116, 118, 119, 127, 130, 133, 139, 203, 205, 215, 223, 227, 261, 263, 304, 311
  *Nightline*, 142–43
  Olympic coverage 1980, 108
  *Primetime*, 123
  Roberts's illness and, 192, 208, 221–22, 223, 225, 226, 227, 295, 303–4
  salary reductions at, 61
  Sherwood as News president, 45, 61, 119, 123, 133–34, 135, 137, 139, 140, 144, 183–84, 197, 221, 260–61, 271, 304, 306, 319, 320
  Silverman as president, 104, 106–7, 108
  Stephanopoulos wooed by, 130–32
  *This Week*, 130
  Vieira wooed by, 30
  Westin as News president, 130–32, 133, 143
Abrams, Dan, 152, 153, 214
Ali, Muhammad, 185
Allen, Woody, 291
*All Things at Once* (Brzezinski), 154
Amanpour, Christiane, 80
Arledge, Roone, 115–16

Barnett, Robert B., 86, 87–88, 95, 97, 234
Barnicle, Mike, 150
Bell, Angelique, 47
Bell, Jim
  background and career, 3, 7–8, 43, 46–47
  Burke and, 7, 43

Capus and, 43–44, 69, 71, 74, 236, 250, 267–68, 287, 297
  Couric and, 58
  Curry as cohost and, 19–22, 35, 42, 44–45
  Curry bashing by, 45–46, 72, 73, 78
  Curry firing (Operation Bambi), 3–7, 10, 44–46, 47, 69, 76–77, 81, 97–98, 100, 234, 250, 267, 275, 277, 283, 292, 298
  Curry's final show and, 96
  Curry's roving correspondent position and, 75–77
  Curry "transition" and, 81–82, 89, 92
  on "the demo," 248
  Fili and, 275–77
  *GMA* race for leadership and, 191, 201, 202, 220, 303
  Guthrie and, 42, 234, 245, 283
  Lauer and, 8, 47, 59, 61–62, 66, 79
  media statement on "the streak," 201
  memo to senior staff, 242–44
  as Olympics producer, 43–44, 46–47, 82, 191, 201, 245, 253, 263, 267, 276, 277, 285–86, 292, 297
  passed over for promotion, 259
  press statements on his firing, 277–78
  ratings drop following Curry firing, 230
  as *Today* chief, 3–7, 17, 29, 34, 43, 46, 78, 120, 123, 149, 266–290
  *Today* sixtieth anniversary celebration and, 51
  Vieira and, 38
Bell, Steve, 106
Besser, Richard, 224, 226
Beutel, Bill, 103, 104
Bianco, Robert, 194
Biden, Joe, 156, 217
*Big Shoes* (Roker), 23
Bloomberg, Michael, 165, 169
Bolster, Bill, 55
Brokaw, Tom, 25, 26, 94, 108, 123, 284
Brzezinski, Mika, 150–163
Brzezinski, Zbigniew, 163
Burke, Steve, 7, 33–34, 36, 259, 298, 316
  Bell and, 7, 43

Curry firing and, 7, 42–43, 44, 59, 60, 86,
    92, 99, 234, 250, 275, 297
Curry hired as cohost and, 35–36
Geist and, 284
Lauer and, 52–53, 59, 61, 64–66, 300, 308
*Morning Joe* move stopped by, 162–63
*Today* ratings slip and, 74
Turness hiring and, 311
Burnett, Erin, 168, 294
Bush, George W., 86, 246

Café Fiorello, 189
Capus, Steve, 7, 25–26, 29, 34, 49, 73, 77, 241
    background and career, 43
    Bell and, 43–44, 69, 71, 74, 236, 250,
        267–68, 287
    Curry and, 19–20, 25, 35, 42–43, 95, 236,
        267
    Curry contract negotiations and, 87–88
    Curry firing and, 66, 75, 82–83, 86, 92,
        94, 97–98, 250, 275, 292
    Curry's final show and, 98–99
    Geist and, 284
    *GMA* race for leadership and, 191, 195,
        201–2
    Guthrie to replace Curry and, 233–34,
        235
    Lauer and, 52, 58, 64–65, 66
    leaves NBC News, 297, 299
    morning show war and, 183
    Nash as *Today* producer and, 286–87
    passed over for promotion, 259–260
    "Rage" nickname, 43, 162
    Scarborough and *Morning Joe*, 160, 161–62
    Sherwood and, 183
    steps down as NBC News president, 292
    *Today* fixing and firing of Bell, 267, 280,
        297
    Zimmerman 911 call and, 70, 71
Carell, Steve, 91
Carlson, Tucker, 284
Carluccio, Matt, 315
Carter, Bill, 183
CBS, 37. *See also This Morning*
    *Captain Kangaroo*, 157
    *CBS Morning News*, 158
    Couric moves to, 29
    Curry at affiliates of, 24–25
    *The Early Show*, 158, 159, 166–67
    *Evening News*, 124
    *Good Morning!* 157

Licht and, 161, 162, 170, 306
    *The Morning Show*, 157
    morning show hosts, various, 158
    morning show war, 113, 157–163,
        169–170, 172
    News, 60, 159
    *Nightwatch*, 167
    *60 Minutes*, 161, 167
    *This Morning*, 12, 165–170, 186, 235, 283,
        293–94, 306–7, 311, 316
    wooing of *Morning Joe*, 158–163
    *World News*, 124, 127, 129
Champion, Sam, 15, 18, 199–200, 207, 214,
    223, 269, 272, 274, 279, 294–95, 301,
    317, 319
    as first openly gay cohost, 269
    leaves *GMA*, appears on *Today*, 319–21
    wake-up time, 188
    wedding, 301–2
*Charlie Rose*, 165
Cherry, Marc, 205
Christie, Chris, 253, 254
Chung, Connie, 249
Cibrowski, Tom, 129, 175, 180–81, 213
    celebration of *GMA* beats *Today*, 207–8,
    247
    morning show leader race and, 185,
        186–87, 188, 200, 201, 203–4, 212,
        215, 230, 247–48, 261, 262
    Obama interview with Robin Roberts
        and, 218–19
    Roberts's illness and, 208, 212, 224,
        272–74, 295
    Robert's return to *GMA* and, 302, 304
Clinton, Bill, 86, 117, 130
Clinton, Hillary, 155
CNBC, 11, 34, 215, 259, 275
CNN, 152, 156–57, 294
    *American Morning*, 156, 157, 310
    author takes job at, 322
    Cooper wooed by Fili for *Today*, 309–10
    *Reliable Sources*, 322
    *Starting Point*, 157, 294
    Zucker and, 294, 322
Colvin, Shawn, 245–46
Comcast, 12, 33, 43, 52, 61, 86, 202
Cooper, Anderson, 161, 309–10
Costas, Bob, 27, 194, 201
Couric, Katie, 19, 26, 49, 51, 66, 114, 227
    ABC talk show, 61, 189, 191
    *CBS Evening News* and, 124

# Index

Katie Couric Week on *GMA*, 63, 65, 190–95
  Lauer and, 18, 39–40, 56
  Lauer reunion proposals, 57–58, 61
  leaves *Today*, 28, 29, 73, 96, 123–24
  *Today* cohost, 26, 28, 55, 76, 112, 114, 115, 145, 179
Court TV, 42, 237, 238
Cox, Ann Marie, 152
Cronkite, Walter, 24, 157
Cuomo, Chris, 130, 294
Curry, Ann, 20, 21, 26, 29, 80, 242
  agent for, 32, 35, 76
  Aurora, Colorado, shooting story and, 252–55
  author's *New York Times* report on firing of, 88
  background and career, 19, 22–26, 31–32
  Bell and, 19–22, 35, 42, 44–46, 72, 73, 75–77, 78, 81–82, 89, 92, 94, 96, 267, 275, 277, 298
  Betty White interview and, 82
  Burke and, 7, 42–43, 44, 59, 60, 69, 86, 92, 99, 234, 250, 275
  Capus and, 19–20, 25, 35, 42–43, 87–88, 95, 98–99, 236, 267
  daily indignities faced by, post-firing, 308–9
  *Dateline* suggested for, 28–29
  faults as broadcaster, 7, 19, 20–22, 39, 45, 88
  firing (Operation Bambi), 3–7, 10, 44–46, 47, 66, 67, 69, 76–77, 81–100, 149, 214–15, 227–28, 233–234, 246, 262, 250, 267, 275, 277, 283, 292, 298
  firing, and contract negotiations, 86–89, 95, 234, 250
  firing, her reaction and analysis, 248–252, 298–99
  firing, viewers' reaction, 5–6, 90, 91, 94, 99–100, 229–230, 235, 251, 262, 275
  foreign correspondent role of, 21, 24, 25, 36, 41, 299
  gaffes by, Gawker video, 72–73
  *gambaru* and, 23, 94
  Guthrie and, 95, 250–51
  Hale column and, 83, 88, 97
  *Ladies Home Journal* interview, 83
  Lauer and, 9, 10, 16, 19, 21, 35, 40, 43, 44–45, 65–66, 74–75, 80, 82, 90, 99, 186, 242, 249, 264, 298
  lawyer hired by, 86, 234
  marriage and children, 24, 249
  Matrix Awards, 73–74
  meanness toward, 80–81, 227–28
  Morales and, 250–51
  "out" clause in contract of, 32, 36
  Page interview in *USA Today*, 97
  popularity of, 35, 75, 85
  publication of *Top of the Morning* and, 307
  reverse seduction of, 69, 75–76, 80, 83, 86–87
  *Today* anchor at large, 95, 241–42, 252–55, 263–64, 293
  *Today* cohost, 9, 16–17, 18, 19–22, 35, 36–42, 71–72, 79, 81, 84–85, 90–91, 94, 95–96, 148, 181, 194, 213, 220
  *Today* cohost, awkward beginning, 38–39
  *Today* cohost, final week and on-air good-bye, 89–100, 229–230, 238, 240, 242
  *Today* lack of chemistry and, 18, 19
  *Today* news anchor job and, 19–20, 26–27, 29, 145
  *Today* ratings slip and, 9, 148, 202
  *Today* sixtieth anniversary celebration and, 50–52
  tsunami coverage of 2004, 21
  Twitter and, 87, 91, 264
  on women in the media, 74

*Daily Mail*, 77
Daly, Carson, 314–15
*Dancing with the Stars*, 171–72, 176, 185, 187, 195, 205, 220
Daulerio, A. J., 72
Deadline.com, 310
Dean, Jimmy, 157
*Death and Life of Charlie St. Cloud, The* (Sherwood), 123, 139
De Leon, Gloria, 179–180
*Desperate Housewives*, 119–120, 121, 205
Deutsch, Donny, 83
Disney (Walt Disney Company), 61, 116, 138
Disney/ABC Television Group, 61, 133, 303
Downs, Hugh, 51

Ebersol, Dick, 28, 43, 46, 111, 112, 115, 277
Edwards, Stephanie, 103, 104
Elliott, Josh, 16, 18, 134, 173, 199–200
  agent for, 138
  family and children, 141, 144
  *GMA* beats *Today* and, 204, 206, 207, 215

*GMA* cohost, 135, 137–142, 147, 173, 188, 248, 269, 317
    Roberts and, 223–24, 225, 272, 279, 294, 301
    Turness meets with, 320
    wake-up time, 188
Ellis, Angela, 175
Entelis, Amy, 139
*Entertainment Tonight*, 144
ESPN, 61, 126, 130
    *Around the Horn*, 138
    Elliott at, 138, 140
    Roberts at, 126, 137, 184
    *SportsCenter*, 138, 140, 141

Fager, Jeff, 60, 159, 160, 162, 166, 167, 168
Falco, Randy, 46
Feldman, Michael, 246, 254
Fili, Pat, 259–260, 275–78, 283, 284, 285, 286, 292, 297, 300, 315, 320
    Cooper wooed for *Today*, 309–10
    replacement for Capus and, 299
    succession plan for Lauer, 309, 313–14
    Turness chosen to head NBC News, 310
Filler, Tammy, 286, 315
Foreman, George, 185
*Fox & Friends*, 11
Fox News Channel, 35
Friedman, Jon, 94
Friedman, Paul, 107–8
Friedman, Steve, 26, 109, 169

Garagiola, Joe, 252
Garroway, Dave, 8, 128
Gartner, Michale, 111
Gawker, 5, 72, 73
Geist, Bill, 284
Geist, Willie, 94, 152, 154, 155, 156, 157, 242, 244, 283–84, 293, 298, 309, 314
Geller, Alfred, 32, 35, 76
General Motors, 79
Gibson, Charles, 116, 124, 127
    as *GMA* cohost, 16, 110, 114–19, 124, 126, 127, 184
    retirement of, 129
Gifford, Kathie Lee, 49
Giordano, Gary, 174, 268–69
Glantz, Michael, 30, 34, 84, 233–34, 235
Godfrey, Arthur, 8
Goldman, David, 178

Goldman, Kevin, 110–11
Goldston, James, 15, 45, 71, 142, 146, 147, 175, 185, 186, 190, 193, 195, 200, 219
    background and career, 142–43
    *GMA* beats *Today*, 205, 262
    Roberts's illness and, 222
Goodman, Jay, 171
*Good Morning America* (*GMA*), 12, 15, 45, 61, 115, 181, 147
    advertising revenue, 11, 271
    Arledge and, 115–16
    booking battles, 174, 177–180, 212–13, 216, 220
    "Botox Mom" story, 178
    Champion and, 15, 188, 269, 317, 319–320
    chemistry and, 18–19, 113–14, 116, 135–36, 141, 188
    Cibrowski and, 175, 180–81, 185, 186–87, 188
    cloning of *Today*, 143, 146–47
    concept of, 105–7
    content of, 14, 15, 16, 71, 78, 106, 107, 137, 268, 270, 282
    contract renewals (2013), 317, 319, 321
    *Dancing with the Stars* and, 171–72, 176, 185, 187, 195–96, 205, 220
    the "demo" (viewers from 25 to 54) and, 216, 219, 229, 247, 257, 260–62, 270, 271, 289, 292, 301, 316
    *Desperate Housewives* and, 119–120, 121, 205
    Elliott as cohost, 16, 134, 135, 137–142, 147, 173, 188, 204, 248, 317
    favorite restaurant of cast, 189
    firing of Curry and, 91, 100
    firing of Lunden, 6
    forerunner of, *A.M. America*, 103–4
    format, 107, 146–47, 214
    Gibson as cohost, 16, 110, 114–120, 124, 126, 127, 184
    Goldston and, 15, 45, 142, 146, 185, 186, 195, 219
    Hartman as cohost, 104–10, 114
    Hill as cohost, 108
    innovations at, 14–15
    Katie Couric Week, 63, 65, 190–95
    KIG (Keep it going) and PYG (Play your game), 317, 321–22
    Lunden as cohost, 6, 107, 109, 114–15
    Maddie the dog on, 172–74, 176, 177, 220

McRee and Newman as cohosts, 116–18

Meow the cat and, 212

*Morning Joe* as competition, 157

as morning show leader, 195–97, 202–7, 211, 215–16, 219, 220, 246–48, 252, 260–62, 265–66, 270–71, 274, 279, 289, 291–92, 301, 306, 315, 316, 318

morning show leader race/rivalry, 14, 16, 27–28, 46, 47, 51, 78, 105, 107, 108–9, 112–19, 181, 183–197, 199–207, 211–220, 228–230, 268–69, 305–6, 316, 318–19

Nielson and, 186

Obama interview with Robin Roberts, 216–19

"Play of the Day," 147, 173

"Pop News Heat Index," 146

problems at, and fall to second place, 1990s, 114–19

rapport at, 16, 213–14, 269, 272–73, 281–82, 283

ratings gap, 73, 136, 147–48, 184, 186, 189–190, 195, 196, 200, 228

ratings increase, 33, 45, 51, 63, 67, 71, 73, 77, 120, 132, 148, 149, 316

Rivera on, 107

Robach's breast cancer and, 317–18

Roberts as cohost, 15, 125–29, 132, 135–36, 137, 181, 184–85, 188, 196, 197, 204–6, 214–15, 247, 317

Roberts's illness and, 221–27, 271–74, 294–96

Roberts's illness and ratings, 227, 243, 274, 279

Robert's return and, 294–96, 301–5, 316

Sawyer as cohost, 16, 117–18, 126, 127–30, 184

in second place, 7, 10, 27, 33, 115, 116, 117, 128, 136

shark fishing exclusive, 247–48

Sherwood and, 119–124, 133–35, 137–146, 178, 183–84, 189, 191, 197, 304, 306, 316–17, 319, 321–22

Silverman and, 104–5, 106

Spencer as cohost, 16, 143–46, 178, 188, 213–14, 270, 317

Stephanopoulos as cohost, 15, 130–32, 135–37, 157, 173, 188, 189, 193, 298

summer concert series problems, 220

typical day, 171–181

viewer demographics, 136, 143

wake-up times of cast, 188

Winter Olympics in Sochi and, 318–19

Zee replaces Champion, 321

Gregory, David, 217, 309

Griffin, Phil, 120, 121, 123, 152, 153, 155, 161, 285

Gumbel, Bryant, 41, 49, 50, 52, 55, 56, 60, 114, 135, 158, 194

reaction to Curry as martyr, 251–52

"what's wrong" memo leaked, 110–11

Guthrie, Savannah, 49–50, 217, 280

agent for, 233–34

Aurora, Colorado, shooting story and, 252–55

author and, 322

background and facts about, 42, 236–39, 246–47

contract price tag, 241

Curry and, 72, 77, 91, 250–51

Lauer and, 235, 244–45, 246, 258, 293, 298

reaction of Curry's fans to, 235

replacement for Curry, 10, 41–42, 44, 59, 73, 79–80, 89, 93, 95, 100, 230, 233–240, 292

Summer Olympics and, 257–260

*Today* cohost, 239–240, 241, 242, 243, 251, 253–54, 257–260, 267, 289, 290

Haffenreffer, David, 143

Hagan, Joe, 308

Hale, Mike, 83, 88, 97

Hall, Tamron, 242

Halperin, Mark, 150

Hanks, Tom, 50

Hartman, David, 104–10, 114

Hartz, Jim, 103, 107

Hill, Erica, 167, 235

Hill, Sandy, 108

Hiltzik, Matthew, 191

Holt, Lester, 309

Hughes, Jerry, 173

Humphrey, Theron, 173–74, 176, 177

Iger, Robert, 61, 133–34, 135

Imus, Don, 151, 188, 284

*Insider, The*, 144, 146

Jackson, Jesse, Jr., 247

Jackson, Michael, 42, 142, 237

Jennings, Peter, 79, 103, 223
Jones, Phil, 158

Kaplan, Don, 303
Kapp, Lauren, 49, 73, 191, 203
Kelly, John, 280
Kelly, Megyn, 35
King, Gayle, 166, 168–170, 307
Knox, Amanda, 86
Kopf, Megan, 44, 49, 66, 73, 84–85, 94, 216,
    246, 263, 288
Koppel, Ted, 142
Kornblut, Anne, 237
Kosofsky, Debbie, 100, 269
Kotb, Hoda, 29, 49, 89, 242
Kotch, Noah, 79, 100
Kristof, Nicholas, 36–37, 87, 92, 249–250
Kurtz, Howard, 307–8

Lack, Andrew, 25, 28, 55
La Grenouille restaurant, 75
Laign, Amber, 305, 321
LaRosa, Julius, 8
Larson, Jace, 253, 254
Lauer, Annette Roque, 10, 27, 31, 52, 65
Lauer, Matt, 135, 157, 168, 280, 322
    agent for, 53, 64
    annual advertisers' luncheon (2013), re-
        marks, 300
    author's New York Times article on,
        299–300
    background and career, 5, 52–55, 63
    Bell and, 8, 289
    conflict with Bell and others, 79
    content of Today and, 268, 269–270, 271,
        274, 282
    contract price tag, 66–67, 93, 241
    contract renewal 35–36, 52–53, 58–64,
        190, 243, 298
    Couric and, 18, 39–40, 56
    Couric reunion proposals, 57–58, 61
    Curry and, 9, 10, 16, 19, 21, 35, 40, 43,
        44–45, 65–66, 80, 82, 90, 95–96, 99,
        186, 194, 242, 264, 308
    Curry firing and, 59–64, 72, 74–75, 89,
        99–100, 240–41, 251, 275, 288, 292,
        298, 307–8
    Curry firing damaging, 75, 92–93, 100,
        275, 292, 293, 298, 299
    extramarital affairs rumors, 10, 52, 58–59,
        93

    GMA beats Today and, 216
    Guthrie and, 41–42, 235, 244–45, 246,
        258
    Hale column and, 83–84
    Nash and, 287
    popularity of, 75, 252, 275, 293
    post-Today job offers, 60–63
    Povich interviewed by, 278
    publication of Top of the Morning and,
        307–8
    Q Score, 75, 275, 293, 298
    resignation offer rejected by Burke, 308
    status on Today, 313–314
    succession of, planned for, 309–10, 314
    Summer Olympics and, 257–260
    Today cohost, 9, 10, 16, 17, 18, 26, 28, 52,
        55–64, 77–78, 83–84, 90, 94, 145,
        181, 212, 253–54, 257–260
    Today management choice and, 286
    Today news anchor, 20, 26, 27, 28, 55–56
    Today ratings slip and, 83–84, 288–89
    Today retirement considered, 10, 47,
        52–53, 58
    "Today Takes On" series and, 81
    Vieira and, 18, 31, 34, 37–38, 40, 51, 56,
        84
    "Where in the World Is Matt Lauer?," 27
    wife and family, 10, 27, 31
    Winter Olympics 2014 and, 297
Leno, Jay, 44, 91, 92, 274–75
Letterman, David, 61
Leuci, Santina, 177
Levin, Harvey, 72
Levin, Jackie, 280
Licht, Chris, 234
    CBS and, 161, 162
    Morning Joe and, 149–150, 151, 152, 154, 156
    This Morning and, 166–170
Lincoln restaurant, 139, 140, 142
Lindner, Ken, 53, 64
Live with Regis and Kelly, 31
Living with Michael Jackson, 142
Lonner, Melissa, 45–46, 80, 100
Luciano, Lilia, 70–71
Luisi, Eddie, 225
Lunden, Joan, 6, 107, 109, 114–116, 226

Man Who Ate the 747, The (Sherwood), 123
Martin, Trayvon, 69–70, 208
Matrix Awards, 73–74
McBride, Martina, 272

McMahon, Ed, 18
McRee, Lisa, 116–18, 249
MDS, 199–200, 206–7, 221–27, 273, 274
Mediaite, 162
Merlis, George, 104, 106
Meyers, Seth, 66
Michaels, Joe, 85
Middleton, Pippa, 196–97, 203
Miller, Amy, 186, 197, 211
Monnin, Sheena, 85
Montag, Sandy, 138
Moonves, Leslie, 159, 160, 168, 169
Moore, Frazier, 115
Morales, Natalie, 29, 42, 50, 58–59, 80, 81,
        93, 98, 235, 239, 240, 244, 257, 268,
        270, 280, 289–290, 314
    Curry and, 250–51
Morgan, Piers, 83
*Morning Drive*, 11
*Morning Joe*, 11–12, 14, 94, 149–163, 284
    beating of CNN ratings, 156
    CBS offer for, 158–163
    content of, 150, 153–54
    Licht and, 149–150, 151, 152, 154
Moyers, Bill, 167
MSNBC, 34, 238, 259, 275, 278
    *Countdown*, 278, 284
    *The Daily Rundown*, 238
    *Imus in the Morning* simulcast, 151–52, 154,
        156
    *Morning Joe*, 149–163
    rivalry with CNN, 152, 156
    *Scarborough Country*, 151, 152
    Web site, 154
    Zucker and, 153
Muir, David, 130
Murdoch, Rupert, 165
Murphy, Jim, 128, 132, 142

Nash, Don, 34, 39, 79, 90, 94, 100, 194, 201,
        244, 259, 268, 270, 285
    Aurora, Colorado, shooting story and,
        253, 254
    fixing of *Today* and firing of Bell, 280
    as *Today* executive producer, 286–87, 289,
        293, 299, 303, 311, 313
NBC. *See also* Bell, Jim; Burke, Steve; Capus,
        Steve; *Today*; Turness, Deborah
    cable channels, 34
    Comcast takes over, 12, 33, 43, 52–53, 61,
        202

*Dateline*, 28, 29, 44, 62, 70, 253
    GE as owner of, 55, 202
    *Meet the Press*, 34
    morning show war and, 108–9
    News, 25–26, 28–29, 34, 43, 66, 70, 111,
        153, 259, 275, 292, 297, 299, 309
    *Nightly News*, 25, 29, 34, 70, 109, 123,
        253, 267
    O'Brien and, 44, 91, 92
    prime-time lineup, 33–34, 120
    publication of *Top of the Morning* and, 307
    ratings, 33–34
    Silverman and, 107–8
    Sports, 43, 45, 112, 277, 285
    Summer Olympics and, 43–44, 187, 201
    *Sunrise*, 25
    *Today* as news profit center, 10–11, 43
    *Today* "slow fade" and, 17, 149, 187
    *The Voice*, 195
    Winter Olympics 2014 and, 297
    Zucker and, 27, 28, 29
NBCUniversal, 7, 259, 308, 309, 315
    Weather Channel and, 320
Neufield, Victor, 143
Newman, Kevin, 117–18
Nielsen, 8, 114
    *GMA* and, 184, 186, 187, 196, 199, 204
    *GMA* and *Today* tie, 260
    *Morning Joe* and, 155–56
    *Today* and, 288
    Zucker manipulating the numbers, 121,
        202
Norville, Deborah, 6–7, 25, 29, 41, 111, 112,
        114, 115, 194, 249, 277
NPR's *Morning Edition*, 128
Nalty, Ariane, 171, 180

Oates, Joyce Carol, 17
Obama, Barack, 49, 50, 155, 216–19
Obama, Michelle, 49, 50
O'Brien, Conan, 44, 91, 92
O'Brien, Soledad, 157
Odom, Lamar, 145–46
O'Donnell, Lawrence, 162
O'Donnell, Norah, 235, 307
Olbermann, Keith, 160, 278
Oliver, Wesley, 212–13
Olympics
    ABC coverage 1980, 108
    Bell and, 43–44, 46, 82, 191, 201, 263,
        276, 277, 297

morning show ratings and, 228–29, 263

NBC coverage, 47, 187, 194

2012 as Curry firing deadline, 74, 86, 250, 252

2014 Winter Olympics in Sochi, Russia, 297, 318–319

Orchard, Mark, 237

Paar, Jack, 157

Page, Susan, 97

Paley, William S., 157–58

Palin, Sarah, 63, 193, 194, 238

Pauley, Jane, 6–7, 28, 29, 50, 110, 111–12, 114, 194

Pfeiffer, Dan, 216, 217

Phillips, Stone, 28, 29

Plepler, Richard, 60

Povich, Izzy, 278, 285, 286

Quintanilla, Carl, 215

Radar Online, 92

Rather, Dan, 249

Reasoner, Harry, 249

*Red Mercury* (Sherwood), 123

Rehrig, Denise, 180–81, 208, 209, 214, 247, 269, 272

Reis, Sean, 90

Rhodes, David, 159–160, 166, 168–69, 294

Ripa, Kelly, 31

Rivera, Geraldo, 107

Robach, Amy, 222, 279, 304, 317–18

Robbins, Ted, 236

Roberts, Lucimarian, 218, 272, 273–74

Roberts, Robin, 15, 35, 45, 63, 125–29, 321

Champion and, 199–200, 207, 223, 272, 274, 279, 294–95, 301–2, 320

"coming out" about sexual orientation, 305, 321

*GMA* beats *Today*, 204–6

as *GMA* cohost, 18, 125–29, 131, 132, 135–36, 137, 181, 184–85, 196, 197, 211–12, 214–15, 247, 302

as *GMA* news anchor, 125

Hurricane Katrina and, 126–27

Katie Couric Week on *GMA* and, 190, 192–93

last week on *GMA*, 271–74, 279

MDS and, 199–200, 206–7, 208, 211–12, 217–18, 221–27, 247, 273, 274, 294

Obama interview with, 216–19

Q score, 222

return to *GMA* after bone marrow transplant, 294–96, 301–5, 316

social media support for, 225

wake-up time, 188

Rogers, Will, Jr., 157

Roker, Al, 11, 20, 23, 26, 81, 84, 85, 98, 99, 145, 176, 201, 239, 267, 280, 289, 290, 293, 301, 314

Champion threatens job on *Today*, 320

Curry and, 38, 265–66

Lauer and, 56, 298

Summer Olympics and, 257, 259

Romney, Mitt, 219

Roosevelt, Eleanor, 87

Rose, Charlie, 12, 135, 165–170, 186, 307

Ross, Brian, 24, 249

Ross, Shelley, 118–19

Russert, Tim, 155

Ryan, Marty, 110

*Saturday Night Live* (*SNL*), 66, 299

Sawyer, Diane, 16, 114, 123, 129, 130, 158, 205

as *GMA* cohost, 118–19, 126, 127–29, 157, 184

leaves *GMA*, 129–130

Roberts and, 126, 274

Scarborough, Joe, 150–163, 284

Scarborough, Susan, 152

Schmidt, Eric, 165

Schneider, Jeffrey, 191, 203, 205, 215, 224, 246, 305, 321

Scott, Willard, 110

Seacrest, Ryan, 61, 62, 193, 242, 258, 260

Shalev, Zev, 158, 166

Shalit, Gene, 110

Shanks, Bob, 105

Shapiro, Neal, 28–29

Shaylor, Jay, 171, 172–74, 175–76, 180

Shepherd, Sherri, 195–96

Sherwood, Ben, 15, 45, 61

background and career, 119–120, 123–24

Elliott hired by, 140–42

*GMA* and, 119–124, 134–35, 137–146, 178, 316–17, 319

*GMA* beats *Today*, 205–6, 208, 215, 216, 260, 261, 262–63, 271, 316

KIG, PYG, and *GMA*, 317, 321–22

morning show leader race and, 183–84, 189, 191, 197, 200, 212, 269, 292

Obama interview with Robin Roberts
and, 217–18
return to ABC, 132–34
Roberts's illness and, 221–22, 273, 274,
304
self-reinvention by, 123–24
sleep deprivation and, 121–22
wife and family, 121, 140–42
Zucker and, 123, 189
Sherwood, Karen, 121, 141
Sherwood, Will, 140–42
Silverman, Fred, 104–5, 106, 107–8
*Sixty Minutes*, 60
Spencer, Lara, 16, 18, 143–46, 178, 207, 222,
270, 317
background and career, 143–44
*GMA* anchor, 143–46, 213–14, 269
Odom analogy and, 145–46
Roberts and, 223–24, 272
wake-up time, 188
Spitzer, Eliot, 238
Sproul, Robin, 216, 217
*Squawk Box*, 11, 12
Stahl, Lesley, 86
*Stardust Memories* (film), 291
Stephanopoulos, George, 189, 246, 302
background and career, 130–31
*GMA* cohost, 15, 18, 130–32, 135–36,
157, 173, 189, 193, 214, 298
*GMA* race for leadership and, 201, 206,
211, 216
popularity, 293, 298
Roberts and, 131, 223, 224–25, 272,
295–96, 302, 304
wake-up time, 188
wife and family, 130, 136–37
Sterling Brands, 280–83
Stewart, Jon, 15
Storm, Hannah, 138–39, 158
Strong, Brenda, 119–120
Sullivan, Andrew, 122–23
*Survivors Club, The* (Sherwood), 124, 140
Sweeney, Anne, 61, 133, 135, 226, 303
Swink, Simone, 209

Tapper, Jake, 168
Tebow, Tim, 196, 205
Telemundo, 70
television
"to do something" euphemism, 4
Sound-Off Test, 283

tape reviews, 22
youth prized by, 30
television: morning shows. *See also GMA;*
*Today*
advertising revenue per 100,000 viewers,
19, 113, 167
alternatives to, 11, 170
booking battles, 174, 177–180, 212–13
the "demo" (viewers from 25 to 54), 7,
11, 200–201, 209, 211, 215, 216, 219,
229, 247, 248, 252, 257, 260–62, 270,
271, 281, 288, 289, 292
as entertainment, 15
history of, 13–14
men as executives in, 4, 6, 125, 187
mock married couple model, 128
morning show war, 108–9, 132–33, 149,
183–197
proliferation of, 11–12
revenues, 11, 12
salaries of hosts, 5, 61, 66, 93, 94, 97, 156,
241
sleep deprivation and, 4–5, 121–22
typical day in producing, 171–181
unwritten rules of, 170
women as viewers of, 4, 125, 136, 187,
225
*This Morning*, 12, 165–170, 186, 235, 283,
293–94, 306–7, 311, 316
TMZ, 5, 72, 77, 92, 94, 222, 251, 266
*Today*, 26. *See also* Bell, Jim; Burke, Steve; Capus, Steve
advertising revenue, 11, 43, 291, 300–301
Aurora, Colorado, shooting story and,
252–55
booking battles, 177–180, 212–13, 216,
220
Brokaw and, 25, 108
chemistry and, 18, 19, 44–45, 56, 97,
113–14, 245, 249, 258, 259
chimpanzee J. Fred Muggs and, 9, 128,
192
chimp attack story, 268
content of, 16–17, 28, 52, 77–78, 79, 85,
241, 268, 269–270, 271, 281, 282–83
Couric as cohost, 26, 28, 29, 55, 73, 112,
114, 115, 123–24, 179
"crashes" increased under Turness, 315
Curry as "anchor at large," 95, 252–55,
264, 293
Curry as cohost, 16–17, 18, 19–22, 36–42,

44–45, 71–72, 79, 81, 90–91, 95–96, 148, 181, 186, 194, 213, 220, 239

Curry as news anchor, 19–20, 26–27, 29

Curry's fans, protests, 75, 92–93, 100, 251, 275

Curry's final week and on-air goodbye, 89–100, 229–230, 238, 240, 242

Curry's firing (Operation Bambi), 3–7, 10, 44–46, 66, 67, 79, 81–100, 149, 214–15, 227–28, 233–34, 246, 262, 275, 292

Curry's firing, repercussions, 5–6, 90, 91, 94, 99–100, 228–230, 262, 288, 300

Curry's first day as cohost, 38–39

Curry snubbed on Diamond Jubilee coverage, 84–85

Curry transition botched, 248–252

Daly as cohost, 314

the "demo" (viewers from 25 to 54) and, 7, 11, 246, 248, 252, 260, 262, 281, 288, 292, 300, 301

Ebersol and, 111, 112

as "family," 4, 11, 17–18, 26–27, 77, 94, 281

Fili and succession plan for Lauer, 309, 313–14

"filters" for show content (coined by Turness), 312

fixing of and firing of Bell, 267–290, 297

format of, 108

Friedman (Steve) and, 26, 109

Garroway and, 8, 128

Geist on, 283–85, 314

GMA beats in ratings, 195–97, 199–209, 211, 215–16, 219, 220, 246–48, 252, 257, 260–62, 265–66, 270–71, 274, 279, 291–92, 300–301, 306, 316, 318

GMA race/rivalry for leadership, 14, 16, 27–28, 46, 47, 69, 96, 107, 108–9, 110, 113–19, 120–21, 183–197, 209, 211–220, 228–230, 246, 260–62, 288, 305–6, 316, 318–19

Gumbel as cohost, 114

Gumbel criticism leaked, 110–11

Guthrie and, 72, 77, 91, 238–240

Guthrie as cohost, 241, 242, 244–46, 251, 257–260, 262, 267

Guthrie to replace Curry, 10, 41–42, 44, 59, 73, 79–80, 230, 233–240

Hartz and, 103, 107

Lauer as anchor of Today in New York, 55

Lauer as cohost, 10, 16–17, 26, 27, 28, 34, 40–41, 44–45, 55–64, 77–78, 81, 83–84, 90, 94, 95–96, 181, 186, 194, 212, 257–260, 288–89, 298, 299–300

Lauer as news anchor, 20, 26, 27, 28, 55–56

Lauer contract renewal, 35–36, 52–53, 58–64, 298

Lauer on four day schedule, 214–15

Meow the cat and, 212

mission statement, new, 311–12

Morales and, 239, 240, 270, 314

Morning Joe as competition, 157

as morning show leader (the streak), 7–8, 10, 33, 56, 63, 109, 115, 119, 120–21, 123, 128, 129, 132–33, 183, 187, 189, 195–97, 201–2, 206, 209, 228–230, 243

Nash as executive producer, 286–87, 289, 311, 313

Norville and, 111–12, 277

O. J. Simpson murder trial and, 115

Orange Room, 314

Pauley to Norville bungle, 6–7, 29, 111–12

problems at, April, 2012, 69–70

rape victims interview, 2002, 179–180

ratings slip, 9, 16, 33, 36, 45, 51, 67, 73, 77, 78, 83–84, 112, 148, 149, 220, 252, 265–66, 288, 291–92, 300

ratings slip causes, 78–79, 230, 267–270, 271, 274, 280–82, 311

ratings tie, 260, 261

Robert's return to GMA and, 303

Roker and, 239, 240, 259, 265–66, 289, 314

September 11, 2001, terrorist attacks and, 27

Silverman and, 107–8

sixtieth anniversary celebration, 49–52

slogan, new, 313

"Steals and Deals," 147

Sterling Brands study, 280–83

studio renovation and graphics update, 312–13

summer concert series, 220

Summer Olympics and, 187, 194, 228–230, 257–260, 263–66

"Today Takes On" series, 81

traveling around the world, 109

Turness and, 310–13, 315–16, 320, 321

as unchanging, 14, 17
Vieira as cohost, 9, 30–31, 34, 55–56, 73
Vieira as "mystery guest," 193, 194
Vieira leaves, 33, 34, 37–38, 147
Wald as executive producer, 27
Weather Channel and Champion, 320–21
"What's Trending Today," 146
"Where in the World Is Matt Lauer?," 27
Winter Olympics in Sochi and, 318–19
Zimmerman 911 call and, 69–70
Zucker and, 7, 26, 30–31, 114, 115, 270, 322
Today.com, 26
Touchet, Tom, 116–17
Townsend, Julie, 203
Turness, Deborah, 310–13, 315–16, 320, 321, 322
author's *New York Times* article on, 310–11
TVNewser, 154
21 Club, 55, 168–69
Twitter, 5, 35, 160, 189, 212, 263
Curry and, 87, 91, 264
Lauer and, 92, 100, 230, 251, 298
Licht and, 306
Roberts and, 225
*Today* viewer comment, 96, 275

USA Today, 97, 179, 194

Van Dyke, Dick, 157
Vane, Ed, 104
Vargas, Elizabeth, 191, 279, 304
Vieira, Meredith, 19, 158, 260
agent for, 233–34
firing of Ann Curry and, 84
Lauer and, 18, 31, 34, 37–38, 40, 51, 56, 84
leaves *Today*, 9, 33, 34, 37–38, 96, 98, 147
on sleep deprivation, 5
as *Today* cohost, 30–31, 73, 76
as *Today* "mystery guest," 193, 194
Winter Olympics in Sochi and, 297
*View, The*, 30, 117, 143, 195, 218
Vlasto, Chris, 261

WABC, 143
Wald, Jonathan, 27, 179
Wald, Richard, 107
Walenstein, Andrew, 93

Wallace, Alex, 267–68, 285, 289, 300
Walters, Barbara, 49, 50, 51, 103, 114, 249
*Washington Journal*, 11
*We Are the Mulvaneys* (Oates), 17
Weather Channel, 11, 12, 319–21
Weaver, Pat, 115
Weir, Bill, 130
Welch, Jack, 55
Wentworth, Ali, 130, 131, 136
Westin, David, 116, 117, 127–28, 130, 131, 133, 143, 205
*Who Killed CBS?* (Boyer), 157
*Who Wants to Be a Millionaire?* 30
Williams, Brian, 25, 86, 94, 253
Williams, Ted, 177
Winfrey, Oprah, 57, 58, 166, 168, 169, 279
Winn, Jeff, 208
WNBC, 55, 56
"Workplace Confidential" (*New York* magazine), 44
Wright, Bob, 28
WuDunn, Sheryl, 36
Wurtzel, Alan, 115
WWOR, 52–53

Zahn, Paula, 310
Zee, Ginger, 321
Zerbest, Kolbi, 212–13
Zimmerman, George, 69–70, 208
Zinni, Mark, 298
Zucker, Jeff, 27, 28, 29, 56, 92
advice to Stephanopoulos, 189
as author's boss, 322
Bell hired by, 46
at CNN Worldwide, 294, 322
fear of *GMA* surpassing *Today* and, 120–21, 196
Lauer championed by, 55
Lauer/Katie reunion and, 57, 58, 61, 64
ousting of, 33, 286
Scarborough and, 153, 160
Sherwood and, 123, 189
as *Today* chief, 7, 26, 30–31, 114, 115, 270, 322
Vieira as *Today* cohost and, 30–31
Zuckerman, Mark, 211
Zurawik, David, 94